STAGE
AREAS
SUMMER
NEW YEAR
1985
I0820855

FRIEND
of the
DEVIL

FRIEND of the DEVIL

My Wild Ride with JERRY GARCIA and GRATEFUL DEAD

LEN DELL'AMICO

weldonowen

for….

Sue Stephens

Veronica Loza

Allison Sullivan

and my daughter,

Kiley, without whose help

this book would not

have been completed,

and her mother,

Laura Kimpton

CONTENTS

INTRODUCTION

This book is not an attempt at a history or a biography of Jerry Garcia or Grateful Dead. There are many books out there that definitely *are* histories or biographies; Dennis McNally's *A Long Strange Trip*, and David Browne's *So Many Roads*, both about the Dead, and Blair Jackson's *Garcia: An American Life* come to mind, and there are also books penned by insiders, longtime members of the family-like tribe that the band really was, even more than it was an artistic effort or a business operation.

This book is nothing like any of those.

Very simply, this book is the story of my relationship with one guy over a period of fifteen years, an incredibly gifted musician and songwriter, embedded within an entertainment-business monster of a shobiz act, Grateful Dead. It's the tale of a man, standing at the vanguard of a complex and highly developed subculture, within the wider context of the American culture, in a unique period in history, the 1980s and '90s, so I've got something to say about those things too.

It is a frank account of my friendship with a great artist, a man who reached great heights of creative accomplishment, fame, and wealth, and was then laid low by serious health problems, a crushing burden of responsibility, and a set of bad habits and substance addictions that landed him in the ICU for three days in a deep coma, with doctors warning family to brace themselves for the worst outcome, and who then fought to recover his memory and mastery of the guitar and his music, and went on to reach towering heights of success all over again. In short, this is the story of a terrible fall and an astonishing comeback, told from the point of view of a friend and collaborator, me.

I'm not a professional writer (though I do write screenplays, a very different animal from a novel or a memoir), so you may find some of my language or grammar unusual or annoying, but I hope also sometimes original or fresh.

I have an entire shelf of books in my office about Grateful Dead and Jerry Garcia, none of which I've read, several of which contain extensive quotes from me. The reason I've not read them is that I have always known (or at least since 1995) that I would have to write this memoir, and I was determined to get down my memories and thoughts in writing, which I did, from 1990

Jerry with acoustic guitar, Squaw Valley, CA, August 1991. Photo courtesy Len Dell'Amico's personal archive.

to the present, without running the risk of being influenced or prejudiced by other accounts of the band and Garcia.

I'd tell myself, "Once you've written your book, maybe then you can read the other books." Likewise, I've always tried to avoid seeing or hearing my own appearances in the mass media (I had to do a good deal of them in connection with promoting the work), on radio, TV, the internet, and elsewhere, and often I'd enlist trusted friends and family to watch or listen and tell me how bad I sucked, and to offer advice on how I might improve. The fact is, the idea of watching or listening to me, myself, was, and is, deeply repugnant to me, due to mysterious and unknown psychological depths that I'd rather not ponder. I can tell you that my mother frowned upon drawing attention to oneself, she was very traditional about modesty, and pitching in for the common good, over self-aggrandizement.

One possible consequence of this strategy of avoiding all other versions of Grateful Dead and Garcia and my own history is that a reader such as yourself, especially if you are a serious fan or scholar of the Dead or Garcia, might find some of my recollections in this book to be in conflict with some other writer's or reporter's, or even at variance from other versions I myself have given. There's nothing I have to say about that, if it happens, just that I have worked very hard in this memoir to stick to facts and report the things that I experienced, heard, saw, and remembered as best as I can. I don't consider it a problem if a given biography or history or individual paints a different reality than I do, even if that individual is myself when I was younger, it's just in the nature of reality. When you are talking about the past, which is gone, and only exists in our minds and in cultural artifacts, you will have conflicting versions; there is no "absolute truth" about the past. In any case, I believe that it's more important to extract from the past that which you find most important and useful to you, rather than obsess on what actually happened, was it this way or that way—that's a fool's errand.

Well, now I've written this book, all these years later, and so maybe soon I'll start looking at one or more of those other books. But probably not, to be truthful. I'm hoping to feel that now I can put my burden down, having fulfilled what I always felt was an obligation I had to tell this story. And maybe now I can stop thinking about this history for a good long while, go for a long walk on a long beach, and not have to think about Garcia and the Dead unless they pop spontaneously into my mind, purely and joyously, or out of a boom box in Mexico or Thailand, as I walk on that long beach, or down a dazzling city street I've never been on before . . .

So . . .

What was the source or wellspring of the love that so many people had and still have for the music of Grateful Dead, and for Jerry Garcia? This question has been pondered for more than a half-century, and I myself feel still deeply involved with it.

Why is it that so many people who have met Garcia, from very different backgrounds over a long period of time, all report about how he was such an amazing person, or a really great guy, or how much they love him? Why is it that so many musicians who befriended him through their work together shake their heads and laugh in profound awe at the effect he had on them?

Why is it that so many people who have never met him, but experienced him only in his concert performances, have such a deep and abiding love for him, whether they've seen a few shows, a few dozen, or a few hundred?

These are questions I hope I can cast some light upon in the chapters ahead.

And, most importantly to me, why do I care so much about this part of my life, Grateful Dead and Garcia? Why do I feel so hugely grateful to have been able to play a part in their history?

I now feel compelled, maybe because I'm entering my third act, a late stage of life, to report on what I learned from my experience. Why have I felt a sense of *obligation* for more than twenty-five years to tell this story? There is a two-part answer.

First, because over the course of my education with Grateful Dead and Garcia, I learned a great deal about the importance of their music in our cultural history, its sources in jug-band, old-timey, bluegrass, rural blues, country-and-western, jazz, and rock 'n' roll music. Through experiencing up close and personal the symbiosis between the band and their fans, over and over via making sixty or so in-concert films, many of which I directed from the mixing and lighting structure in the middle of a stadium surrounded by 70,000 or so delirious fans, I came to understand the underlying dynamic of this phenomenon: The shows were fundamentally a spiritual experience, more like going to church than any other musical act I have ever worked with.

"Uncle John's Band," "Scarlet Begonias," "Estimated Prophet," "Eyes of the World," "Throwing Stones," "Bird Song," "Cassidy," "Lady with a Fan/Terrapin Station," "Box of Rain," "Brokedown Palace," "China Cat Sunflower," "Dark Star," "Franklin's Tower," "Let It Grow/Weather Report Suite," "Playing in the Band," "Ripple," "Sugar Magnolia," "U.S. Blues," "The Wheel," and of course "Not Fade Away" . . . and there are as many lists like this as there are ardent fans out there, all different from mine.

I think of these songs as "the liturgy" at the very core of the whole Grateful Dead/Garcia phenomenon. If each concert was mostly like a church service or a spiritual revival show, these songs were the part of the concert that actually contained the singing out loud of the deep-seated and motivating spiritual feelings and beliefs, created, and transmitted by the band, and deeply held by the fans. They were the meat and potatoes of the whole experience and worldview of the subculture, the fans.

Yes, there were lots of fun rock' n' roll moments in a typical show—up-tempo originals and covers of old favorites, romantic love songs, some funny tall tales, and a variety of Dylan tunes (the Dead and Garcia's side bands were the number one and two Dylan cover bands of their time)—but the truth is, fans bought tickets and came for the uplifting songs and improvisations that, first and foremost, moved them in their hearts and souls.

So, I came to understand the importance of the Grateful Dead phenomenon in our cultural history, and I came to feel that the Grateful Dead juggernaut is at least as much a spiritual movement as it is a musical act, or just a part of the entertainment industry.

The second reason I feel obligated to tell this story is because in the fifteen years I knew him, Garcia was the closest thing to a mentor I ever had. I used the lessons I learned from him to build my own career, and to seek the life I imagined, and to enjoy an amazingly big hunk of fulfillment and happiness, and to end up now, somewhat late in life, feeling like one of the most fortunate people I know, and feeling like I owe it to a large degree to the lessons learned from Garcia.

I'm indebted to Garcia and the Dead for the role they played in my career and my life, and for the friends and lovers I encountered along the way, for the sheer amount of fun I had with all of them. For all of that, I feel a tremendous sense of gratitude.

INTRODUCTION

My goal here is to try to give you readers a sense of who Garcia was as a person, what it was like to be with him in person, in a lot of ordinary situations, and in some weirder ones too. I try to answer the question I've often been asked, "Yeah, I know a bit about him, but what was he really like?"

And now, if you turn the page to Chapter 1, I will turn you over to the person I was many years ago to start the story I want to tell you, to try to reveal what he was really like, and who knows, maybe something about me as well.

Jerry as Chef in Straight Arrow Cooking, *video production still from* "Ticket to New Year's" *pay-per-view broadcast, December 31, 1987. Photo courtesy Len Dell'Amico personal archive.*

Chapter 1

HOW I MET JERRY

So I found myself somewhat dazed in the back of a cab on my way from SFO, the San Francisco airport, to a theater unfamiliar to me in downtown SF called the Warfield. Dazed because when I woke up that morning in Brooklyn, whatever plans I had were tossed aside and instead I was put on a plane to San Francisco, and because I was sick with some kind of cold or something, and in denial about it, and also jet-lagged, and to be truthful I was pretty frightened about whatever situation I was now agreeing to put myself in. It was September 25, 1980, and I was twenty-nine.

The driver took me to the backstage door of the Warfield and helped me get my carry-on bag and attaché case (a thing that replaced the briefcase in those days) out of the cab. I glanced around at the peculiar scene: It was twilight, excitement in the clean, fresh SF air as showtime was approaching. There were a dozen or so wild-looking young men and women, happily twitching and gyrating to music from a boom box, possibly due to the substances in their bloodstreams. They were flanking both sides of the holy backstage door, actually just a grim gray metal door, forming a kind of two-sided funnel made out of weird half-naked dancers that visitors, such as me, would have to navigate. Before I realized in my addled state what was happening, a scraggly bearded guy got in my face, grinning maniacally, "Hey, you got any extra passes?" I just looked at him, dumbfounded. The crowd had immediately sized me up as a likely guest-list person. Other greeters moved toward me, talking, gesticulating. The cab driver nudged me, put my bags down, offered a receipt. I came back to reality, paid him, and he shook his head and gave me a look of pity as he turned to go. I had a half-formed feeling of "wait a second" as I watched him retreat, but it was too late, he was gone.

I summoned an ounce of courage, turned to face the grim metal door, the backstage entrance to a Grateful Dead show, the hugely hyped first show of an historic two-week run in their hometown. I ignored the shouts coming from the gatekeepers and knocked on the door. Nothing. The people around me laughed and clapped. They weren't threatening, really, but in my bewildered state I felt a wave of panic and I pounded on the door, hard, thinking, "What the *fuck* am I going to do if this door never opens. The cab is gone, I've got luggage, Jesus fucking Christ."

Sue Stephens, Garcia's personal manager, had directed me via phone before I got on the plane to go straight to the Warfield instead of a hotel, which would have been more what you might expect when summoned to a meeting with a major rock band, but I was eager to make professional headway, and in no position to ask questions. She told me that I would be met at the backstage door by Steve Parish, the Grateful Dead stage manager in charge of Garcia matters, and that Steve would take me to meet with him.

I suppress the panic. I have no choice but to pound on this door until it opens.

Then suddenly the door swings open, and there is a bearded, long-haired guy in a cowboy hat lunging out, looking around angrily, brandishing a long black metal flashlight in one hand like, Who the fuck is pounding on this door? I try to look nonthreatening, shrinking back, luggage by my side, not sharp enough mentally to realize the crazy fans were probably pounding on this door every few minutes. After a moment, his eyes land on me.

I shout at the guy, "Sue Stephens said I should ask for Steve Parish." The guy looks me up and down, moves back, slams the door behind him. The little crowd resumes their jeering and merriment at my expense. A long minute passes, then the door swings open again, and there is "Big Steve" Parish himself, tall and large, black mustache, an intense gaze. The crowd recognizes him immediately and shrinks back in awe and respect, falling into a murmuring silence.

I'm like, "Okay . . ." I have never been in this situation before, kind of like a PBS nature documentary, where you see firsthand how a specific tribal society works, in this case, the interface between the adoring ecstatic fans and a living person, Big Steve, who symbolizes the object of their adoration, Grateful Dead. He suddenly appears, and they shrink back in humility and quiet excitement, like plants that close their leaves in the presence of direct sunlight.

I know of Steve from many earlier shows of the Dead and the Jerry Garcia Band that I had seen him at, both of us workers, he for the band and me for the promoter. My job is putting video images up on the big screens so everyone at the show, even those who were far from the stage, could see the musicians, the rock stars, their idols, in close-up. In the late 1970s into the 1980s, we called this *video reinforcement,* a new technology that would make huge arena and stadium tours possible and is now of course a normal part of all large shows.

To my great relief, Steve waves me inside and summons someone to grab my bags, and then leads the way into the backstage area of the Warfield. I'm concerned about my bags and the seedy-looking guy who was taking possession of them, but Steve just keeps moving, and I'll be damned, but I do end up in a nice hotel room at the end of the night, with my bags. Grateful Dead may look like an out-of-control circus, but it isn't. I have absolutely no memory, possibly because I was about to become extremely high, of moving from the Warfield to my hotel that night after the show, or how I am reunited with my bags, but I know it all happens smoothly.

I have passed over into the hands of Sue Stephens, Big Steve, Garcia, and Grateful Dead.

Backstage is a warren of corridors and spaces and rooms, filled with cigarette and marijuana smoke, happy people going in both directions in the narrow corridors, lots of chatter and laughter, people in weird outfits, a guy in a full clown suit with the red nose, kids of all ages, laughing, running, and you could hear the excited hum of the full house of fans upstairs, invisible from here, but waiting to explode very soon when the band came on. I just follow Steve.

We arrive at a door. Steve turns to me and indicates, okay, you wait here. He pushes open the door and a huge cloud of pot smoke comes pouring out of the room, right out of a Cheech & Chong movie, an overwhelming blast. I've plenty of experience with smoking pot by this time (I'd first smoked weed, of much weaker potency, thirteen years earlier), but in this moment I'm tinged with fear: I'm backstage at a Grateful Dead concert, about to have a meeting with Jerry Garcia, which I know is actually an audition for the job of directing the band's first live mass-media event, using untested technology to reach their fans all across America, something that had never been done before, and deliver a top-quality audiovisual experience. What could go wrong?

I stumble into the room, so thick with smoke you can't see across it, and hear a voice to my left. It's Garcia, welcoming me. "Hey, man!" I look at him, seated, looking up at me, and handing me the largest joint I've ever seen. "Here, have some of this!" The burning joint in his fingers is inches from my face, framed entirely by his big, smiling face. Garcia is a big man with a big head and an unruly penumbra of thick black hair and a full salt-and-pepper beard, always wearing his signature aviator-style glasses. He has dark eyes and animated, dancing eyebrows, a prominent nose, and big cheeks puffed out by a semipermanent grin. While performing, his movements are smooth and relaxed (except for his fingers, of course), but offstage he seems to crackle with electricity. If there isn't a joint in his hand, there's most likely a cigarette, unfiltered. He is missing the top two joints of his right middle finger, the result of a childhood accident (Django Reinhardt, another great guitarist, also played with the use of just eight fingers). And he always seems to be wearing the same uniform: nondescript shoes, dark pants, black tee shirt, and a plaid, long-sleeve flannel shirt, always unbuttoned, over the tee.

Confronted with the huge joint Garcia was offering me, I know immediately this is one of those what-the-fuck moments. I could say, "Oh, no thank you, I'm not feeling great, I probably shouldn't," or I could just run out of the room and out into the night yelling, "No, I didn't sign up for this, I'm just a tech-type nerd from New York, not some kind of swinging psychedelic adventurer."

I look Garcia in the eye and take the joint from him and smile and thank him and take a big toke from it. It tastes great; the quality shines through. Then I look around to my right in the haze and find someone to pass it to. There are no familiar faces, maybe eight people sitting on chairs and a sofa and upturned road boxes. They note my arrival, but quickly go back to their chatter and laughter.

Garcia waves me into the room, "C'mon in, sit down!" I smile and nod and quickly realize there is nowhere to sit. Steve, still in the doorway, notices as well, and he suddenly barks at this big, scowling Hells Angels guy sitting on a road box beside Garcia. "Hey, Tiny, give him your seat!"

Holy shit! Now I'm really alarmed. The Hells Angel turns his head to look at me, his scowl deepening, then slowly gets up, grumbling menacingly.

Inside, I'm shouting, "No, No, I don't need a seat, don't do this to me, please, please," but I keep my cool, nodding politely to Tiny as Steve takes him outside and closes the door.

As soon as I sit down, Garcia turns to me with that big, happy grin, and makes a sweet greeting, "Glad you could make it, good to meet you, how was your flight?" I'm relieved that he does in fact know who I am and that I'm here at his behest, and he seems like a really nice guy.

The giant joint goes between us again, and the weed begins to hit me; my God, this is not like what we smoke in New York. I try to relax into the high. I've been directing film and video of rock bands for five years, and I'm accustomed to the backstage world and the shenanigans of successful musicians, the wild drug-fueled partying, the groupies, as they were called then, and naturally I know that Grateful Dead has a hard-won reputation for on-tour excess. On the other hand, as a professional, I'm also well aware of their reputation for demanding the best technical standards in everything they do, and they treat their crews and their fans very well, keeping ticket costs down and the quality of their sound way up.

Garcia explains to me that tonight is the first night in a fifteen-show run at the Warfield, and that they are adding an acoustic set at the start of the show, something they haven't done in a long time. Their fans are all worked up about it. After the Warfield run, the Dead are booked to play some shows at the Saenger in New Orleans, and then move to Radio City Music Hall in New York, where they will do another eight-show residency. The last show will be on Halloween, and it will be televised via a closed-circuit broadcast to twenty or more theaters across the United States, something that has never been done before, and also simulcast across the nation on FM radio. He's articulate and speaks quickly as he briefs me, while making sure I'm keeping up with him. Fans will buy tickets to see the band on huge color screens in theaters equipped with state-of-the-art PA systems—good and loud. And I start to understand why I am sitting here with him: Because I am someone who can help make this happen.

I mention to Garcia that I recently filmed a live concert of the Meters and the Neville Brothers at the Saenger Theatre in New Orleans. The Meters are well known for their improvisational playing, which can be difficult for film directors to capture, and which Grateful Dead are of course famous for—lots and lots of improvisation. Garcia smiles and nods knowingly, as if he has seen some of the footage already, or maybe he has spoken to Art Neville about it, or maybe he's just signaling, "Yeah, you just filmed the Meters and the Nevilles, two of the greatest bands ever, and somehow you got that gig, and I heard it went well, and so that qualifies you to be sitting here." I'll never know.

I am now firmly in the grip of the weed. It's like I'm watching a movie, another Fellini movie maybe, a movie that I'm also in.

Bob Weir pops in suddenly, acoustic guitar slung around his neck, laughing, the sound from the venue above surging until he shuts the door, then the revelers in the room greeting him. He strikes me as a very relaxed, outgoing guy, male-model good-looking, athletic, in marked contrast to Garcia. He makes a reference to the impending disaster of the acoustic set, Garcia returns the jocular repartee, and it's clear that doing an acoustic set is Garcia's idea and everyone else is going along with it. Then Weir refers cryptically to the director auditions going on for the Halloween broadcast: "Is this one of the guys?" referring to me (we had not formally met). Apparently, there may be one or more other directors, maybe already come and gone, or maybe still lurking about, and my previous East Coast insecurities calmed by talking with Garcia are suddenly inflamed again. Weir exits, still laughing. Jeez! What am I in for?

Parish ushers someone else out of the room, brings Tiny the Hells Angel back into the room, and gives him the seat. Tiny glares at me.

Garcia seems to notice my . . . shall we say slight discomfort—I'm so high my head is spinning—but he presents that warm, reassuring smile, signaling that all will be okay. I had no idea then, but over the next fifteen years I'd grow accustomed to his ability to make others comfortable. Even in that moment, I could see he was a warm and gracious man. Something of a charm machine.

My brain fog lifts gradually as we fall back to talking about the Radio City shows in New York and the closed-circuit theatrical event on Halloween. The subject of hosts for the broadcast comes up. Garcia and the band like Franken and Davis, the hot *Saturday Night Live* writing and performing team, and yeah maybe we should prerecord a bunch of comedy skits to fill out the band's thirty- or forty-minute breaks between sets, and I point out that this meant that, yeah, we'd have to move fast if we were going to shoot this material here in San Francisco. D-day was only a month away and they'd be too busy to shoot comedy by the time they got to New York.

He understands immediately and nods enthusiastically, and says, "So we should get Franken and Davis here right away so we can get to work!" I nod along, but then feel a rush of, "Woah, Nelly, this is moving fast"—I haven't been hired yet. He picks up on my sudden, slight blanch—this is my first exposure to Executive Garcia—and he leans in a bit and softens his tone, as if reassuring a child, and says, "Just tell Sue the plan, it'll get taken care of." I'm impressed, and I think, "It's good to be the King."

Even through my deep weed fog, I can feel and am impressed with his honesty and his deep understanding of what I will need to know in order to figure out what my role in it would be and if I would want to do it. And the *it* was the job of directing the band's first live mass-media event, an audiovisual experiment really, in transmitting a live multicamera show to two dozen or so theaters all across the country. In 1980 there was no other way to play live to all your fans; there was no cable, no satellite TV, and the three major networks were not interested.

Garcia turns away from me with a hand-up, give-me-a-second gesture, and smiles and nods at Tiny and leans toward him, "Hey, man, so tell me, what's up? How're you doing?" You could see Tiny's eyes widen a little. He sits up straight, puts his hands on his knees, clears his throat, and starts to speak. "I come tonight with a message for you from Mr. Sonny Barger, the president of the Oakland Chapter of the Hells Angels. He sends you his warm regards and his best wishes for the first show of this historical acoustic big run that you start tonight at the Warfield, and he regrets that he cannot attend in person . . ."

Garcia laughs delightedly, nods appreciatively to Tiny: "Thanks, man, that was great! Listen, would you send a message back to Sonny? Just tell him I was really, really glad to hear from him tonight, okay?" Tiny bows his head briefly, much relieved, and returns to his earlier statue form. I learned later that Barger had recently completed a prison sentence, but was still under house arrest, and so couldn't make the show tonight.

Parish pops in suddenly and yells, "Ten minutes!" Tiny and a few others get up and shuffle out, so now it's down to me and Garcia and two or three others who apparently know they can stay; Garcia reassures me with a hand gesture, so I make no move to leave. He picks up his giant Martin acoustic guitar and starts to strum.

Someone pokes their head around the door and asks Garcia if he wants a boost from the Doctor, apparently an injection of unspecified but certainly benign ingredients meant to enhance your imminent performance. Garcia declines, politely but firmly, and the guy leaves.

Now he starts playing, with some focus, improvising, obviously warming up for the show. I sit back, feeling like the talk time is over, and feeling comfortable and happy, this has gone well, and this guy is knowledgeable about the project we are planning . . . and that he is really sweet and smart.

Parish pops in to announce, "Five minutes!" He holds the door open. You can hear the sound of the crowd now, even down here in the bowels of the theater, you can feel their anticipation. Almost as one, the visitors rise to their feet and bolt for the door, and I get up to join them. This is obviously the time for Garcia to be alone. But he glances up at me and says, "No, sit down," without missing a beat in his playing. I sit. Parish closes the door.

Now it's me, Garcia, and his music. I am high—and how, yes. I am momentarily confused by what has just happened, but I am also able to just let it go. This music he's playing is beautiful, he wants me to stay, so "Shut up" I say to my mind . . . and I let go . . .

What follows is a gorgeous, intimate musical journey, one of the greatest guitarists of all time playing his giant Martin in this little room with no one else here but me. He's playing rapid arpeggios, as you'd expect in a warm-up, but also melodies were weaving in and out, bits of songs, pieces of ethereal music, going deeper and deeper . . .

Now I'm not just high from the weed, I'm definitely getting off on his playing. I have no thoughts, only feelings, and it feels really, really good.

Time stands still. He's not paying any attention to me; he's just doing his thing. I'm basically just tripping on the music, now hypnotized, wandering off into another dimension . . . I'm not aware of who I am or where I am anymore . . .

Suddenly, the door flies open, the spell is broken, and you can hear and feel the roar of the crowd, a huge crescendo, responding to the houselights-out cue, the band is about to come out, the building is vibrating. Parish yells forcefully, "Now, now, now, let's go, let's go!"

Garcia snaps to, jumps up, Martin in hand, and exits the room, Parish pulls the door shut behind him. I am shocked back in to the present.

I'm left sitting there, suddenly sealed in this little room, by myself, all alone, high as a fucking kite. Wait, where am I? I work my way back to reality, step by step, and it's good, okay, but what am I supposed to do now? Something tells me I'm in no shape to just wander around backstage or into the theater. For one thing, I have no backstage IDs or band-only laminates to grease my way. So, I decide to just sit there for a while, breathe, I'm safe and sound. I can hear the thunderous roar of the crowd as the band takes the stage and eventually starts to play.

After a while a young woman steps delicately into the room, all smiles, carrying some passes for me. Softly she approaches, probably sensing my condition, and sweetly offers to escort me to my seat. I nod once for yes, and follow her through the narrow corridors, passing Tiny as he comes the other way. I swear he growls at me. I smile back politely, edging closer to my escort.

Now, looking back forty years, I am still touched by how well the band treated me. After all, someone must've eventually said, "Hey, where's this Dell'Amico director guy we're supposed to take care of?" And they went and found me.

My seat was in the first row of the balcony at the Warfield, the best seats in the house, right next to the lighting director and the sound mixer, the legendary pair Candace Brightman and Dan Healy. When I got there the band was already well into their acoustic set, and it was an awesome scene. The sound and lighting were fantastic, the crowd was ape-shit happy, and the band sounded and played great.

And that's how I met Jerry Garcia.

When I look back now on that day at the Warfield and wonder why Garcia had gone to the trouble of seeking me out, I realize he had *always* taken a keen interest in visual and sound recording technology and mass-media developments, and how the Dead could and should interact with this evolution. On that day, he was just doing his thing, playing his role in imagining and bringing about whatever the next new thing might be, for him, his band, their extended family, their legion of fans, their subculture. It had been in his DNA all along.

He'd established himself as a thought leader in a two-part cover-featured interview for *Rolling Stone* in the '60s, he'd pushed for the Dead to participate in the Richard Lester film *Petulia* (1968), he'd provided original music for Michelangelo Antonioni's mind-blowing 1970 film *Zabriskie Point*, and he was the chief advocate for the notorious *The Grateful Dead Movie*, shot in the early '70s and privately distributed in 1977.

CHAPTER 1

When I came into Garcia's world in 1980, maybe he was looking for some good tools for their immediate needs, to help facilitate the brand-new idea of electronic-theatrical distribution of their music to their subculture, and strengthen and build that subculture, and maybe also to ready themselves for the new world that the looming debut of MTV, finally born in 1981, and the arrival of home video technology (Betamax, VHS, then later laser discs and DVDs) might create. And maybe Garcia decided after spending a little time with me that I might be a good tool, and what happened that day at the Warfield was a bit of a seduction, bringing me into his and Grateful Dead's gravitational field, and ultimately their orbit.

Jerry and Phil Lesh, pay-per-view broadcast, Radio City Music Hall, NYC, Halloween 1980.
Photo courtesy ©Jay Blakesberg/Retro Photo Archive.

Chapter 2

THE HALLOWEEN 1980 SHOOT

The day after that first Warfield show, I was asked to stick around for a while, come to the shows so everyone can talk, get to know each other, see some more shows at the Warfield, all expenses paid, relax, while the band decided what they were going to do. Like I'm gonna say, Nah, I got something better to do? These people were very intriguing.

I got the directing gig. Al Franken and Tom Davis, the hot writing team and sketch comedy artists on *Saturday Night Live,* would host the closed-circuit broadcast from Radio City on Halloween, and they were brought in during the Warfield run (September 25 to October 14, 1980) to work with the band and me to produce a bunch of sketch comedy bits to use as roll-ins during that live performance broadcast (a *roll-in* is a prerecorded segment of a live broadcast that is designed to be played back and blend in seamlessly to give the production people a chance to breathe and prepare for the next events).

From that day in September when I met Garcia to Halloween, when the first national closed-circuit broadcast by a musical act in the United States was a done deal and over, my life was an amazing blur of activity. My first job was to direct the comedy bits written and acted by Al and Tom that would be filmed in and around the Warfield, and which would be played back a few weeks later as if they were live from Radio City (the Warfield standing in for Radio City). Franken and Davis, dressed in tuxedos, would be hosting the live Halloween broadcast as if it were a telethon called Jerry's Kids, to benefit the neediest of the young people who liked to follow the band around. My second job would be the three-day shoot beginning October 29, including the live broadcast on October 31 at Radio City. Many comedy bits that we put in the can for later use on Halloween were only just backups, in case of technical problems during the live broadcast, and were actually reshot live during the Halloween broadcast. I'm proud to say that you couldn't tell the difference between the roll-ins from the Warfield and the real live pieces from Radio City when you were watching the broadcast, or *Dead Ahead,* the home video version that was released later.

I had no time to reflect on what this might demand of me or mean for my career or anything like that. I had to get busy to make sure that it was actually technically possible for us to rent two dozen or so theaters across America, put in top-notch rock 'n' roll sound systems and giant color video projectors in all of them, and distribute via satellite a broadcast-standard signal of a multicamera video shoot from a bunch of trucks parked outside of Radio City, one of the largest and most beautiful legit theaters in the world (in other words, one fully equipped to host huge theatrical events, with an enormous stage to hold many sets for different acts of a musical or play, a vast loft space, flies above the stage for lowering and pulling up props and huge backdrops in a matter of seconds, endless lighting pipes and fixtures, movable parts of the stage, trapdoors, and so on). Much of the credit for the event goes to technical director Thom Drewke, whom I'd been working with for five years at the Capitol Theatre in Passaic, New Jersey. I continued to rely on Thom as technical director for much of my work until the end of the century.

I realized quickly that once Garcia and the band set their mind on doing something, they don't fool around, when Franken and Davis appeared in San Francisco almost instantaneously. Those guys were wicked smart and funny. You could tell from the get-go they had been best friends forever and were as close as any two people I've ever met in show business. We got on well, all of us New Yorkers around the same age, and they were big Dead fans and already close with the band. And they knew that because this would be a closed-circuit broadcast—that is, private, for ticket holders only—there would be no rules governing content, no FCC oversight, and we could do whatever the fuck we wanted, basically. I could see the gleam in their eyes about that, particularly Davis's, which was a little worrisome to me, as he was the wilder of the two.

While the band was playing fifteen shows at the Warfield, Franken and Davis, along with me and a lot of production staff, were staying in a hotel in San Francisco. Al and Tom were writing, and I was coordinating production gear and crew and liaising with the band, their office and crew, and the Warfield staff. Almost all the comedy sketches—and there were a shit-ton of them—involved members of the band as actors, and I was always trying to simplify the bits or shorten them, because in my experience, musicians, rock stars, are not necessarily able to cope with stuff like learning lines, hitting marks, doing an excruciating number of takes, showing up on time . . . y'know, movie and television stuff. But Tom and Al were just irrepressibly positive and gung ho. We'd schedule filming with band members either on their days off or on afternoons before their nightly shows. We got a huge amount of very funny stuff, most of it used during the Halloween broadcast and seen only by that audience in those theaters, and then a smaller part of it was used on the follow-on 1981 home video release *Dead Ahead* and the 1982 Showtime TV special called *Live Dead!* But it's all in the vault, to this day!

Tom and Al were accustomed to working very fast and at very high budget levels as veterans of *SNL*, a weekly hit network show. It was hard for them to accept any limitations on their creativity. They were so goddamned excited to be working with the Dead, and their energy was infectious. At some point I realized that there was basically a huge open spigot of money funding all this insanity, and I just had to ride it. The Halloween concert broadcast generated a lot of income, of course, and after the home video sales run of *Dead Ahead*, a lot more money came in. *Dead Ahead* was rereleased several times over the decades, so I'm quite sure the band and everyone else did quite well in the long run.

After the Warfield run and the comedy filming ended on October 15, I relocated to my home in New York City, where I had exactly two weeks to recover and prep for the Radio City shoot, October 29–31, which involved rehearsing and shooting more comedy, and of course the live concerts. And did I mention that Radio City had never before hosted a live multi-camera production?

CHAPTER 2

My main takeaway from that whole experience, from meeting, or auditioning, with Garcia through to the Halloween broadcast, was how amazingly game the six guys in the band were to undertake this wild, risky theatrical broadcast concept in the first place, quite obviously because of Garcia's leadership and advocacy, and then how game they were to put their energy into filming the comedy bits. It wasn't that they were simply submitting to the demands of their commitment to a live event that would require material to fill big chunks of downtime while they took breaks between their three sets. Knowing that the audience in theaters out there would need to be entertained, they were actively participating in it, adjusting their acting to notes from me and Al and Tom for the next take, and the one after that. None of them ever complained or acted put-upon; they just went with the flow, it was amazing. I came to understand that it was in their historical DNA, given their roots in the Kesey Acid Tests in 1965 and '66, to just step right into absolutely unknown territory, to take big chances, do stuff that had never been done before, damn the torpedoes, all while having a good time. I came to understand that the Garcia ethos seemed to be, "Why would we want to do something if we weren't going to have fun?" in contrast to the more generally accepted show business response: "For the money."

Just to give you an example: Al and Tom came up with the concept of a big frame for the Halloween broadcast. It would be a satiric take on Jerry Lewis's annual Labor Day telethon (a huge broadcast network event Lewis hosted from the mid-1960s into the 2000s) to raise money for kids suffering from muscular dystrophy, who came to be known as "Jerry's kids"—only Jerry's kids would be Garcia's and not Jerry Lewis's. All the details would be vague, but the entire Halloween broadcast was framed as a "Jerry's Kids" telethon, an obviously provocative premise, arguably in very poor taste. But that is my point: We all did it anyway, and the comic possibilities were endless.

We pretended that the right middle finger Garcia had lost in an accident when he was a kid had been kept on ice all these years, and it would be offered as a prize for the largest donation to our live Jerry's Kids Halloween telethon. I was there when Garcia heard about this idea, and the film production that it would require: He'd show the finger, in a cotton-lined wooden box, to Al, using one of his own functioning fingers, which he'd wiggle a bit, and then later the finger would escape the box and be seen running around to the ominous sounds of the theme from *Jaws*, and it would have to be captured. He just loved it, went with it, acted his part for it. I would think that the average or typical musical genius making big bucks might shy away from spotlighting a physical deformity that resulted from a traumatic family accident for the sake of what some hired creatives thought would get some laughs, but not Garcia.

Thus far in my early showbiz career, I had never seen such a willingness to go with wild and crazy stuff just to see what happens, but also never since, after my work with Garcia and the Dead ended in the 1990s. The methodology of Grateful Dead, if you could call it that—it might be better understood as an *anti*-methodology that could either end in chaos or stunning creative progress—was clearly rooted in the early and mid '60s psychedelic evolution and the Acid Tests that were its first flowering.

My experience working with Garcia in 1980 and the years following changed me profoundly. It opened me up to possible ways of doing things, of working in film, television, the entertainment business: how to laugh in the face of pressure and adversity, having faith and belief in ourselves to achieve our goals, not betting against ourselves (for example by saying "we can't do that, that's overreaching, so it's better not to try, since we could fail"). I was in many creative planning or production meetings with Garcia, and when he sensed some "unevolved thinking," he'd lean forward and say, "Hey, wait. We *have* what we need." He meant we have the technological tools, we have the desire and the will, *and* we have creative thinking. If we can't see the way to a particular goal right now, we just have to figure out a different route. The key is to not give in to our insecurities or fear of failure. He seemed to think of this view as self-evident, axiomatic. Like, "How do you think we humans got to this point?"

Do it or don't do it, but if you decide to do it, then start from the premise that we are all working together toward a common goal, everyone has a right to their voice and fair treatment, park your ego and your weird sensitivities at the door, learn how to give up your fears and anxieties, and learn how to embrace the goal of *having a good time* as at least as important as creating "a professional product," or coming in on time and on budget. And if you treat people right, and everyone buys in to the premise that we are all working together, fear and anxiety fade away, and the positive joy of creating something can grow and grow, and we all end up doing much more and much better than we previously knew we could, and *that* experience, that knowledge, that the enjoyment of what we're doing as a first and primary goal is not just a desired side effect, but it's also one of the best guarantors of a positive outcome, a great show, a great film, a great broadcast, can be life-changing. And also, you will find that as the project moves forward, you will attract amazing positive input from new people, formerly strangers, who will help you along the way. And if it doesn't work out as well as we hoped, well, there's always tomorrow—plus, we had a good time!

I adapted my approach to producing and directing for the rest of my working life from what I learned from Garcia and working with the Dead and found that it helped me tremendously. Film production can be a stressful, tense environment. There's a lot of money on the line, no one knows if the project will be a hit or a flop, and there are dozens or hundreds of people involved, most of whom don't know each other and haven't worked together before. A lot of interpersonal friction is possible, head butting (especially among the males of the species), power games, on and on. You've got the studio or the money people or the clients over here, and the writers and actors over there, and the crew, the people who actually make the film, lighting, camera, production design, costume, hair and makeup, special effects, picture and sound editors, composers; it's just amazingly complex. As filmmaker Jean Cocteau once put it, "A great film is an accident." Most of what we work on turns out to be either not very good or not profitable. Just the way it is (except for the work of Stanley Kubrick, and arguably, the Coen brothers, Bergman, Buñuel, Kurosawa, Antonioni, and a few others).

I learned the concepts of deflecting negative thinking or prophetic fear, letting go of anxiety about what could go wrong, floating in some sense with everything that's going on in any large production, having faith that the thing we're working on will manifest itself, with all of our participation. And if we're lucky, it will happen at that moment when we are going live into a lot of homes, or onto film or videotape. The idea that the thing will manifest *itself,* rather than be forged out of the intent or force of will of a director or an entire production team, was a revelation to me, but it resonated strongly with my own spiritual development, which in turn had been greatly shaped by my experience with the Halloween pay-per-view event and the making of *Dead Ahead.*

By 1980, the time of our Radio City broadcast, the technology had evolved to the point that live electronic distribution into theaters was theoretically possible, and Garcia led the way, leaving films shown in theaters in the past.

That pay-per-view event and subsequent home video *Dead Ahead* pointed the way, for Garcia. The Dead were making nice money right up front and playing live to their fans, and then making more money from the back end, the release to home video. They were doing what they'd always done, playing live concerts, only now two new revenue streams had been added at virtually no cost to the band, simultaneously growing their audience and promoting their ability to bond together in the future, toward any goal of their choosing.

There was a wild party at the hotel where everyone was staying following the Halloween broadcast. It was a huge suite, two bathrooms, a mountain of food and booze set out on a big, long table. A lot of the production crew were there. Weir put in some time, which meant an accompanying entourage of beautiful young women. Garcia was there. Al Franken and Tom Davis were there, still in their tuxedos as I recall, now disheveled, but clearly elated because the show went so well—their live bits and the roll-ins went down great, and their introducing the Dead to the crowd at Radio City remains one of the most electrifying and hilarious moments I've ever experienced.

At some point, well into the proceedings, a bunch of us, maybe a dozen, were seated around the long table, smoking, drinking, and nibbling. Garcia and me were at one end, across from each other, and everyone's in a really good mood. Tom Davis came in and put a hand on Garcia's shoulder and addressed us all ceremoniously: "Great night, good show." He then pulled a business-size envelope out of his inside jacket pocket, pulled an empty plate toward him, and dumped an enormous pile of cocaine onto it. Everyone was stunned, cheering; Garcia giggled. Tom then with a flare stuck two finely cut straws into the pile of blow and moved it carefully, directly in front of Garcia. I had seen a lot of the behind-the-scenes lives of rock stars up to this point in my life, but I gotta say this was something I hadn't seen; I was impressed. That mountain of cocaine, already finely cut and ready for consumption, was maybe several ounces—it was a shitload of blow. I noticed that Al made a hasty exit at that point; it was clear that he didn't always agree with Tom's behavior.

There were lots of oohs and ahhs and laughter at this wonderful ceremonial moment (it was the dawn of the '80's, people). Garcia enjoyed the moment, and after Davis moved the plate in front of him and stuck the straws into the sparkling little mountain, Garcia leaned over it, grinning, looked around at all of us, and placed his elbows on the table surrounding the plate, pulled out a straw, and did a huge hit. Applause all around.

Time passed. It seemed obvious the plate of blow would be passed around the table—that's just standard etiquette—but that was not happening. Instead, the plate remained in front of Garcia, who partook of it occasionally, but not excessively, in no apparent hurry to share the party favor.

I was of course pretty high, booze and weed and friends and coworkers partying, loving the afterglow of a risky and daring plan coming together successfully, but I remember observing Garcia's behavior as somewhat odd. He must have been aware of all these other people present who would love to have a big snort, but . . . was he toying with them? Toying with their obvious desire? Or was he somehow unaware that if he did all of that blow himself he would certainly die, or best-case scenario suffer cardiac arrest and a trip to the ER? I didn't know him that well at that point, but I'm sure he knew what he was doing. I think he wanted to see who had the guts to treat him like a regular person and ask him to share.

A member of the video crew seated next to Garcia finally said to him, "Hey, do you mind if I have some of that?" Garcia just grinned and said, "Sure," and pushed the plate down the table, and that was it. Was it performative? Was he conducting a private social science experiment to see who would break the wall of pretense and *ask* him to share? And if no one would make that move, was it really incumbent on *him* to offer to share? I know it sounds somewhat far-fetched, but from my experience with Grateful Dead, if this scene had been set within the confines of the Dead family, others would have swarmed him immediately after his ceremonial first snort and shoved him aside to get their own hits, and everyone would be laughing. But this setting was not just Dead family members exclusively, and many of the broadcast and video-production crew were unknown to him by name—he'd gotten used to everyone because we were all around him onstage during production. Maybe he was trying to break down some kind of barrier . . .

I remember coming to at dawn the next morning. I was sprawled on a couch and most everyone had gone. I opened my eyes to the half-light, still half asleep, or more accurately, semiconscious, and I could vaguely make out these two gorgeous young women standing over me, looking down, having a smoke, and quietly chatting, wondering what to do with me in my helpless state. They were wide awake, taking care of business, and they helped me to my feet and guided me to my room.

Above: Len and Jerry at the San Francisco news conference and press premiere of So Far, *September 1987. Photo courtesy ©Susana Millman.*
Center: Jerry, Len, Bobby, and Clive Davis at the NYC news conference and press premiere of So Far, *September 1987. Photo courtesy ©Susana Millman.*
Below: Jerry and Len at the NYC news conference and press premiere of So Far, *September 1987. Photo courtesy ©Susana Millman.*

Above: Jerry, Len, Allison Sullivan, and Bobby, with foot on tiger, celebrating the wrapping of filming for official music video of "Hell in a Bucket," August 1987. Photo courtesy ©John Werner.
Below: Jerry and Bobby offering The Duck a drink, on the set of official music video for "Hell in a Bucket," August 1987. Photo courtesy ©Susana Millman.

Above: Production still from official music video for "Hell in a Bucket," Brent Mydland at piano, Phil Lesh with ringmaster hat, and Duck. Photo courtesy ©John Werner.
Below: Len directing cast of Grateful Dead family members and office staff for the music video of "Hell in a Bucket," August 1987. Photo courtesy ©John Werner.

Above: Len directing Mickey Hart, Jerry, and Bobby on the set of official music video for "Throwing Stones," Oakland, October 1987. Photo courtesy ©Jay Blakesberg/Retro Photo Archive.
Below: The band in front of the mural, shooting of official music video for "Throwing Stones," Oakland, October 1987. Photo courtesy ©Jay Blakesberg/Retro Photo Archive.

Above: Len with Jerry on a break, on location for official music video for "Throwing Stones," Oakland, October 1987. Photo courtesy ©Jay Blakesberg/Retro Photo Archive.
Below: Len directing Robby Taylor (stunt double for Bill Kreutzmann), Brent Mydland with daughter Jessica, Jerry, Bobby, and Phil, on set of official music video for "Throwing Stones," Oakland, October 1987. Photo courtesy ©Jay Blakesberg/Retro Photo Archive.

Above: Bob Dylan performing with Grateful Dead at RFK Stadium in Washington, D.C., July 7, 1986. Photo courtesy ©Ebet Roberts.
Below: Carlos Santana and Garcia, Coliseum Arena, Oakland, January 26, 1993. Photo courtesy ©Susana Millman.

Above: Robert Hunter and Jerry in Grateful Dead office, San Rafael, CA, January 31, 1991. Photo courtesy ©Jay Blakesberg/Retro Photo Archive.
Below: Bobby, Bill Graham, and Jerry backstage, January 23, 1988. Photo courtesy ©Jay Blakesberg/Retro Photo Archive.

Above: Len and crew in production truck, PPV Broadcast, Shoreline Amphitheater, Mountainview, CA, June 1989. Photo courtesy ©Susana Millman.
Below: Bobby, Len, and Jerry at the NYC news conference and press premiere of So Far, *September 1987. Photo courtesy ©Susana Millman.*

Gold DVD plaque for the 2005 re-release of Dead Ahead. *Courtesy Len Dell'Amico personal archive.*

Chapter 3

THE ZEN OF JERRY

I was back in Marin County, California, November 1980, following a bit of recovery in Brooklyn, ready to start editing with Garcia the footage we'd just gotten from the Halloween Radio City broadcast for a home video version. I was comfortably ensconced in a nice motel right on Highway 101 in Corte Madera, in the heart of Grateful Dead territory, a mile from their office and studio in San Rafael, ground zero for all things Dead. My motel had a full-time restaurant, a cocktail lounge with a firepit (again, it was the '80s), pretty girls bringing drinks, a swimming pool, and other amenities. All of it very California, much of it new to me.

On my first day, I visited the Dead office to ask Sue Stephens, "When can we get to work?" (meaning me and Garcia on the editing project). She gave me one raised eyebrow, leaned back in her executive chair behind her large executive desk, tapped the ash off her cigarette, and said, "Len, why don't you take a few days to get acclimated, y'know, take it easy, slow down a little bit. Things around here don't move so fast . . . You smoke dope, right?" I said, "Yeah," eager to promote any behaviors that might align me with the subculture of my new clients. Sue tossed a baggie of weed over to me, "Here, this will get you started."

I probably came off as a little lost. Sue said, "Hey, they have hot tubs over at your motel, right?" I nodded. "You ever been in a hot tub?" I said, "No,

I'm from New York." She said, "Well, so you should go back to your place, get high, order some food from the restaurant, and get into that hot tub. You're going to like it."

I was assigned a temporary desk in her office for me to do my work, so I had a ringside seat to Sue's formidable demeanor and reputation within the Dead operation that she'd built in her longtime capacity as Garcia's personal manager. She could drink and do drugs right along with the bad boys, while never losing sight of what her duties and obligations were. While on the job, she was like Edward G. Robinson in the 1944 film *Double Indemnity*, if he had been a beautiful Irish woman in her early thirties with bright blue eyes and long dark, curly hair, smoking cigarettes and rocking in her executive chair while talking on the phone or dealing with the queries and entreaties from her coworkers and other odd members of the Dead scene who seemed to come and go in an endless flow through her office door.

I came to understand over the years that Garcia had her in this position because she was a person of great integrity, 100 percent trustworthy, someone who would never even *think* of taking advantage of her position for personal gain, someone who knew what the rules were regarding her boss and the band, and how to stick to them. I observed many a hapless approach from someone thinking they could handle her or bullshit her to get her to help them in whatever it was they were after, only to be put in their place—as gently as possible, yes, but without a doubt. In the entertainment business, the person who does this for a major player is called a gatekeeper.

But when she tossed me the baggie of weed and advised me to get in the hot tub, I, still very much a newbie to the Dead scene, felt the need to remind her of a few things. So, I said, "Oh. You do know that I'm getting my full fee of $1,000 a week ($3,500 in today's dollars), plus all my expenses, hotel, rental car, and a per diem, as long as I'm here?" She looked at me indulgently, took a drag on her cigarette. "Uh-huh. Just go back to your motel and take a hot tub, Len. We'll let you know when it's the right time."

It took a week or so, during which I worried over whether these people understood how much they were spending on me but were not asking me to do anything, and several after-hours parties in her office that Sue invited me to, where I met other Grateful Dead workers and friends and learned how to party the way they partied, before I finally understood the message: You are in our world now, and we want you to relax, and we'll let you know when we decide that you're relaxed enough.

I remember an after-hours party where the girls of the office, as they sometimes called themselves, asked me to roll a joint and handed me the weed and the papers. I got to work while they returned to their jocular banter, wanting me to demonstrate that I knew how to do it. When I proudly handed them my joint, they stopped conversing, leaned forward to examine it, squinting, perplexed. Then they all broke into uproarious laughter, slapping their thighs, throwing their heads back. Sue took pity on me, "Len, we call that a *pinner* here." I got the message, my pinner might be what we did in New York, but around these parts it was pathetically skinny and light. Everyone reassured me that it was okay; they liked me, it was just funny. Then one of them took over the job and took twenty minutes carefully tamping the pot into the joint, to fashion what I would call a small cigar—heavy, dense, like a German car.

I did my best, as a New Yorker through and through, to adapt. I remember appreciating the incredible fresh air coming across five thousand miles of the Pacific Ocean, as opposed to the air in Brooklyn, which came from New Jersey. I remember noticing that nobody here beeped their horns while driving, which I did at first, just by habit, like everyone in NYC.

I smoked dope, went in the hot tubs—wow, this is great!—did what work I could on my own, such as cataloging footage and assembling notes. I visited Sue in the Grateful Dead office every day, just to politely remind her of my presence, and to remind myself that this was not all an illusion.

One day I was told: You will be meeting with Garcia at his home tomorrow at noon, where it has been decided the editorial work will take place. "Oh boy," I thought, "finally, okay, this will be great!"

I drive up to a ridgeline in San Rafael, to Garcia's place on Hepburn Heights Road. It's a bright and sunny day, perfect temperature. I'm dazzled by the view of Richardson Bay. I park in the modest carport, get out of the car, and notice I'm actually a little nervous. I'm in a business relationship with the Dead, but I also have a personal connection with Garcia after the Radio City event, and now I'm going to spend time working with him in his home. I suck it up, do my usual mantra of just remembering that all the stars I work with are really just people like me (and, if I have to, picture them sitting on the toilet, as each and every one of us must do), and this grounds me.

CHAPTER 3

The house is poised on the top of a ridge. It's kind of hidden in greenery, deceptively larger than it looks at first glance. I follow a short laneway from the carport down toward the front door, a lush garden surrounding the path in front of me. Suddenly a person pops out of the foliage, announcing, "Hi, I'm the gardener!"

I can't make a judgment right away as to whether this person is male or female, but they are dressed in work clothes and appear cheery and eager to befriend. I might be in Grateful Dead's world, but the New Yorker in me is still guarded against embracing anyone too quickly, and having never encountered a gardener before, I say hello as briefly as I can and try to get to the front door. I take a breath and knock strongly on the door, aware that the gardener is hovering in the foliage ten feet away, watching.

I am relieved that the door opens pretty quickly, and I'm greeted by Rock Scully, whom I know as one of the managers of the band, a tall, thin, energetic man, dressed as usual in a florid hippy style, always exuding positive, inclusive vibes. He was the one guy in the Grateful Dead scene at that time who had highly developed, extroverted outreach skills to deal with record biz execs, concert promoters, stoners, fans, journalists, VIPs, and professionals like me. He steers me inside to say hello to Garcia, who is equally welcoming.

It's a nice home, with a big, sunken, wood-paneled living room area where we'll be working, lots of easy chairs and a sofa, with a big TV to look at our footage. There's a large deck off the living room with a spectacular view of the bay.

As small talk, I mention that I just met their gardener on my way in, and Rock and Jerry glance at each other, take a beat, and then say, "We don't have a gardener," and look at me blankly. So, I have to cope, and I hem and haw, thinking, "Okay, so there's a person outside who *thinks* they are the gardener, or these guys just don't know that he or she actually *is* the gardener, and they're not pursuing the subject, so maybe they think I was just hallucinating, which may be a typical occurrence in their world, I don't know. So maybe I should just move on conversationally," which is what I did, but it may have left an unfortunate impression with these two gentlemen that, well, really, maybe I didn't meet a gardener, maybe causing them to wonder why I thought I did, or why I would say that I did . . . I eventually discovered that the gardener was what we would now call a stalker, but at that point in time, Garcia and Scully may not have known of her (she was a she), and I also learned that Garcia had a peculiar way of dealing with these types of fans (remember, *fan* is short for *fanatical*, isn't it?), preferring to treat them kindly and gently rather than call the cops or hire security or otherwise freak out. I would learn more about this trait of his as time went by.

The rest of the top floor of the house on Hepburn Heights includes a dining room, a big kitchen, and two or three bedrooms and one or two bathrooms down a hallway. It is apparent that Rock and his longtime partner, Nicki, share this house with Garcia.

Having brought me into Garcia's sanctum, Rock wishes us well and takes off. Garcia and I move into the sunken living room and settle in. It's quickly clear that he is more interested in conviviality than work, and that's fine with me, so we end up talking about our shared interests and history; we'll get around to looking at the footage eventually. I mention my reaction to being in Marin with time on my hands, my home in Brooklyn, my fear of flying—maybe a dumb thing to bring up, since I will obviously be doing a lot of flying in order to work on this project, but that's who I was back then, not very skilled in presentation—but Garcia is quite interested and leans in. He says he had been afraid to fly, too, but he learned to get over it. He implies, "Would you like my help?" and I say, "Yeah, sure."

So, the work we are supposed to be doing is just put on pause, while he engages me in an extended tutorial and dialogue. He starts by pointing out the obvious factual and statistical data that shows that travel by air is far safer than any other type of transport, by whatever metrics you might choose. Then he says, "Nothing happens when you're cruising at thirty or forty thousand feet, six or eight miles high, because you're completely above almost all weather; there's no stress on the airplane, it's just cruising, and there's no air traffic around you, it's not congested like it is around big city airports, and the air traffic controllers meticulously direct everything, and so what we're really talking about with fear of flying is the ascent and descent, the takeoffs and landings, and the occasional turbulence at cruising altitude."

He goes on, "Y'know that extreme acceleration at takeoff? It makes a lot of noise and vibration, and you can feel the g-forces in your body; it's scary for anybody. Here's why they do it that way: The pilots don't push the gas pedal gradually, like in a car; no, at takeoff they move the throttle from Off to Full On in one move . . . so now the engines are at full output and the plane starts moving down the runway at increasing acceleration, throwing passengers back in their chairs, and frightening many of them. But the pilots do this so they can examine all the avionics, the behavior of the engines and all the systems that feed them, at full blast, over the next minute or two, and be sure that everything is totally optimal before they commit to takeoff, while they still have time, and runway, to abort the takeoff in case something is off.

"To put it another way, they need the engines to be at full blast for at least a minute so that they can read all the gauges, the oil and fuel pressure, and go through a checklist, the engines are all hitting the proper protocols, the jet is roaring down the runway while everything is a big *go*, and then they release the brakes and commit to takeoff."

He continues, "And there are always two pilots up there, and they both have one hand on that single throttle between them, one hand on top of the other, in case one of them has a fatal heart attack during the takeoff, which is the most critical four minutes of the flight, so the other can smoothly take over until they are safe and sound, and everything will be fine. (You'll just have to deal with the dead guy next to you in the cockpit.)"

He's enjoying this and so am I; I'm learning stuff I didn't know. He goes on to talk about the sounds caused by the stowing and deployment of the landing gear and wheels during takeoff and landing, which people find scary; and the sounds of the moving parts of the wing surfaces during ascent and descent, which are loudest if you are seated over the wings; and the choices to make in seating, because if you hate turbulence, seats over the wings are the calmest, but they are also subject to those noises; how the quietest seats are toward the front, and on and on, with sidebar lessons on how jets are actually kept aloft by the force of air rushing up to fill the vacuum created by the curved shape of the wing, the history of aeronautical engineering, and other related topics.

Now you may ask, "Why am I going into such detail about this?" (And believe me, I'm leaving out a lot.) It's because it made a big impression on me. Garcia happily interacted with my little neurosis and took the time to try to help me out, an overt generous act of kindness, something I'd had little experience with before in my short professional life in show business.

That one conversation cured my fear of flying, and I have repeated the tutorial many times over to anyone I know who has told me of their fear of flying (and some of them have reported positive results too). This was a lesson to me about the value of knowledge and rationality, facing up to your fears and dealing with them rather than hiding them, pretending everything is great. Part of the Zen of Jerry.

That is when Garcia and I really got to know one another. And eventually, we did get down to work, installing an ad hoc editing system in his living room at the house on Hepburn Heights, where we could do our work. We'd look at the stuff we'd shot, two whole shows of music, plus all the comedy bits, both the roll-ins from the Warfield and the new bits recorded at the live Halloween show at Radio City, making selections, most critically from all the music the band had performed, for inclusion in the *Dead Ahead* home video released later in 1981.

A typical work session was us making judgments about what was good and what was not so good, pretty much uninterrupted by phone calls or visitors, with me taking voluminous notes; then we'd take a break and get back to what I'd call serious bullshitting.

We quickly identified many shared important influences: We both loved Laurel and Hardy and Buster Keaton, from watching their black-and-white shorts on TV when we were kids, and Abbott and Costello, especially their films *Abbot and Costello Meet Frankenstein* (1948) and *Abbot and Costello Meet the Mummy* (1955). We also loved *The Day the Earth Stood Still* (1951), with the first use of a theremin in a soundtrack and the giant robot, Gort; *Forbidden Planet* (1956) and the monster of the id; *This Island Earth* (1955), with the aliens with very high foreheads and their amazing interocitor, a big triangular video communication device. We got pretty excited remembering how our young minds were influenced by those very B movies. And then there were the movies so truly bad that they were great because they were funny, like *Robot Monster* (1953) and *Plan 9 from Outer Space* (1957).

We discovered we both had a huge love of comic books from the 1950s and '60s, and he named the Donald Duck series as one of his faves, and I chimed in with, "Yeah, and my all-time favorite was the one where Donald lets his Uncle Scrooge take charge of Donald's nephews for an afternoon!" Now, Scrooge McDuck was the fabulously wealthy patriarch of the family, an eccentric character, a bit of a scoundrel, and there were three nephews: Huey, Louie, and Dewey. Scrooge takes the boys to visit his gigantic personal vault where he keeps all his wealth, and they all take great joy slipping and sliding down mountains of gold coins and jewels, and swimming in oceans of hundred-dollar bills, tossing loot in the air and having a great time.

CHAPTER 3

Garcia grinned big, agreeing about how great that comic was, and then he said, "Let me show you something," turned away to stub out his cigarette, and then moved fast, as was his habit, and I had to scramble a bit to tag along. He was heading toward a staircase that led to another floor of the house beneath where we'd been working. I said something like, "Where are we going?" and he cheerfully informed me that Rock and Nicki lived upstairs, in what I had assumed was Garcia's home, and that he lived downstairs in his apartment, where we were headed.

The downstairs had a far smaller footprint than the upstairs. It still had a view of the bay, but compared to the floor above it was kind of cramped, and the upstairs deck cast the downstairs in shadow.

Garcia's hang-out room was very spare. It reminded me of a college dorm room: plain white walls, a TV, stereo, coffee table for drug paraphernalia, ashtrays overflowing with cigarette butts, piles of books and records, a disused kitchenette, dirty dishes. It was a bit shocking to see the disparity between how he lived compared to how his manager above lived. I would come to understand that Garcia genuinely and thoroughly did not give a fuck about luxury or the trappings of money, or any material means by which we humans typically signal our status (with one exception: his BMWs). He was all about experiencing things, as he put it, and not about having things, or maintaining appearances. So, the guy at the very center of this operation that generated huge amounts of money didn't actually care at all about money.

He took me around the place quickly, and we passed by a walk-in closet, door open, and I swear to God, what I saw was this: ten or so standard dark-colored tee shirts on hangers, a half dozen standard long-sleeve plaid flannel shirts on hangers, and a few pairs of pants, also on hangers . . . and that was it. Then he parked me in the living room while he rummaged in a storage area.

He came back with an obviously well-curated collection of comic books, preserved in plastic covers, and showed me an original copy of the very same Scrooge McDuck book we were just talking about, wherein Scrooge entertains his three nephews inside his vast vault of treasures. I was kind of blown away by this, both by the unexpected confluence from our pasts, and by the obvious rigor and care that he applied to tangible objects from the past that he really did care about, in big contrast to his total lack of interest in the physical surroundings that he lived in.

It seemed a little uncanny that he and I would share such similar influences. Looking back from decades later, I must admit that despite how well we were getting along, I had this dim feeling, possibly originating from my mild autism at that time, that maybe he was humoring me, trying to be nice rather than sincere, as a part of handling me. After all, he was universally loved by everyone who had ever met him or worked with him, his intelligence and warmth and creativity were legendary, even in 1981, and so it wasn't a stretch to wonder, "Is our interaction part of his practice of his art and his business, and maybe I should not get carried away with what felt like a burgeoning friendship?" That is, is it possible that he is just very adept at making people like him, by finding common interests?

Sure, I was relaxing into the role, Garcia made that easy. I was naïve back then, but I had a vague understanding that I was being courted for my professional skills. I was also dimly aware that Grateful Dead, the band, but more importantly their complex tribal family business, might possibly have feelings and ideas about my new emerging role within their world.

We settled into a comfortable schedule of work for the next months, me commuting from NYC with my yellow legal pad. We had a pretty cool playback system installed in the living room, great video and audio, and we were mostly uninterrupted. I recall Caroline Adams Garcia, aka Mountain Girl or MG, visiting occasionally, one or both of their daughters in tow, Trixie maybe five years old at the time climbing over the furniture and her father. MG struck me as a very solid, supportive presence in Garcia's life—calm, good-natured, intelligent. They weren't married at that time (that would happen later, at the end of 1981), but they had Annabelle and Trixie together, and they raised Sunshine, who was MG's daughter with Ken Kesey.

Garcia was very consistent about enjoying the work we were doing, repelling any outside input that might get in the way or cause stress about deadlines, and I fell right into that mindset, having been initiated into the Grateful Dead way in the month following the productions at the Warfield and Radio City: "Be here now, live in the moment, pursue the positive feelings, banish doubt, have fun while you can."

We'd take breaks and talk about various things. We lamented Reagan's election on November 4, 1980. He filled me in, with surprising detail, about how bad Reagan's political rise had been for California, and how we needed to be concerned about him becoming president; about Reagan's reactionary and authoritarian responses to the changes many Californians wanted, the students, minorities, and progressives who just wanted a better society for everyone. I was struck by Garcia's knowledge of California and national politics, and how articulate he was; this was not the norm in my life in NYC. The people in the industry, the recording artists and the businesspeople surrounding them that I worked with, were not noticeably interested in politics or the state of the nation . . . their lives were keyed toward working hard, trying to make money, their career, hustling, partying, and doing drugs.

I sometimes muse that the responsible center of the postwar American consensus was lost in the 1980 election. The following decade saw the birth of celebrity culture and the contemporary corporate vision of consumerism, the dominance of *People* magazine, *Lifestyles of the Rich and Famous* on TV, and the idea that greed is good, which set the stage for the full-blown, late-stage capitalism that we now live in.

President Carter was of like mind, consistent with all the previous presidents since FDR, a traditional patriotic guy (okay, maybe not Nixon so much), a Navy commander of a nuclear-powered submarine who wore his morality on the outside, proudly. Meanwhile on the other side, Lee Atwater fine-tuned the southern strategy popularized by Nixon (the strategy was basically racism) to move southern states from the Democratic coalition into theirs, and they colluded with the ayatollah in Iran to delay the release of American hostages held there until after the 1980 election, in return for arms that Reagan would give them, or arms that Reagan's people could redirect from their Nicaraguan rebel army to Iran . . . all subsequently revealed illegal behavior. In other words, treason, colluding with a power hostile to the United States to impede our country's official policy and strategy.

All of this was going on in the background while Garcia and me worked and hung out, in late 1980 and on into early '81. We mourned John Lennon's murder on December 8, 1980, together.

During one of our gabs, the subject of Edgar Allan Poe came up. We got all bubbly when we discovered he was one of both of our favorite writers, and we went down that rabbit hole for a while, discussing his poems and short stories, until we landed on "The Cask of Amontillado," agreeing and grinning and nodding vigorously that this was Poe's best story, or at least our all-time favorite. At that moment, I felt a faint reminder of my doubt—do we really have these common touchstones, or is he just more of a master people person?

I was suddenly swept away by the moment and began quoting from the last paragraph of the story, loudly proclaiming, "Montresor! For the love of God!" And Garcia immediately chimed in: "Yes! For the love God!" we shouted together, and then collapsed in laughter, and in that moment I let go of all my neurotic inhibitions surrounding my relationship with him. He was as real and authentic and honest as anyone I'd ever met, and I never doubted his motives or methods ever again.

It was during those work-break gab sessions that we really began to bond, perhaps facilitated by our mutual opening up about the dark things going on in our country. We talked about movies a lot. He already knew that Michelangelo Antonioni's film *Zabriskie Point* (1970), featuring Grateful Dead music and also Garcia's own original commissioned solo acoustic music, was a huge influence on me, because I had used his acoustic solo in my NYU student film *Wharf Rat* (1973), which I'd told him about.

The more time I spent working with him, the more I liked him; he always firmly and quietly rejected any sense of urgency or fear of deadlines or fear of failure, because obviously your best hope of doing something original and good creatively is if you do not fear failure at all, but rather embrace it as the necessary cost of pursuing the better. More . . . do more. More is better . . . better to try and fail than not to try . . . fail better (as Samuel Beckett put it). Don't give up, don't look back . . . don't let a big clam (musician lingo for a mistake) in the intro to a song hobble the rest of the song. The audience is there to support you; you can't let them down. Plus, there's always editing, if you're recording everything.

We finished the editing and mix-down for the home video *Dead Ahead* by mid-'81, and the same for *Live Dead!* for Showtime by early '82. With that, my commuting between New York and Marin came to an end and I would resume my other, regular life.

During our last conversation before I flew back to NYC, I got a little sentimental with Garcia, like, "Garsh, it's been a lot of fun working with you." (I had no notion that we'd be working together again in the future.) He grinned and nodded and laughed, "Yeah, we try to have a good time around here." I said something like, "I'm gonna miss Marin, I've kinda fallen in love with the clean air and sunshine and the birds and the deer, the hillsides dotted with the lights of houses, kind of like the Shire where the Hobbits live . . ." He slapped me on the back as he said goodbye, "Well, who knows, maybe you'll end up living here someday!"

Chapter 4

THE CABOOSE

I had to get up earlier than I usually like on Friday, August 10, 1984. My girlfriend, Veronica Loza, was already at her parents' house in Jackson, down on the Jersey Shore, maybe a two-hour drive from our apartment in Brooklyn, where we would be celebrating her birthday later. But I had to wedge in a business meeting—or was it personal?—in eastern Pennsylvania, in the opposite direction, before I could head south for the family get-together. Veronica and I had met ten years earlier, at NYU Film School, working together as a team of film editors, began cohabiting shortly thereafter, and joined forces again in John Scher's start-up video operation at the Capitol Theatre in Passaic, New Jersey, me as a director and her as a camera operator and editor.

I hastily made breakfast, drank some coffee, fed and said goodbye to the two cats, then hit the street and found my ten-year-old Audi—my first car, and I loved it—and headed to Moosic, near Scranton, Pennsylvania, where the Jerry Garcia Band was playing that night.

But I wasn't going to the show (I would be at Veronica's birthday dinner that night). I was going to meet with Garcia at his hotel room before the show. As I was driving, I tried to resolve the tangled thoughts in my head, my recent experience, and the gossip I was hearing, which were the motivations behind my asking for a meeting with Garcia.

CHAPTER 4

In all the time we had spent together working and hanging out, talking, and laughing, between 1980 and '82, often for many hours straight, I had not registered any telltale signs of addiction from him: mood swings, trouble keeping appointments, frequent breaks when the addict needs to be alone to feed the beast, not to mention the obvious compulsive substance use, nodding out, excessive sweating, and other things. While I thought it was definitely possible that he might have fallen into something scary in the time since I last saw him, mainlining (injecting substances directly into blood veins using a hypodermic needle) seemed highly unlike him. He had recently turned forty-one, so not a kid in his twenties going crazy over a new substance du jour. He was an old hand at this; he understood how to walk the line. I knew that from my own sixteen years of experience with a wide variety of substances, and the troubles they could cause if you didn't exercise good judgment, and I'd been eight years in show business, film, television, mostly rock 'n' roll, with plenty of close-up experience with the often-bizarre behavior of some very successful performers.

In early 1984, I heard the gossip that Garcia was in serious trouble with drugs, but it didn't match up with the person I knew, or thought I knew. I have always tried not to make judgments about other people, both in my personal life and business life, especially the talent, the people all of us behind the camera depended on for our work, our careers, our income, regarding their personal affairs, their love lives, their substance use, and so on. My job was to just hone in on their work, their music, and try to do the best I could to embody it in the new visual media.

Sometime in early summer of '84, I went to West Orange, New Jersey, to meet with John Scher at his office. I'd been working for him for ten years as a freelance camera operator and director in his pioneering video-reinforcement team, putting images on big screens for people in the cheap seats. It was at his Capitol Theatre in Passaic, New Jersey, and his venues in Asbury Park and various other gigs that I learned to shoot multicamera rock concerts without rehearsal or even a set list. I had shot hundreds of acts, some of them multiple times, by the time our business relationship came to its end, due to the fact that I was developing a lucrative career, and his sandbox was getting a little small for me (it was Scher who promoted the Dead's historic Radio City stand in 1980 that included their first theatrical pay-per-view event, described in Chapters 1 and 2).

THE CABOOSE

The pretext for the meeting was to make an amicable parting of ways. I owed John a lot. He handed me an opportunity to learn my skills, but possibly I was still a bit too autistic at that time to express it. In truth, I was there to learn what he might know about Garcia's condition, given that his company routinely promoted Grateful Dead and the Jerry Garcia Band in the eastern half of the United States, and his people had a lot of day-to-day contact with the Garcia camp.

John and I had an at times tense but mostly civil chat about our shared history. To wrap up the meeting, I casually mentioned Garcia. John sincerely cared about the Dead and Garcia, and I could see he was pained by what he saw as the situation. The thing is, a lot of people in the business imagine they are closer on a personal level to the talent than they actually are. There's a perceived sexiness in our current culture that attaches to you if others believe that you know, or know something about, what we now call a celebrity, what used to be called stars, and before that actors, singers, musicians, writers, playwrights, and so on. The talent understands the dynamic and uses it to help them in their negotiating positions with the nontalent, the suits, 1980s and '90s lingo for the PR people, the press, the agents, producers, promoters, lawyers, and so on. So, you end up with people in the business who believe they know everything but have no actual idea what is going on in an artist's work and life. Here's how the conversation went:

Me (offhandedly): So, what are you hearing about Garcia?
John: Ah . . . it sucks. He's all fucked up.
(Pause)
Me: What do you mean?
John: He's using again.
(Pause)
Me: Uh, using what?
John (a bit perturbed): Smack! You know, heroin!
(Pause, so John can calm down)
Me: Wow . . . How . . . is he . . . doing it? What have you heard?
(Pause)
John: Ah, he's shooting it . . . (shakes his head in despair)
Me: Oh, that's not good . . . How is his health; is this life-threatening?
John (exasperated): Ah, who the fuck knows.

CHAPTER 4

Me: But he's out there playing, right?
John (calming down): Yeah . . .

I stewed on what I had learned from my meeting with Scher and stayed in touch with Sue Stephens at the Dead office, but by July '84 I hadn't seen or talked to Garcia in person in more than a year. By then I knew, in my bones, that I had to go see him and talk to him and find out for myself what was going on with him.

Back in our Brooklyn apartment while taking a bath, I had an epiphany. There was only one way to interpret what I was feeling. I loved the guy, and for me to just turn away and proceed with my life as if I hadn't heard the many rumors that I had in fact heard was cowardly. Probably it was more convenient for me to not get involved, but it just gnawed at me. Despite what Scher had said, I knew for a fact Garcia was not shooting smack, because Garcia and I had talked in depth about our mutual fear of needles, plus he invariably performed in a tee shirt (which most intravenous drug users would not do, because their arms are where they put the needles, and the tracks would show). Garcia did not strike me as the kind of person who cleverly figures out where to make injections that were always undetectable; he was one of the least self-conscious people I have ever known, and completely disinterested in his appearance or what other people thought of it.

I asked Sue if she could arrange a meeting with him, and she came up with August 10 at a Jerry Garcia Band show in Pennsylvania, where she told him I wanted to talk to him about possible projects. The Jerry Garcia Band was playing one show only at Rocky Glen Park that night, in Moosic, Pennsylvania. We would meet in his hotel room in the early afternoon.

I arrived at the hotel in the early afternoon, tried to banish all the stuff swirling in my mind, and resolved to do what I always try to do: get in the moment and stay there. I was there to find out what was really going on with my friend.

Garcia's hotel turned out to be a strange concept motel, a collection of train cars and cabooses repurposed as an amusing place for tourists and travelers—especially those with a love for locomotives, I guess—to spend the night. If Garcia had a love of trains, I'd never heard about it. It was disorienting for me, trying to find the right caboose in this weird fantasy environment, but eventually I did. I climbed up on the little rear platform that people in cabooses might hang out on, listening to the sound of the engines and the clickety-clack of the tracks as they gaze out at the receding countryside, which was now just a silent, still picture of a parking lot on a blindingly sunny day.

Garcia opened the door energetically and invited me in with a big smile and a hearty greeting, typical of him, which I did my best to reciprocate, given my smaller personality compared to his, and my secret knowledge of my mission. Though I was very aware of my mission, I really had no idea of what I might say or how I might proceed.

He was in a good mood, apparently happy that someone would want to visit with him here in the middle of nowhere. He seemed open to whatever I was there to present.

Once he closed the door and we did the usual chitchat and sat down, I noticed that his room was almost entirely dark, every window covered, with a couple of light bulbs the only source of light. The room was, y'know, the interior of an old caboose: eight feet wide, light fixtures with elaborate shades sticking out, a weird, curved ceiling, heavy red cloth and pillows all around—kind of a Victorian horror movie vibe.

We smoked a little weed. It felt like a nighttime meeting pretty quickly. He may have gotten in very late the night before, and this might still *be* that night for him, or it could be the next morning for him. Life on the road is an unending series of disjointed, disconcerting changes in weather, time, hunger, eating, and accommodations.

I remember thinking, "What the hell am I doing here? Did I get him out of bed for a meeting . . . about what? Why is he in a caboose in Bumfuck, Pennsylvania, when he's a major part of one of the top grossing bands in America?" About this last question, I would later form a conclusion that he loved to play for an audience above all else, and that drove him to tour and play basically all the time. And I also came to understand that despite his key role in the Grateful Dead juggernaut, he refused to leverage that into a larger share of the income from the massive group operation. He may have thought of himself as only a cog in that machine, but given his relative fame and his outsize role in Grateful Dead, that stance left him earning far less than an onlooker might have guessed.

So, I launched into an idea that I'd improvised while looking for his caboose: Maybe we could produce and sell a live concert video of the Jerry Garcia Band, with a number of guest artists joining them. He was receptive to the idea, even a little excited, and we moved on to discussing JGB's repertoire and which guest players might match up with it, such as Los Lobos, Dylan, Santana, and Willie Nelson.

The conversation went back and forth for a while, and then the moment of truth: He produced what we used to call in those days the works; that is, the tools and paraphernalia associated with whatever ritual substance use you were into at the time. He did this without any sense of self-consciousness. Something that was never public between us suddenly was, and that has made me wonder, decades later, if in fact he *did* have an inkling about why I was there, talk about future projects aside, and that he had already decided to let me in and be honest with me.

While we chatted he nonchalantly unfolded a heavy-duty chunk of tinfoil about the size of an open book, then put a fairly stable blob of something black maybe a half inch across in the middle of the tinfoil, then produced a short metallic-silver pipe, like a straw, then lit a Bic lighter. He held the flame beneath the tinfoil, the foil in one hand, the lighter in the other, and the heat turned the black blob into a liquid. He put the pipe into his mouth, holding it with his teeth, and then returned the lighter to heating the blob, and when the blob produced smoke, he leaned over and put the pipe close to the smoke and inhaled it. After a moment, he seemed to be done.

I was learning fast what I wanted to know. You might think this moment would be awkward, but it wasn't. The two of us were able to relax and be very honest with each other, maybe under the influence of the weed, or our shared work experience, or maybe because we were oddly alike in certain ways. Or maybe he knew why I was there and was leading me through it.

I could have deferentially ignored what he was doing, but that would have denied my purpose in being there. So, I said, "What is that?" pointing at the black blob on the tinfoil. Cheery and reflexively honest as always, he said, "Well, it's a thing called Persian smoking powder. It came over to our scene, the San Francisco Bay Area, when the shah of Iran was on the run from the revolution over there, and a big chunk of the rich ruling elite class were moving to the US, and some of them liked Tiburon, and they brought this smoking powder with them." I nodded. Somewhere deep inside I knew it was a crucial moment. Would his explanation that it's "Persian smoking powder" be enough for me? A force within me demanded that I ask the obvious question: "What's in it?" He replied, matter-of-factly, meeting my honest question head-on with an honest answer, "It's a combination of something like smokable morphine and freebase cocaine," and then went back to work for another hit, assuming, correctly, that I would understand what he was talking about even if I'd never heard of it before.

For the curious, or anyone new to this subject, the natural (as opposed to synthetic) opiates are opium, derived from the poppy plant flower, and morphine and heroin, which can be derived from opium by a process of distillation (as higher-proof alcohols are derived from lower-proof alcohols). Morphine is stronger per unit mass than opium, and heroin is stronger than morphine, and all of these substances are commonly known as downers, and scientifically known as central nervous system (CNS) depressants. On the other hand, the coca plant is commonly used throughout Central and South America, especially by Indigenous people, as a medicinal stimulant. The leaves of the plant are chewed or used to make tea, which helps the people at high altitudes in the Andes Mountains live with low levels of oxygen and work under cold conditions, sometimes lacking enough food or water. Cocaine is derived from the coca plant, is much stronger per unit mass than ingesting just the leaves, and is typically inhaled—snorted intranasally—by people looking for a stronger, more sudden, stimulating high than they can get from drinking the tea or chewing the leaves of the plant itself. It's considered very entertaining by a lot of Americans and other wealthy people throughout the Western world. It is, of course, much more addictive than drinking the tea or chewing the leaves. Freebase cocaine is a further distillation of cocaine, and it has the additional quality that it can be activated by heat and then inhaled directly into the lungs, bypassing the slower barrier of the nasal tissue, and delivering a hammer blow higher than snortable cocaine. Crack is a variant form of freebase cocaine and played the lead role in the war on drugs of the '80s and '90s, a classic example of race-based political theater creating fear and insecurity within the dominant white population.

I'm sitting there in this dark caboose while he's taking another hit of this Persian smoking powder, and I'm thinking, "It's a combo of morphine in a smokable form, not much different from heroin, and a smokable powerful form of cocaine." It hits me, he's chasing the dragon, also known as speed-balling, slang from the 1980s for combining a powerful upper and a powerful downer, which needless to say sends an enormous mixed message to the brain and central nervous system, and in turn to the heart. It's what famously killed John Belushi at the Chateau Marmont in LA in 1982.

I'm kind of reeling inside from this, but good at hiding it. And then I think, "He could die at any moment, doing this. This is much worse than just being a heroin addict. He could just die while I'm sitting here." The pause in conversation grows. His silver pipe reflects a rainbow of colors from its sinewy twisted surface, like a vine.

I say, "That's a beautiful pipe." He turns it in his hand, admiring it, "Yes, I made it myself, out of tinfoil."

I feel myself beginning to panic. I'm still pretty naïve about a lot of stuff, so I think maybe I should try to calm down; after all, he seems pretty okay, behaving normally. In fact, in all the time I spent with him, all the times I'd seen him consume large quantities of controlled substances, and also alcohol and cigarettes, sometimes sharing with him, I never once noticed any change in his behavior; sometimes I wondered how this could be. Was it just a lot of experience, or a large tolerance, or some very hard core of mind or character that he possessed?

He puts the tinfoil down and turns to me, and with classic Garcia generosity and inclusiveness, offers me the pipe: "You want some?"

That was when it all came together for me. I was suddenly in the terrifying now, the inescapable present. I could feel the hair on the back of my neck standing up, the total fear that he was toying with death, and I recoiled involuntarily: "Uh, no, no, that's okay, I'm good, I've got somewhere to go after here. I don't think that's for me." I struggled to appear normal, unflappable. He smiled graciously and put the works down and busied himself putting it all away. It occurred to me that a lot of people in his circle might have routinely taken him up on his offer, and there might be lots of other people, what you might call hangers-on, who would have eagerly shared this high with him, since it was after all on him, at his expense, which I'm sure was considerable.

In that moment I decided, in my nerdlike reflexive way, that my best move here would be to bring out my own works and join him in a substance ritual using my own stuff. I had a small glass vial of cocaine, with a little cork stuck in the top, and a single-blade safety razor. I asked for a hard surface, and he handed me a CD or something, and I tapped out some blow onto the CD and started chopping it up with my little razor. He observed, somewhat bemused, and I became uncomfortable. I asked, "Would you like some of this?" He said,

"No, no . . ." I kept chopping; it was a pretty laborious method for making a very fluffy, snortable powder out of a chunky crystalline substance. Finally, he said, "Let me show you something." He asked me for a credit card, took the CD with the blow on it from me, and expertly proceeded to crush it under the pressure of the edge of the credit card, with no errant pieces of crystal popping away to be lost in the carpet, very fast and efficient. And then, proud of his work—or his abilities as a substance-use teacher—he handed it all back to me with a big smile. It wasn't exactly, "It is better to teach a man to fish than to give him a fish to eat," but in the substance-drenched show business of the 1980s, it was pretty good.

I felt a sudden embarrassment once again at my naïveté. As an afterthought, he added, "So you don't need to carry a blade, and you might want to consider not carrying a straw or a little bottle—you can replace the bottle with a paper bindle." He offered to show me how to make one, but I told him I knew how—a lie—and he went on, "So this way you have no evidence on you, and you can swallow the bindle if you have to." I made some comments about dollar bills, and he said something about always having a little pad of Post-its on you or nearby, for use as snorters.

I instantly knew I had nothing to say to him in the way of advice or warning, or anything like that, regarding his just-revealed habit of chasing the dragon. I always knew, from the moment we met to the end of his life, that there was nothing that anyone could say to him about the current research or the known medical risks, or his own behavior, that he wasn't already aware of. He had a voracious and voluminous mind, constantly reading and talking with eggheads and other big minds, and over time built up a huge font of wisdom. I've come to believe that a lot of us who are relatively healthy get some relief from our worrying about our less fortunate loved ones and friends by giving them a stream of advice, most of which we've picked up from mass media and self-help books, most of it con jobs propounded by wealth seekers—y'know, snake-oil salesmen—instead of just investing more of our time in being physically present with them, to better understand them, to experience what their lives are really like compared to our own, to provide companionship.

We said our goodbyes and agreed to continue a discussion about the JGB project, and I exited the caboose back onto that little caboose porch, blinded by the sudden bright sunlight. I managed to find my Audi and jumped in and sped off to Jackson, New Jersey, for Veronica's birthday dinner. I vaguely remember being discombobulated during the drive. Looking back, I'm like, of course; I'd just gotten the truth that I'd been looking for about my friend. Oh, and I'd also committed to opening a new file with him to produce a home video, *and* I had to slow down and acclimate to a birthday dinner with my girlfriend and her folks.

I found myself thinking in terms of helping this accomplished musician and rock star, eight years older than me, more intelligent than me, and vastly wiser. Seriously, I was going to help him? The concept seemed like a juvenile fantasy . . . and yet, whenever I put my urges, my improvisational ways of dealing with his situation, into practice, he seemed to get better, he seemed to appreciate it, understand it. It might have been as simple as two artists in adjacent fields (music and film) finding each other, relating, and then working together to help themselves move into the future.

It came down to this: He knew what he was doing, and the question for me was, did I know what I was doing?

I stopped at some town on the way to look for a birthday present for Veronica. I don't remember what I ultimately selected, maybe a stuffed animal. I hope it was appropriate and kind; I think it was. The thing I most recall is that I had a full-on panic attack in the store while paying for the present. I had to struggle to get a grip on myself while I staggered out of the store and back to my car. I have only had two other such events in my life, and none in the last four decades. I got hold of myself in the car, got some water and food, and then drove to Jackson.

Chapter 5

SO FAR, PART ONE

Shortly after my meeting with Garcia in the caboose, he had Sue Stephens send me a set of board tapes, audiocassettes made by the concert mixing crew, of the band's recent set of shows from the Greek Theatre in Berkeley, California. I interpreted this overture from Garcia as an invitation to play; that is, our meeting in Moosic wasn't just hot air—he was interested in doing something. And when I listened to those board tapes I heard the Weir-Barlow song "Throwing Stones" for the first time and found it . . . intriguing, to say the least. Sue and I set up a new meeting with Garcia close to NYC while he was on the road back east.

We met in his hotel room on October 9, 1984, my birthday, in Worcester, Massachusetts. His Persian smoking powder kit was visible in his open attaché case, but he put it away a little sheepishly, because he now knows that I will not be sharing it—which implies, if not disdain or disapproval, a certain . . . distance. He knows I respect and admire and like him a lot and that I would not judge him, and he also knows I am a professional. That from my perspective he is a potential partner or client, and that I can be totally trusted to be discreet about everything that goes on between us. Those are part of the rules of show business. After ten years of working with rock stars, I'd seen, if not everything, a whole lot. I mean, we're talking late '70s and early '80s here.

CHAPTER 5

We resumed our conversation about the proposed Jerry Garcia Band concert film from a month earlier and reviewed a list of potential guest artists that would enhance it: Dylan, Van Morrison, Willie Nelson, Los Lobos, Santana. We went over the repertoire of the Garcia Band and which songs would suit each possible guest, which new songs we might want to bring in, and so on. It was a good meeting and we agreed to schedule another one shortly, also on the road. I was tasked with floating trial balloons of the concept with a few potential buyers.

At that next meeting he got right to the point: For "political reasons," we were going to have to do another Grateful Dead film project first, before we could do a Jerry Garcia Band solo film project. I was a bit thrown by this, but it was no big deal; if he wanted to lead the Dead through another mass-market broadcast or film release, it was fine by me. I was struck by his use of the phrase "political reasons"; it wasn't the kind of thing I'd ever heard from other artists I'd worked with. It signaled a sophisticated understanding of the complex interplays in the entertainment business, stuff that I associated with managers and agents and record and studio executives, but not with the talent, which is how all those people referred to those who actually created the stuff they were selling. His statement signaled that he was more of the business mind behind Grateful Dead than I had previously known. It was an understanding that would grow over the time that I knew him.

I saw Garcia as being in a unique situation throughout his musical career, which became more and more problematic for him as Grateful Dead grew in popularity and ticket sales. As a solo artist, participating in numerous side bands, producing, and contributing to other artists' work, and with many other side projects going on (film and television scoring offers, his artwork), he could reliably earn a good living outside of Grateful Dead, but the other members of the band were less well positioned to do that, Bob Weir being a bit of an exception. Garcia had to constantly weigh his devotion to Grateful Dead and his perceived position as the golden goose against all the other stuff he could, and wanted, to do. He had a political problem more or less all the time. How would he cope with the financial demands of the sprawling Grateful Dead business, family, and tribe that frankly fell more heavily on him than all the others? This tension was a burden on him that, among the other band members and within the entire enterprise, only he felt.

I came to understand over the next ten years that his devotion to Grateful Dead, as a band, as a concept, as a subculture, was absolutely crucial to him. He was there when it was conceived in 1965, he would never consider turning away from it, and he was also totally committed to the idea that Grateful Dead—the band, the guys who founded it and owned it, plus the guys who were added and currently played in it—was a true democracy, everyone with equal say and votes in artistic and business decisions. He did not ever, in my experience, try to throw his weight around.

The other big burden Garcia carried is that the other band members and everyone in the Dead family organization seemed to know that he was the smartest person in the room, meaning the wisest, most knowledgeable, most articulate, and most importantly, most principled person among them, and he also could not escape being aware of this. And yet he absolutely refused on principle to be considered the leader of the band in the eyes of the world, but also in the eyes of the other band members and the entire family business. I was in many band and family meetings over my time with them when a question would be posed from staff or management, and there'd be a silence while everyone waited for what Garcia would say. I could tell that this irked him, but what could he do? He *was* the wisest person. He'd offer an opinion, and everyone would fall in behind it.

In 1984, Garcia invited me to come to San Francisco for Grateful Dead's New Year's show and suggested that I should bring my mate and business partner, Veronica. Garcia was familiar with Veronica from the post-production of *Dead Ahead* and *Live Dead!*, which she edited. She and I could then stick around for a while. I'd have a meeting with the full band and management, and could make my proposal for a deal, and hopefully we could reach an agreement.

Veronica and I got the royal treatment, which I admit was a little mystifying to me. We were greeted at the gate at SFO by a black-suited driver holding a sign with our names on it, whisked away in a white Rolls-Royce limo, and installed in a motel just blocks from the Dead office at the corner of Fifth Avenue and Lincoln in San Rafael. The New Year's shows were a lot of fun; it had been maybe two years since I'd been in Marin, so I got reexposed to my friends in the Grateful Dead scene: Sue Stephens and her friend Annette Flowers, who ran the royalty distribution part of the band's publishing operation, Ice Nine, and other people. Then in the new year, 1985, Veronica went back to New York, and I had my meeting with the band.

So, I show up at the Dead office right on time on the appointed day in the first week of January to pitch my proposal to the band for a new Grateful Dead home video. I'm feeling pretty good. I'm comfortable presenting to all six guys because we have a track record and I feel like I've learned their methodology. Hah! What a conceit.

I'm ushered into Grateful Dead CFO Bonnie Parker's corner office, a sunny room with lots of windows, and I find all six guys already there, seemingly waiting for me. I'm impressed; this is a serious meeting. Chitchat, and then I make my pitch: I would be contracted on a nonexclusive basis to produce and direct; I would not be an employee. I would approach financial partners, home video, and cable distributors, such as HBO, and be responsible for raising the money for the production and for the band's up-front fee for the rights they were selling to the money partner. I foresaw no problem in securing financing because of the band's recent track record in attracting viewers and buyers and turning profits. The deal would grant the band sole ownership of the copyright and the master recordings, which would mean the back-end income would be all theirs, for all time. And it would give them artistic approval over the final cut, a hefty up-front fee for their signing, and a generous production budget for all the costs of creating the new product. I would be paid out of the production budget and also receive a percentage of the back-end income (a royalty from future uses), and therefore it would cost them nothing up front. In short, there was no better deal for them than this, although it was only aspirational when I pitched them, but I saw no reason to think they couldn't get it.

All six guys are extremely attentive while I speak. I remember being impressed by their apparent straightness at the time. There's a short pause, and Garcia took a pull on his cigarette. Finally, he exhales some smoke, leans forward, and says, "How about this: Instead of you working independently, you partner with us, and instead of looking for outside financing, we pay for it ourselves, and when we're happy with the finished product we then take it to the market and sell it to the highest bidder or to whomever we have confidence in." I take this in and respond, "And of course you'd have complete artistic and copyright control." Everyone nods, and there's a pause as they await my response. Before that moment, I had been used to a model where the artist would prefer to have no financial risk or exposure at all, but these guys have a different approach; they have the cash on hand, and they understand that if they really want to have complete artistic control, they have to be the banker as well. I think fast . . . I say something like, "Well, I'm DGA [Directors Guild of America], so GDP [Grateful Dead Productions] would have to be a signatory. We'd have to sign a contract." There's some nodding, like, so what? I think to myself, "Holy shit, this is a great deal for me." I'd be getting paid by them instead of having to negotiate my up-front fees from a buyer; I don't have to expend huge energy preselling the project to anyone; and I'm glad to be subject to their artistic approval and method of working, having done it before. I notice the six guys are waiting for a response, and so I say, "Okay, great!" Everyone relaxes and has a moment of chuckles and camaraderie.

There's a moment among them of "Okay, that's done," and maybe they have other things to discuss, but I have to say, "But just a minute here, you guys are the artists, and now you're going to be my client, and it's not a good idea for me to negotiate my terms directly with you. I need to do business with a business representative of yours, to keep business and art separate . . ." Garcia thinks for a moment and says, "Okay, go upstairs, the middle office on the right, and there's a guy there, Danny Rifkin, and make your deal with him." I'm a bit staggered. Okay, no lawyers, no delay, not what I'm used to, but there's nothing about this group that is like the rest of the industry.

Before I get up to go, Bill Kreutzmann, one of the two drummers, a loosey-goosey, regular, friendly kind of guy, demands my attention. He makes direct eye contact with me and says, "Hey—you're going to be working for the six of us." I nod, like I got it. I'm used to working with multiple people in the food chain above me, but he wants a bit more from me. He says, "All six of us," and points around at the other five guys, the clear implication being that on anything important I am going to have to get six sign-offs. I say yes, I understand, and then Garcia chimes in, "That's how it works for us. And also, you are going to discover that there are a lot of people around here who think they are in charge—." A couple of the guys chuckle. "They are going to try to tell you what to do now and again. Don't listen to them; your relationship is with us, and no one else."

I leave the meeting; the door closes behind me. I'm standing in the hallway, thinking about the instruction, "It's the six of us, don't listen to what anybody else tells you," kind of . . . perplexed, and now I'm supposed to go upstairs and talk to Danny Rifkin about our deal.

I enter Danny's office, which is more of a communal workspace with several people working within it, doing management stuff. Danny is on the phone. I give him a wave and he acknowledges me and hangs up presently. I know him slightly. I'd interacted with him over the years when the Dead passed through the Capitol Theatre in Passaic, when I worked with John Scher, but I doubt he knew me much, other than recognizing me. Anyway, we shake hands. He's busy, doesn't offer me a chair, so I get right to it, thinking, "Well, this isn't going to be settled right now. We're going to have to draft an agreement, lawyers, it will take time." But I want to give him the overview while it's fresh in my head.

I run down the bullet points, and he just nods at each deal term. When I pause, he says something like, "Well, all right." I'm kind of stunned, but I press on. I tell him I could go on a retainer of $1,000 per week (about $3,500 in 2024 dollars), starting now, plus all travel and living expenses (housing, car, per diem), which would give Grateful Dead the first right to my time, provided they gave reasonable notice. I imagine that the project might take several weeks to several months to complete, depending on the band's artistic concept, but Grateful Dead have final say on how much it would cost and how long it would take. He thinks for a moment, then stands, offers his hand, and we shake on it, and then he wants to go back to work. I'm like, wow, I can't believe it, but this is how these folks do business, and they were very successful with it. I left feeling humbled and thankful and excited.

Garcia was in charge of all things visual for the band because he loved film, TV, and mass media, and also had an excellent grasp of the technological advances taking place, the possibilities for Grateful Dead, the invention of the future. He had spearheaded *The Grateful Dead Movie* (1977) and the 1980 Halloween event and home video *Dead Ahead,* and so he was my contact with the whole organization. I answered to him, and he represented the band to me.

It became clear in the next few weeks of working with him on our new project that he wanted to flip the whole paradigm of music video production. I learned about his concept for what we were about to embark on, which was much more than just shooting a live concert. It was an idea totally new to me in relation to the current state of mass media and popular music production and distribution. He wanted to make a film by recording the soundtrack first and then creating the accompanying visuals second. That's the way you would make an animated feature film, like Disney's *Fantasia* or today's Pixar films: Record all the music and dialogue and then create the animated visuals to match the dialogue and music. Further, he wanted to record the music of the Dead playing ensemble on a soundstage—essentially live, but without an audience. That wasn't at all how records were being made in the 1980s, when it was the norm to record multiple takes of a song, with different musicians at different times, and then methodically combine all of it into a finished audio product. In Garcia's vision, the Dead would be free to do as many takes of a given song as they wanted to, stopping, and starting, fooling around, because there was no audience. And he wanted to avoid overdubbing, the substitution of pieces of solo performances or vocals for the original live recordings. We would film all of this live recording with a state-of-the-art broadcast-quality, multicamera production, so that in the final edit of the finished film we could always choose to use either the actual real-time visuals of the band's performance, confident that they would be of the highest technical and artistic quality, or we could instead use what we called cutaway visuals, so we could substitute all kinds of imagery—special effects, animation, stock footage, you name it—for the visuals of the band playing the music of the soundtrack. The band playing the soundtrack on the soundstage would become just one option among many visual choices, which we would develop and create over the next several months.

I remember the conversation that we had that finally culminated in me understanding his concept. There was a moment of silence, and I said, "Jeez, I'm gonna be spending a lot of time here." He laughed and nodded and said, "Yeah, you should get yourself a place here; you're gonna need it." With that, I got a real estate agent and rented a house in San Anselmo, and officially became what was known back then as bicoastal, having a place in New York and a place in California. I was getting used to dealing with a group of people who essentially had unlimited resources and were fully committed to pursuing their creative goals, provided only that "it would be fun."

Garcia's concept was totally original and fascinating to me, and I eagerly started working with him at the Hepburn Heights house. First we assembled a list of target songs to film for the project from the Dead's huge repertoire, now understood to be the filmed music from which to draw the final soundtrack.

Maybe twenty songs would be put in the can, and then we could choose maybe ten or so for the final edit. Then came the tantalizing idea of creating a visual envelope, or possibly a plot-driven story, that could encompass or contain the songs selected for the soundtrack. And even more far-out, compiling a huge wish list of visual imagery from multiple sources that we could call upon spontaneously in an imagined final multitrack picture mix-down. Garcia wanted to replicate the process of mixing a record in the process of making a film! "Oooh, instead of using images of forests for the chorus of, Uncle John's Band, which we have on picture track number 8, let's try using images of mountains, which we have on picture track number 12!" It sounded like a wild idea, but that is what we eventually did.

It would be three and a half years before it was done.

It's easy to forget that Garcia loved to draw and paint and was a gifted visual artist, because he was so known and identified as a great musician, singer-songwriter, and counterculture guru. Starting in 1958, while still a teenager, Garcia spent some time at the California School of Fine Arts to study drawing and painting. This was prior to him joining and leaving the Army in 1960. Shortly thereafter, he survived a terrible car crash that killed one of his friends, and this experience led him to make a choice to pursue music over art.

As long as I knew him, he was constantly doodling on napkins and envelopes, sometimes during meetings, and he'd leave his work behind after the meeting. He also carried pencils and markers and notebooks on the road and maintained his hobby at home with an easel or large sketchbooks always nearby. In the late '80s he discovered airbrushing and experimented with that for a time into the '90s, and he was an early adopter of using computer software to make digital art. Later in life he had solo shows in New York and San Francisco, and published several high-quality books of his work, like *Jerry Garcia: The Collected Artwork* (2005, Insight Editions), a big coffee-table book. He took private art lessons from the artist and teacher Roberta Weir in the East Bay in the early 1990s, and ultimately his artwork was taken seriously, even more so after he passed away, and it continues to this day. Today it's fascinating to look back at his artwork and think about how it connected with his musical career and may have reflected his lived experience in general.

When we started work on *So Far* (the 1987 home video release) in 1985, Garcia made it his job to make sketches and drawings of the many ideas we were tossing around for the visuals that would be in the film that were *not* the band playing the music on a soundstage. We pursued a variety of crazy worlds, and I've included some of those drawings in this book to demonstrate his wild imagination and artistic skill. He made the storyboards that would define the production design of the possible animated portions and created sketches and color impressions of specific props and characters. In the end, though, we decided to abandon a complex and expensive storyline in favor of a simpler concept; we were going to have the band playing the soundtrack as a visual source, and we would cut away to all kinds of imagery and special effects that were less complex and expensive.

Garcia was also a big, big movie buff. When we first got to know each other in 1980, we bonded over conversations about the movies we both knew and loved. My BFA was from New York University, where I first enrolled as an art history major, and then switched to the film program. I had learned a lot about film history and was an avid filmgoer as well as a filmmaker, but I was struck by how much he knew about film and how much he loved it—pretty much more than anyone else I've ever known.

Grateful Dead worked in and around film from early in their career. There were film crews at the Acid Tests, and they appeared in the Richard Lester movie *Petulia* (1968, with George C. Scott, Shirley Knight, Richard Chamberlain, and Julie Christie) playing the house band in a scene shot in a club in San Francisco. Lester was famous for making the lighthearted Beatles movies *A Hard Day's Night* (1964) and *Help!* (1965), but by contrast *Petulia* was an intensely contemporary and serious tale, and it was Garcia who pushed for the band's participation and ultimately made it happen.

Then Garcia worked on Michelangelo Antonioni's film *Zabriskie Point*, released in early 1970, contributing a long and beautiful acoustic guitar instrumental to accompany a surrealistic group love scene shot in Death Valley, once again teaming up with a big-time avant-garde director on a very cutting-edge film. The film's soundtrack was revolutionary, using contemporary music playing on your car radio, including songs by Pink Floyd, the Rolling Stones, the Youngbloods, Patti Page, John Fahey, and a good bit of Grateful Dead's "Dark Star" from their recent album *Live/Dead*.

In one of my early meetings with Garcia, I mentioned to him that *Zabriskie Point* was the film that flipped the switch in my head, helping me decide that filmmaking would be my calling, and I immediately changed my major at

NYU from art history to film. When I told him that my senior thesis film at NYU, a thirty-minute short called *Wharf Rat* (inspired by his and Robert Hunter's song), included his guitar solo from *Zabriskie Point,* he seemed both flattered and slightly mystified. Embarrassed, I blurted out that there was never any income from the film, it was not a commercial product, just in case he might be thinking, "Oh, I don't recall approving any such deal about that . . ." Silly, dorky me, it was obviously much more likely that he was wondering, "What the hell is this guy talking about?"

On January 18, 1985, I got a call from Sue Stephens telling me that Garcia had been busted in his car in Golden Gate Park holding illegal white powders, clueing me in to a crisis that would obviously cause a pause in whatever work plans we had. In the aftermath of the bust, a hangdog-looking picture of Garcia appeared on the front page of a local newspaper. I stopped by the office to chat with Sue a few days later, and she was in her usual high spirits behind her desk, smoking a cigarette, laughing about the vagaries and absurdities of her job and the whole scene. She said, "Get this. Tomorrow I have to take him down to the DMV, because his license was suspended, and his car was unregistered. So, I have to do the driving! That'll be a scene, standing in line. Ha!" I thought for a moment and said, "How could his car be unregistered?" And she chuckled, "I dunno, I think it's cuz someone just gave him the car." Okay . . . a new 7 Series BMW? Costing maybe $160,000 in today's dollars? Someone *gave* it to him?

A day or a week later, the first time I saw Garcia after this event, he was a bit sheepish, but basically unaffected. I tried to sympathize, as a person who was in on his substance habits, trying to help as best I could, given that I knew he already knew all the arguments about health outcomes. We had a relaxed chat about a three-day high-end shoot at the Marin Veterans' Memorial Auditorium in San Rafael in April 1985, starting the production of *So Far,* working from the list of twenty or so songs that Garcia and I had agreed on. The band had never done this before, playing for six cameras and the ultimate multitrack audio, essentially recording live performances with no audience. The first two days were . . . okay, but I have to admit I had my doubts about the concept. We were doing a lot of takes of a particular tune, like Weir and Barlow's song "My Brother Esau," but no particular take seemed to jump out and grab us. We were spending a huge amount of money per day, the band's money, so it was natural to feel some anxiety. On the final day of the shoot,

I wanted to be the first one there, so I arrived at the venue before my call time. As I got out of my car, Garcia pulled in aggressively and parked next to me, his tire hitting the curb at 10:00 a.m., just like me. He clambered out of his Beamer and greeted me, full of vim and vigor, and said to me, "I feel like we're really gonna get it today, I can feel it." He was radiating positive energy, and I was like, *wow, okay!*

On that day we recorded two takes each of an "Uncle John's Band"/ "Playing in the Band" medley and a "Throwing Stones"/"Not Fade Away" medley that were simply awesome, and it was obvious to everyone. Even though we were all supposed to be not there, as film crews are taught to behave, when the band finished the second take of the "Throwing Stones"/"Not Fade Away" medley, the entire crew and everyone else present broke into spontaneous cheering. Because this was the last day of the shoot, the breakdown commenced immediately, all the different crews swarming to get everything out of there. It was the normal chaos, but the people who could have just left right away, like me and the band, instead lingered, floating around in the chaos, because the feelings in the air were so positive, satisfying. I saw band members chatting and laughing with camera operators and grips. Garcia and me just stood next to each other, grinning.

We did another shoot at Marin Veterans' Memorial in November to see if we could get more songs, and we did get a bunch, and some other stuff, like a cool session of the band huddled around the piano searching for the right vocal arrangement for "Tons of Steel." We also did a New Year's Eve broadcast coupled with an FM-radio simulcast, kind of off-the-cuff, on the USA Network, "harvesting" some more potential music, but in the end *So Far* was made up mostly from what we shot on that one day in April. (See Appendix B: Fun Facts About *So Far*, on page 248 for more information.)

Chapter 6

COMA AND RECOVERY

I was called in by the Dead to direct a live segment of their show in Buffalo, New York, a remote feed that would contribute to Willie Nelson and company's second Farm Aid live national telecast on July 4, 1986. When I got the call I was busy working on a concert show for HBO, built around Fats Domino. We had just completed the live shoot in New Orleans and were moving into postproduction, but I saw that I had a break in the schedule, and I could go up to Buffalo.

Buffalo is my hometown, and I've always known how wildly appreciative the Dead fan base is up there. It's a working-class kind of place, like a lot of the strongest markets for the band, cities like Boston, Philadelphia, Chicago, Baltimore, Washington, D.C., and New York City, places with a much larger demand for concert tickets than anywhere in California, including the San Francisco Bay Area.

My mother, Shirley Ellis Dell'Amico, was very musically talented. She read music and played piano, guitar, and recorder, she had a beautiful singing voice, and she was an avid collector of LPs (long-playing phonograph records, now making a comeback) of country blues and urban blues (Lead Belly, Howlin' Wolf, John Lee Hooker, Robert Johnson, Muddy Waters, Willie Dixon, Etta James, Bessie Smith), and also the explosion of folk music in the 1960s—Woody Guthrie, Pete Seeger, Joan Baez, Judy Collins, Bob Dylan.

CHAPTER 6

She turned me on to Dylan when he was an acoustic folk musician, from 1962 to '64, when I was twelve, thirteen. My father, Fred Dell'Amico, also loved music. He favored opera and classical stuff: Brahms, Mahler, Verdi, Puccini. So they were both very open to and accepting of my work filming musicians. My mom especially, I think, understood Grateful Dead.

I floated the idea to Garcia of him joining me and my family at my parents' house in a suburb of Buffalo for a late lunch on the band's day off on July 3. To my surprise, he accepted. I broke the news to my mom gently, as in, "You know, this probably won't happen, because it's rock 'n' roll, but it might, so I just want you to be prepared, and understand that you, and we, should not get bent out of shape about the idea, or go to any great effort to put on a great lunch, cuz it probably won't happen, so we should just remain casual and roll with whatever happens, maybe be ready to make some sandwiches and a salad." I reminded her that Garcia was just a regular person, someone who relished being treated as a regular person, and that he might appreciate her musical interests more than her interest in him.

When the day of the visit came around, I woke up in my ancestral home eighteen years after leaving it. It was like 9:00 a.m. or so, and I came down the stairs in search of coffee. Immediately I was hit by the powerful smells of cooking. My mother was already hard at work preparing stuff for a meal that was set for six or eight hours later. I gathered my wits and gently tried to talk to her about what she was doing, but I eventually realized that it was to no avail. She was on autopilot fixing to put on an incredible spread—and by the way, she could do it, she was a great cook. By early afternoon I got the word that Garcia was not going to make it to the luncheon, and that he wasn't feeling well, something about a tooth problem.

I was not surprised at the cancellation, but I was slightly concerned that he was ill, if in fact he was, and it wasn't just an excuse.

The next day, the Fourth of July, I went and did the shoot at Rich Stadium (known these days as Highmark Stadium) for Farm Aid. The Dead played well. If Garcia was feeling poorly, I couldn't tell. The crowd was ecstatic, with lots of American flags waving. The band played a memorable set, including (always special) "Uncle John's Band," which we shot and recorded on a brand-new high-definition format (analog, not digital—this was well before the digital revolution). The local producer was Richie Namm. (The last I heard of Richie, he was working as a producer and director in Los Angeles in case anyone out there wants to research available archival sources or assets. He might have the master tapes, if anyone does, or may know where they are . . .)

A few days later, in early July, I was in Austin, Texas, working on the new music special for HBO, called *Fats & Friends.* We were doing the final mix-down of the sound for the picture. Once completed, this work would lead to what has always been one of my favorite stages of making a film: marrying the final sound mix to the final picture. In terms of a natal chart, this is the actual birth moment of any film or audiovisual piece of art. I've lost count of the times I have sat back in a dark mixing studio and watched and listened to the first playback from beginning to end of the married final sound and final picture, at top volume, best conceivable audio and video technology all around and in front of you, and thought to myself, "This is fucking awesome, man. How is it that I get to be here?"

Fresh out of film school and cab driving in NYC in the mid-'70s, I started out as an assistant editor and then an editor, and I soon grew to love the editing rooms and recording studios where all the work of the previous months and years on any given film culminated: the postproduction, everything shot, all the sound recorded—it's all there in that editing suite, so the feeling of all things coming together was strong. This is in contrast to the other end of making a film: conception, writing, fundraising, shopping for partners—all of it so amorphous and spread out through space and time. And at that point nothing is real at all; there's just a person or a few people who have an idea, and the idea itself keeps changing, depending on the web of new, or departing, partners. In postproduction, yes there's stress, because now there are very real deadlines, and the expectations of everyone who's at risk on the project, including investors and studios and other people whose reputations are in play. But I love that kind of pressure. You just bear down and do the work, uninterrupted if you're lucky, and have faith in the skills of everyone involved to make a good product.

The *Fats & Friends* project was dreamt up by executive producer Dave McBurnett and commissioned by HBO and starred three of the first four keyboard players inducted into the Rock & Roll Hall of Fame: Ray Charles, Fats Domino, and Jerry Lee Lewis (the fourth was Little Richard, but we couldn't get him), plus Paul Shaffer (of Blues Brothers and David Letterman fame) as musical director. Shaffer recruited a band, including Ron Wood (of Rolling Stones fame), to back up the stars. When *Fats & Friends* hit everyone's TVs a few months later, it was a solid hit for HBO, and my star rose in the firmament as a concert film director. Naturally, I have had a warm feeling in my heart for HBO ever since then. HBO was the gold standard in cable and broadcasting for my entire time in the business, inventing the subscription business model, no commercial interruptions, generous budgets, and treated the creatives really well. It peaked with *The Sopranos,* continued strong through *Game of Thrones*, but now, sadly, is slipping into the twilight of its life, subsumed by its offspring, Max, part of the eternal evolution of the entertainment business.

We were in the studio to analyze the multitrack audio recordings from the live shoot, the first step in mixing them down, listening to the trap kit, musician talk for the drum tracks. There seemed to be a problem, which Shaffer was handling. Technical director Thom Drewke was sitting on a couch during a little break, reading the newspaper. He said, "Hey, Len, do you know anything about this? It says here that Jerry Garcia is in a coma in a hospital in Marin . . . "

Talk about whiplash. I went from a place of total serenity and joy to sudden alarm and fear in an instant. I remember taking the paper from Thom and skimming the piece for myself, and then bolting for the door. We were still pre–cell phone then, so I stepped out to the little sitting area they reserved for the clients, where I could use the phone.

I quickly got through to Sue Stephens in the Grateful Dead office in San Rafael, and she filled me in. Yes, he was in a coma in Marin General. He'd gotten back from the grueling road trip of summer stadium concerts two days before, collapsed at home, and went into the hospital the next day. Diagnosis: diabetic coma. My guts were kind of churning inside, a feeling of dropping, dropping. In between my other work commitments, I went to several shows on the tour, as a fan, and it was great to see the Dead playing well, to huge ecstatic crowds, with Tom Petty and the Heartbreakers accompanying Bob Dylan as a co-headliner act. I mean, wow! Garcia had worked to break from the Persian smoking powder habit all spring and summer, and our work together on the postproduction of *So Far* was going very well—better and better, in fact. I had only great expectations for his health and our work. But now suddenly this! What the fuck?

Sue told me that Carolyn Adams (MG) had flown in the day before and taken charge and suggested that maybe I could check in with her, which

I did. I knew MG from the 1980 to '82 period, when Garcia and I were working on the Halloween broadcast and the *Dead Ahead* edit at the Hepburn Heights house, where she visited with their daughters, Annabelle and Theresa (Trixie). Though they were not married, it was clear to me how important an influence she was on him, for the better. By nature, she was quite formidable, very intelligent, and when I spent time with her and Garcia together, it was obvious why they were drawn to each other. They were both strongly centered people, not much subject to insecurities or neurosis, with a good idea about what is important in life: try not to hurt anybody, be kind, have fun, that sort of thing. I like to think that MG may have trusted me to some degree.

She told me on the phone that the first indications from the doctors were that it didn't look good. He might come out of the coma, or not, and if he did there was a high likelihood of some brain damage from the lack of oxygen after his collapse and before the medics got to him. The idea that he might ever be his old self again, let alone play guitar, could be remote.

I had that visceral, sinking feeling. MG was being very straightforward and honest with me, describing the worst scenario along with better scenarios, which I greatly appreciated.

Paul Shaffer plunked himself down on the couch next to me. He was obviously agitated about something, but he could also tell from my words and demeanor on the phone that something was badly off with me too. I hung up the phone. Shaffer said, "Len, we don't have discreet tracks from the trap, only the live mix-down done during the shoot." How do we do a mix-down of the drums without these tracks? I looked at him through a bit of a fog. Paul was crazy-happy to work with Ray and Fats and Jerry Lee and had done an incredible job on this project.

I might have said something like, "Are you sure? No tracks? Well then I guess we're going to have to use the live mix-down. It's always sounded pretty good to me. The mixer we hired was good, as I recall," like I was far, far away. Paul looked at me, like, what's wrong? I guess he hadn't heard what Drewke had read from the newspaper in the studio. I told him I'd been on the phone with the Grateful Dead office in Marin, that Garcia was in a coma. Shaffer's demeanor changed. He was and is a musician's musician. He knows and has worked with everybody, is universally revered, and he also knew the importance of Garcia in the contemporary music scene and revered him.

CHAPTER 6

Paul went from professionally upset to empathetic on a dime when I told him I would likely be heading back to Marin immediately. "Okay, sure, I get it, man," he said. We'll deal with it here. Do what you have to do." I told him I was confident that between him and the team we were working with, they'd do great, and I'd be back as soon as possible.

As a DGA director, I had an obligation and responsibility to oversee the mix-down and creation of a final master for release, but I could also delegate these rights and duties if all the relevant partners agreed. Paul went back to work in the studio, and I went back to work on the phone to get back to Marin as fast as possible. There was no thought process; I just felt compelled to be there, even though MG and Sue Stephens had warned me no one was allowed into the ICU at the hospital, and there wasn't much anyone could do to help him.

I flew that night from Texas and got in late to my place in Marin. I felt pretty shaky when I got up in the morning and thought about what I was going to do, which was face down my fears and go to the hospital and offer whatever support I could. As far as I knew, Garcia was in a coma and might survive, but probably not recover his former self. My best strategy was not to think about it and just move forward on autopilot.

I already knew not to expect to actually see him. No visitors were allowed, and he was still attached to tubes and stuff. I was directed to a small, hushed seating area near the ICU, and there I found MG and Annabelle, and possibly others, maybe Trixie and Garcia's brother, Tiff. It's a dim memory, because of the moment. I'm deep breathing, trying to be calm, and there was hugging. We sat and commiserated. I do remember that MG was her usual true self: deftly coping, strong in the face of adversity. MG told me she would call me if he came to or there was any other significant change, good or bad. I sucked it up, wished them well, and went back to my house and slept.

A day or two later I got a call from Sue Stephens telling me Garcia had come to. He had emerged from the coma, and MG said I could go over to Marin General.

I was supercharged as I headed to the hospital. Oh my God, this was fantastic; he was conscious, he was back, great news, he was out of danger of the vegetative-state diagnosis. But then I felt the doubt and fear: What if he wasn't who he used to be? The concept of what a loss that would be to me, to his family, and then, somewhat weirdly, what a loss that might be to all of us, to humanity.

I was feeling very roiled when I arrived at the hospital, emotional. I'm normally a very centered kind of guy, preferring calm and equanimity, so when I feel strong emotions, I know it—it's unusual.

For the second time in a few days, I greeted MG and everyone else in a waiting room area, this time outside the private room that Garcia had been transferred to from the ICU. It was a different mood entirely from my last visit: hushed but hopeful, a little excited. Maybe things would work out?

MG told me Jerry was visiting with his older brother, Tiff, at the moment, and suggested we give them some time before I went in. I sat down and settled in. She filled me in that he was awake, fully able to speak, but that it wasn't at all clear yet if he had suffered any brain damage or memory loss, and if so, how much. Time passed. MG checked Garcia's room, then quietly motioned me to go ahead inside. I had a big moment of sucking it up, getting a grip on my feelings, before I went in.

It was dark in the room, to keep sensory stimulation to a minimum, I guess. Garcia was visiting with Tiff; they were close together, Garcia propped up a bit, lying against pillows in a full-on hospital bed, Tiff in a chair pulled up next to him, talking quietly. I found a chair in a corner to sit in, trying to just be still, to respect the moment. I don't think they were aware of me. Presently, I realized that they were reminiscing about old memories of their father, Jose Ramon Garcia, a Spanish immigrant, musician, and bandleader, who drowned in a fishing accident on a family vacation when Garcia was five.

To be honest, I felt like Garcia was not obviously frail. This was not a broken man; he was animated and lively in talking to Tiff, despite the rather grim warnings from the doctors. Then he kind of noticed me there, and I tried to be cheery. He knew who I was. The old grin was still there, and that's pretty much all I needed. I went over and patted him on the shoulder, got close enough so we could smile and nod our heads at each other, and then I went back to my chair in the shadows.

I was thrilled out of my mind, having to control tears, that he was awake and conscious and speaking, and wasn't going to die. He went back to reminiscing with Tiff. A short time later MG came into the room carrying a small acoustic guitar. She approached his bedside and handed it to him, awkwardly, because he didn't seem to know what it was. I felt suddenly anxious, like, "Oh no, what if this ends badly?" But MG is an adventurous person: move forward, try things, be fearless—in this sense just like Garcia. Slowly he took the instrument, trying to figure out how to hold it, looked around at all of us, and after a moment it was clear he didn't know what to do with it or what we expected him to do. But without any sense of fear or disappointment, he handed the guitar back to MG.

MG just accepted the guitar back when he offered it to her, like no big deal. Tiff and I just smiled and kept stiff upper lips, at least that's how I felt. I was *not* going to start crying or any other obvious emotional shit when this man was just coming back to life, clearly unsure about everything going on around him.

MG appeared to have a plan. It seemed like she was controlling the flow of people into his room in order to best manage what might best help him to recover, one or two people at a time, then rest periods, and we were being encouraged to be positive with him. He seemed to have very little memory of the past or who he was or who some of us were, but he was awake, and could talk and smile. She encouraged visitors to try to reminisce with him to help awaken his memory. This is what Tiff was doing with Jerry, talking about their dad, and why MG had placed a guitar in his hands.

I had weirdly mixed feelings as I said my goodbyes. I arrived home feeling drained, fighting off a feeling of despair, and then I was suddenly elated that it looked like he might actually recover, and certainly would not die on us. Also, I was confronted by some weird philosophical questions. How could someone so gifted and important to the well-being of so many people be suddenly struck down by . . . what? An act of God or nature? Substance abuse, which I thought was in remission? Over time I would learn that Garcia had a tooth infection that went untreated (causing him to cancel our lunch date in Buffalo); coupled with extreme heat and dehydration as the tour ended, it led to a diabetic coma.

I went back to work and finished the Fats Domino HBO show, and kept in touch by phone with Sue Stephens and MG. By the time I got back to Marin, Garcia had been moved to a private room in the cardiac care part of the hospital, a lower-key, things-are-improving kind of situation. My third visit to the hospital was a world of difference from the earlier two. MG may have been there (she seemed to manage to be near him around the clock for all this time—at least that was the impression I got), or it may have been Annabelle or Trixie who greeted me and took me to his room.

The room was brightly lit, it was daytime, the window was open to the outside. Garcia was sitting up in his bed, maybe connected by one or two monitoring wires, but otherwise unencumbered. He greeted me by name, grinning, happy to see me, and boy was I happy to see him so much improved. He just seemed to be his same old self, except sitting in a hospital bed: positive, articulate, talkative, witty, humorous, laughing. We had an animated chat about what he had been through. He told me about the nightmarish coma memories, about feeling like insects were crawling through his bloodstream, about what it was like to gradually recover memories and mental powers. I wanted to tell him about what was going on in the outside world, the outpouring of emotion and love in the Grateful Dead community, everyone wishing him to recover and get better. He seemed a little mystified, but he nodded and commented that he did actually feel that he was receiving some kind of a flow of spiritual support while he was in the coma and during his convalescence. I said, "Well, lots of people are praying for you," and he kind of conceded that it was true, but he was also kind of befuddled. I was struck by this and fell into a reverie as we sat in silence for a moment.

In that moment when he mentioned feeling a kind of energetic support coming to him during his coma and convalescence, and I mentioned prayer—a stand-in for the idea of concentrated energetic or spiritual support—he seemed to be slightly staggered at the implication that he might have actually been a recipient of what some would call a supernatural force. It didn't stagger me, because I have never been famous or a gifted artist, or the focus of a large and growing community based on a set of spiritual values, but I myself was praying for his recovery. So, to me, this was not a surprise, but to the person, the actual human being who might be the subject or the recipient of this kind of massive psychic support, it might have been a hard thing to contemplate or accept. Perhaps ultimately humbling.

Over the previous five years, we had talked a bunch of times about theology and Joseph Campbell and religion and spirituality versus Western enlightenment, rationality, and contemporary physics, two long-standing worldviews that seemed to be converging in our own time toward the Eastern take on consciousness and the ultimate nature of reality. But nowhere in all those explorations did I ever get the impression that he was actually religious, at least not in the sense of being a member of a given church or faith, which would include accepting the truth or centrality of a given oral tradition or written text, such as the Bible or Koran. It always felt to me we both assumed we were fundamentally agnostic about religious beliefs. I think we both preferred to see rationality as the best ground to stand on, but we also loved the excitement offered by a wide variety of points of view and belief systems. For instance, the obvious knowledge we had of psychedelic experience, the weirdness of UFOs, or the possibilities offered by any number of fringe subjects, like the work of Terence and Dennis McKenna, David Bohm, and Rupert Sheldrake, or the late-night cable preacher Dr. Gene Scott. And there was the mainstream stuff, like the work of Fritjof Capra (*The Tao of Physics, The Web of Life*), novelist Nikos Kazantzakis, author of *The Last Temptation of Christ,* and Kurt Vonnegut, who wrote *Slaughterhouse-Five* and *The Sirens of Titan* (which Garcia had optioned for a possible film).

Breaking the brief but meaningful silence, I brought up the film project *So Far* we had been working on as a way to get back to regular conversation. He did remember it, getting happy and excited about the possibilities once he got back on his feet. But I was not about to steer this visit into a work or business meeting, so we just basically shot the breeze, small-talked, beaming happy vibes back and forth. I was truly elated to see him this way, and I'm sure it showed, and he was glad to see me too.

I came away greatly relieved, a weight off of my heart, but I still had no idea what the future would hold. Would he recover enough to return to his role at the center of Grateful Dead and its large and complex subculture? The leader of a huge live-concert draw, once again one of the great songwriters and guitarists of all time? And as for our project, *So Far*—would it ever be finished? Who the fuck knew?

In August and September 1986, I was living in Marin as a home base, but also commuting to my home in NYC. Garcia checked out of the hospital and returned to the house on Hepburn Heights, but the people previously sharing the house, Nicki and Rock Scully, were now gone, and MG and their kids were living there, at least part time, reassembling a family that had not been together in a long time.

I visited the Grateful Dead office regularly, staying in close touch with Sue Stephens. She gave me updates and gave me clearance (presumably from MG) to visit Garcia at Hepburn Heights when the time was right. The mood around Deadworld was tense. The office managers, administrators, and secretaries, the employees at the recording studio and the warehouse, where the stage crew hung out, all the people at the merchandise operation, the ticket office—all were on the payroll, and now in limbo. For many of them, their future was suddenly a great unknown. The majority of them seemed to me to be true believers, and at least now they had reason for optimism, but it was tough for them.

I met with the CFO of Grateful Dead Productions, Nancy Mallonee, and told her I wanted to put my retainer fee on hold, pending the outcome of Garcia's recovery and the determination of any further need for my services. She was a bit surprised, but it made sense. I was the only one in the operation who was a freelancer and not an employee, and I had other sources of income that she had no reason to know about. I would go back on the payroll in early 1987, once it became apparent that Garcia was in the middle of an incredible recovery. By then, *So Far* was very much back in production, and the band was making a record that would require music videos and planning a stadium tour that would require video support.

I knew everyone in the scene was being kept at arm's length from visiting Garcia, for the sake of his recovery, and that his old friend Merl Saunders had taken the lead in the effort to try to restore his memory and his musical knowledge and skill. Jerry and Merl were very close musical collaborators, going back to a small San Francisco club, the Matrix, in 1971. They had made three albums together in the 1970s, took a band or two out on the road, and then continued to cross musical paths for many years, producing, among other things, the world-music classic *Blues from the Rainforest* in 1990. I knew Merl only casually from backstage mingling, but he was obviously a very empathic and spiritually evolved person, as well as a gifted musician.

Following Garcia's release from the hospital, I was pretty stoked emotionally for my first visit to the Hepburn Heights house. The last time I'd seen him was in the cardiac care unit at Marin General. From all reports it was clear he was getting better, but my optimism was mixed with fear. The time I'd seen him before that he hadn't recognized what a guitar was, so it was still by no means clear to me how or when his hoped-for recovery would unfold once he was back in his home.

I walked down the familiar garden path that I'd first traveled in 1980 to the Hepburn Heights house. But here I was six years later, after a lot of different experiences with this man and his world. And just like that first visit in 1980, I had no idea what to expect from this visit, only that I was encouraged to visit, and welcome. I felt some pride that I had been judged and found a good prospect for giving a boost of support to Garcia and Merl without running the risk of any drama or negative distraction.

I found Merl sitting at the piano in the sunken living room, and Garcia was at his side, holding an acoustic guitar gingerly, tentatively. Just the two of them, no one else around, sunlight pouring in through the giant windows; it was peaceful, quiet. They took a pause in what they were doing to give me a warm greeting.

We had a happy moment of chitchat, lots of smiles and chuckles, as if nothing were wrong. Positivity is its own reward, straight from the Garcia playbook. I asked if I could hang out until they wanted to take a break from their work, and they happily agreed.

Merl was showing Garcia a chord on the piano, and then helping him finger the same chord on the guitar. When it sunk in that this was what they were doing, I felt momentarily overcome by a wave of emotion, and had to get it under control. Here was this much-beloved and hugely talented musician humbly facing the fact that he had to relearn the most basic facets of his life's work and experience, and here was his best-friend musician there to help him do it. Merl showed no hint of any dismay or fear about the task at hand; he was just being the positive, joyous man he always was.

Part of me, the realistic part, was thinking it didn't look good. Oh my God, if Garcia had to learn chords all over again, how likely was it that he could ever return to his previous, astonishing levels of musical performance? But this thought was quickly washed away by witnessing this act of love on Merl's part, an act of faith that it was possible for Garcia to relearn what he had previously known or be returned to his earlier self. Merl was just going to do whatever he could do to help, ignoring the dismay or the fears he might have about his friend's recovery. He would stay in the moment, conjure joy. And because they were so well attuned to each other, Garcia, for his part, also didn't show any anxiety or stress about what he had lost or how much he would have to recover. True to his character, he showed no indications of self-pity or suffering. He was who he always was, determined to be happy.

Chapter 7

NEW GEORGE'S

In my new bicoastal mode, still maintaining an apartment in Brooklyn, I returned to Marin in late October and dropped in on Sue Stephens at the Grateful Dead Productions office to catch up on things. She told me Garcia was continuing to recover, even playing shows with the Jerry Garcia Band at the Stone, a San Francisco club he favored, and that he and MG had moved to a new house in the San Rafael Hills.

Since the coma, postproduction on *So Far* had been suspended indefinitely. I had put my retainer from GDP on hiatus until further notice because I had income from other work, but the people of GDP did not. I was not going to raise the question of resuming work on *So Far* with Garcia or anyone else until the right time, if ever . . .

I went up to Garcia and MG's new house for a visit. The place was bright and cheerful, with a pool, a nice view, a warm, friendly atmosphere, familial calm. There was a kid or two around, as I recall. The mood was so much better than it had been back at the Hepburn Heights house. MG was clearly in charge, thank God. She was such a reassuring, dependable presence, as she had been since the coma crisis. Garcia himself looked healthy, in good humor, and was really relaxed and positive. He seemed to be making a remarkable recovery, happy to be with his family.

CHAPTER 7

I got invited to dinner there a few times, with MG's home cooking, and boy, did it make me feel great to be welcomed there by two of my favorite people. Garcia even mentioned wanting to go back to work on *So Far* early in the new year, and it filled me with hope, because truthfully, I was still afraid, reasonably, or not, that my friend might not ever be his old self again.

On November 11, 1986, I went to a Jerry Garcia Band show at the Stone, feeling a little queasy about it. I didn't go backstage, thinking the less commotion back there the better—I didn't want to be another distraction. It turned out to be a half-decent show. Garcia was clearly not on his game, but then that happened every twentieth show or so even when he was healthy. The crowd was very happy to see him there, alive. They were enthusiastic, but clearly not driven mad by the music. On the drive home I was thinking, "Well, he'll either get better or he won't." If I were less neurotic I might have considered the fact that twelve weeks ago I'd watched him struggle to hold a guitar properly, and that actually his progress in the intervening weeks had been astonishing.

A few days later I found out that Los Lobos, a hot band with a hit album, *How Will the Wolf Survive?*, would be playing soon at New George's, a popular club in San Rafael. I loved their music and I had recently done a job with them, and Garcia and I had talked about them often pre-coma, and he was a big fan too.

I had the idea that maybe it would be good for him to get out and about after his period of pain and recuperation. We could go see Los Lobos, and I could go with him and make sure he stayed out of trouble (as if!). I floated the idea to Sue Stephens, and she got the okay from MG, with certain conditions MG laid down. Sue and her friend Annette Flowers would accompany us to the show.

Sue made the arrangements with Los Lobos and the club, so they would know what was going on. And with some trepidation, but a larger excitement, I drove up to the new house in my new rental, a big gold Thunderbird (still a sexy car in the '80s). I'd gotten the car after Garcia had severely razzed my previous tiny cheap rental, because he had to spend time riding shotgun and told me to get a bigger car. I knew I'd be the designated driver for the night.

I found him and MG in the kitchen waiting for me. Garcia was acting a little sheepish. He was smiling, clearly happy to be going out, obviously deferential to whatever MG had in mind, but also a little nervous and giddy.

MG laid it out for us, especially me: no drinking (remember, he had been in a diabetic coma), first show only, then right back home. "Len, you're gonna keep an eye on him, right?" I was a little surprised by her directness, like, wait, *I'm* in charge of the big guy here? But I didn't say anything, just nodded vigorously. "It's *your* responsibility, Len; no drugs, no drinking, right back here after the first show." I was like, "Yes, ma'am." Jerry chuckled.

Just as we were about to leave the house, Garcia said, "Wait a sec," went into the next room, and returned with a blue-and-white Fender Stratocaster, a beautiful symbol of the advent of rock 'n' roll in the 1950s. "I had Parish bring me this from my collection," he said.

"I'm gonna give it to Hidalgo." I'm like, wow, what an amazing gesture. Dave Hidalgo was the driving force behind Los Lobos—songwriter, lead vocal, and guitar. He and I had met, but I knew he and Jerry had never met; at least neither of them mentioned it to me if they had, but I'm guessing their admiration was mutual. Garcia's dad, Jose Ramon Garcia, was a Spanish immigrant, as well as a horn player and bandleader, and Los Lobos is a Mexican-American rock 'n' roll fusion band.

We drive to New George's in downtown San Rafael and meet Sue and Annette at the front door. Other ticket holders passing by are surprised to see Jerry there, but they keep moving as if in disbelief—after all, word on the street is he's supposed to be at death's door. We get a nice table in the back for the four of us and the guitar, safe and sound. There is a whole dance floor between us and the stage. A lot of people don't notice us as they go by, but there are some double takes and the occasional "Jerry! Good to see you!" Sue, Annette, and I form a protective bubble around him, as most of the house starts to realize he is there, but mostly they leave us alone. Garcia seems genuinely happy.

Los Lobos plays a great show. A waiter visits our table (which I didn't anticipate because I'm stupid). She asks for drink orders, and of course Garcia asks for a white Russian faster than I can react or say anything. I have a little tremor of fear, knowing that he was standing there when MG was making *me* responsible, and he was agreeing not to drink . . . Damn you rascal, Garcia! So, I have a nice stiff drink to calm my nerves.

Toward the end of the set, I make my way backstage and touch base with the band's people to arrange for a Garcia visit after the show for a meet and greet. They are all on board and in the know. I return to our table for the encore, which is great, and then the houselights come on and the place empties out, everyone very happy. We wait at our table for a bit, and Sue and Annette say that they'd hold it down while Jerry and I go backstage. He tells me to grab the Fender and off we go.

We plunge into the cramped backstage area. It's suddenly really dark. I park the Fender against the wall, see the band, and introduce Garcia to Dave Hidalgo. It's surprisingly emotional, but I've seen this happen before when great musicians meet. Then the rest of the band shake hands with Jerry, and they all chat happily. I'm so happy to just relax and try to disappear into the wallpaper. It's a role I'm good at—I've never been eager to mix with the stars or anything like that. I'm more comfortable seeing myself as a person who helps musical and performing artists achieve their goals in visual media. That is what makes me happy.

Garcia waves for the guitar, and I hand it to him. He turns to Hidalgo and makes a little speech, then gives it to him. Hidalgo is very moved, a little overcome, and thanks Garcia profusely. Everyone applauds and shouts. I'm just amazed to be there.

And then Carlos Santana walks in.

I've never met him before, but obviously I know who he is. I don't know to what extent he and Garcia, these two master musicians who emerged in the '60s and '70s as icons of the San Francisco sound and sustained artistic careers ever since, have actually known each other before, and the sad fact is that sometimes fame and success can isolate people from each other.

Santana and Garcia see each other, each a little bit shocked, and their faces light up. Then it's like a dam break of emotions: There's an outpouring of hugs and affection and laughter, and then the two of them and Hidalgo and the other musicians form a huddle. I'm just glad that things are going well, and I can hang back. I'm thinking I can't believe I get to be there while this is happening. (A few years later, in 1989, I was able to bring Garcia and Santana together in an HBO show, *Caliente y Picante,* along with Linda Ronstadt, Tito Puente, Rubén Blades, and Celia Cruz.)

It gets to be time to prep for the second show, so we have to skedaddle out of there, the plan being that Jer and I would head back to his house—the plan unfortunately being only in my imagination. We get back to our table, where Sue and Annette are patiently awaiting us. The crowd for the second show is already streaming in, more boisterous than the first show crowd, which is to be expected. Some of them notice Garcia and are at first stunned and then delighted to see him, shouting out greetings, and Garcia grins and nods.

I suggest we should get going, but Sue and Annette are partiers first and foremost. They are happy and in no hurry, and Garcia just shrugs, like, "Whatever." He is very obviously happy, in a comfortable bubble with me and Sue and Annette around him. I feel a glimmer of unease as I realize we are staying for the second show.

The band comes out, starts the second show, and somehow I lose track of my responsibility. It isn't on Sue or Annette, who are having a great time, and it sure as shit is not on Garcia, never a guy I associated with the word *responsibility*.

In due course a waiter appears to take drink orders, and of course Garcia asks for another white Russian. Sue and Annette and I order, and I'm just kind of . . . lost. He is drinking, it's the second show, goddammit!! I'd promised MG I'd have him home by now. But soon enough Los Lobos is cranking it out, the entire club is ecstatic, I'm carried along, and there's a kind of euphoria about it.

Suddenly, one very excited, high, and irrepressible young lady breaks through the bubble of our table and invites Garcia to dance with her, and he doesn't hesitate at all, as I hoped he would, giving me a chance to intercede and point out that maybe that isn't a good idea. He's out of his chair and gone with her, and they disappear onto the dance floor, out of sight of us, and I am like, "What the fuck? What the fuck have I done?"

Sue and Annette are laughing, perfectly fine with what is going on. But me? I'm still that nerdy outsider, neurotic, thinking, "She could be some crackhead who's gonna have him out in her pickup truck in five minutes and we'll never see him again." Maybe I'm worried when I shouldn't be, but then, I'm not a lifelong member of this Grateful Dead tribe, so what the fuck do I know?

I look into the crowd, can't see Garcia or the girl, and I am alarmed. I look back to Sue and Annette, who are of course slightly inebriated, and they look at me like, "We don't know, what the fuck. What can you do, he's gone, but he's a big boy. He'll be fine, and everyone's having a good time, so we're not going to worry about it." Then I know I am on my own, out on a limb of my own making.

The show progresses and Garcia is still missing. The band stops the music to announce, "Please welcome our good friend Carlos Santana to the stage." Santana does a great short set with the band and the crowd loves it. He finishes his guest turn, takes a bow, and starts to take off his guitar, when suddenly there is Dave Hidalgo welcoming Jerry Garcia to the stage. Garcia climbs up, Santana hands his guitar to him, and he straps it on. No one in the crowd at that moment had any idea that this might be happening when they bought their ticket or came in the door that night, and they go ape-shit.

Now imagine you're me: I've spent twelve years filming live rock 'n' roll, chasing and living for moments like this.

I leave our table and move toward the stage.

It's a screaming, jumping, ecstatic crowd, happy beyond belief. The musicians join the mayhem, and the whole thing just transcends anything else I have ever experienced. It moves into a whole other dimension; there isn't anyone in control of it, anything could happen. You can get addicted to that feeling, and I did, starting in 1974 and lasting right up to the mid-'90s. There is nothing else like it, and I drank from that cup, to quote Robert Hunter.

I am so excited and delighted to see him up there, because he isn't drinking or doing drugs with that girl, so I am thinking I might be okay with MG. But I'm also afraid that this might not go well; he's never played with Los Lobos before, he's playing a guitar he's never handled, he might be high from something he got from the girl . . . I don't fuckin' know. And if it doesn't go well, it will be my fault. That's insight into my own worldview, as distinct from the Grateful Dead worldview—me still being a neurotic transplant from NYC.

The band and Jerry go into a nice up-tempo jazzy jam. It's really good, the crowd loves it, and I'm about as happy as a person can be. Then the band suddenly shifts gears into "La Bamba," the classic rocker, signaling the end of the show. Garcia is rocking along, the crowd still going ape-shit, dancing wildly. I look back at Sue and Annette—they are grinning, the picture of no worries. The big guitar-break solo comes along in the song and the band turns to Garcia. He catches it with gusto, and rips out a beautiful, soaring solo, dropping it in, perfectly in sync with the band. The place goes nuts.

I find myself in another state, with no worries, no thoughts. I'm just fully and totally in the moment, one of the most amazing moments of my life. I'm crying, it's just so beautiful.

Looking back now, that moment was the happiest moment of my life up until then and is still one of the happiest of my life. He was back. I knew it to my very core at that moment, he was back.

The second show ends right after the "La Bamba" closer. The lights go up, everyone starts to leave, and Annette and Sue and I are sitting at our table, beaming. I'm personally kind of exhausted after having to adapt to things not going how I thought they would: a quiet night out on the town with a beloved rock star. But where is Garcia? We talk, deciding he must be backstage hanging with Santana and Los Lobos, so we wait. The club workers are respectful as we sit at the table, and soon the club is almost empty.

Suddenly I remember my promise to MG to intercept drug and alcohol offers (which Garcia had tacitly agreed to up at their house) and to bring him home after the first set, so I jump up from the table, announcing to Sue and Annette, "I'm gonna go check for him backstage. Could you stay here and watch for him coming out?" I look and find empty rooms, cleanup staff, and ask random people, "Did you see Jerry back here? Know where he is?" I go outside under the marquee and watch as stragglers leave the club, but no Jerry. I'm starting to feel anxious. I go back inside and check in with Sue and Annette, who are much more sanguine than me. They are feeling that, well, he isn't in the club, he isn't there, he's gone somewhere, so we should probably get going ourselves, what the fuck, see what happens . . . they get up and shuffle off, wishing me luck.

And I'm in my head yelling, "No, you don't understand! I made a commitment to MG, and Garcia and her and I, we had an agreement. He's still fragile. You're leaving me here alone?" But Sue and Annette are happy and high, and they are lifelong members of the Grateful Dead family, and probably have total faith in Garcia that he'll be fine. But they don't know the deal I'd made with MG, and they haven't had the experiences I've had over the last six months, or six years, seeing firsthand how he'd had to work to get back to where he was. And there was my neurotic fear that he was more fragile than anyone realized.

So now I go into a full terror-mode panic attack: "OMG, where the fuck is he? He ran off with the crazy dancing girl and they're doing meth somewhere, and it's all my fault. What the fuck was I thinking?"

I remember this moment of extreme clarity, standing in New George's near the front doors, the work lights on, workers moving by me, heading home.

I look around: The place is rapidly emptying out; the cleaning crew is hard at work. I've looked everywhere, and everyone's gone. I have a moment of panic. I thought I could help, give Garcia a positive human experience, and it seemed to have gone really well there for a while, but now . . . what the *fuck* was I thinking? I made a promise to MG, I took him out into the world . . . and *I'd fucking lost him*! What the fuck, that sinking feeling that you are in deep, deep doo-doo . . . sinking, sinking . . . I'm not used to this sensation. I've always been a person who stays calm, rational, moves ahead, leads, keeps the faith—traits that have served me well in producing and directing . . .

I know he'd had one or two drinks, maybe more? Maybe that girl took him home to her trailer and is doing meth with him right now? Holy shit!

Finally, I give up. He's not here, anywhere. We looked everywhere; he's not here. I head outside onto Fourth Street. Cool air hits me in the face. I look around, under the club's marquee . . . and there is Garcia, standing there, happily bouncing in place, chatting with fans leaving the show, smoking a cigarette, I guess waiting for me to show up to take him home.

Enormously fucking relieved, I can't tell you, I hang back for a second as he says goodnight to a young couple. I overhear a fragment of dialogue: " . . . we are *so* happy that you are all better." Garcia thanks them and wishes them a good night, they depart, and I come up to him and say, "Hey, we been looking for you." He's glad to see me, jolly even. He clearly has no concept that his disappearance could have been a problem for me or anyone else, and he is fully his normal relaxed and happy self. We go back to my car and get in. Once in the car, with me in the driver's seat, turning the ignition, him next to me, slamming doors, I am so relieved. I take a few breaths, relaxing, reentering normal reality. All of it had been no big deal; it was all in your mind, Len . . . I am so relieved to see him, so it's just, "Hey, let's get going."

As we are driving back to his place, he seems really happy, deeply happy. I make some comment about how I was surprised and amazed that his guitar solo sounded so much like *him*, even though it was not his normal guitar, just the guitar Santana had handed him. He just laughs good-naturedly and says with faux sarcasm, "Hey, it sounds like me, because it's *me* that makes the sound, it's not the guitar." I just nod, kind of playing the innocent, and he keeps the ball in play. I say something about how we thought we might have lost you there, after the show, couldn't find you. And he's like, "Yeah, I was outside waiting for you guys. There were so many people passing by, they were just so friendly, stopping to talk to me . . ." He pauses, and I feel he is searching for words, so I just keep my mouth shut. He goes on, "I had no idea so many people were so . . . concerned about me, they knew about all this health shit. I've never had such an experience of love coming from strangers; it was amazing."

I am staggered by this. I can feel myself getting emotional, but I squeeze out a comment like, "You didn't know how beloved you are to a really large number of people?" And he actually hears me, thinks about it, and says, "Hey, I've been separated from regular people for a long, long time. I got really isolated, and I had no idea how much regular people seemed to . . . care about me, even though I don't know why they care so much."

There was a pause, then I say, "How did that make you feel?" He breaks into a big grin and says, "It made me feel great, I just never knew . . ."

At that point I choke up, finding it hard to speak, and have to work to get it under control. I'm thinking, "Really? You had no idea about how these people, thousands and thousands of them, feel about you? And I share their feelings; we all love you."

I made some actual verbal statement about it, I can't remember what exactly, but the emotion hung there in the air, and he just smiled and nodded. He seemed as happy as I could ever remember, and I dropped him off at his house and drove home. I plopped into bed and had a great sleep, knowing that was the happiest day of my life (up until then).

Platinum certification acknowledgment for video So Far, *1987. Courtesy Len Dell'Amico personal archive.*

Chapter 8

SO FAR, PART TWO

Throughout 1985 and into '86, before and after Garcia's coma and recovery, he and I were thinking up what imagery we wanted to have to play with during the final edit of *So Far.* Ann Leslie Uzdavinis and Larry Lachman were brought into the project as postproduction specialists to find and license the stock footage and special effects providers to help realize our wish list. By early '87, Garcia seemed to have finally wrestled his substance problem to the ground, to the point where he could go with me to LA and spend ten-hour days in high-end postproduction facilities working with special effects editors without any breaks. I like to think that by helping him work on a project that truly engaged his incredible mind, he could escape the pull of the substances.

It was great to go into these very expensive edit places, like the Post Group in LA, which were very set in their ways. They had high expectations from the engineers and technicians about what their clients were planning, what they wanted, like, "What's the script here?" To be confronted by me and my team, and by Jerry Garcia in person, must have been a culture shock for them. We were saying, "Hey, guys (yes, they were all guys), we're all about improvisation and having fun, and we know that you guys know what your tools can do much better than we do, so we want to let you into our process. We want to see what you can do to improve on our ideas," and you'd see their jaws drop. They're like, "OMG, these hippies from SF have no script! Don't they realize how much this is going to cost?" Garcia was physically there and participating, and we all had to overcome the difference in expectations. The workers had to be liberated from their straitjackets, which was Garcia's specialty.

Now, I'd already been indoctrinated into the Grateful Dead approach, so I was just tickled by Veronica's reply to their question, "Well, where are we going to get all this imagery?" Veronica, our editor in chief, just said, "From this set of ten one-inch video reels full of what we might need, and my index by time code of where every image is." At that point, Garcia sat them down and smiled and explained that we wanted them to just relax and have fun with this and be our partners (not our slaves). Show us what they could do with their gizmos, show us stuff that they know they can do that their other clients don't ask for. It was magic to see what happened. The straitlaced, disciplined, subservient technicians flowered into creative, liberated participants, and they, the people who actually knew what their technology could do, dove into the job, and we all had a great time. Garcia was having a ball watching all this stuff go down. The two years we'd spent recording the band at the Marin Veterans' Memorial Auditorium, putting together the imagery we would need, and now seeing the special effects coming in was finally paying off.

The staff engineers were not used to having someone like Garcia sitting next to them in front of the vast array of monitors and mixing boards and switchers, all of us in our ergonomic chairs on wheels so you could roll back and forth. At one point we were confronted with a need to shorten a soundtrack piece to make the thing work. With only poor options, I suggested to Garcia, "Well, we could cut one or two verses of your guitar solo—that would do it." (I was being purposefully provocative.) There was a silent pause. Then Garcia said to me, "Yeah, or I could rip your head off and use it as a soccer ball." The two engineers flinched in fear and rolled their ergonomic chairs away from us, thinking that he meant it, that all hell was about to break loose in their edit room. Garcia and I played it out with a tense pause before we both burst out laughing. A highlight of my career.

Once these guys were liberated, their contribution to what we were doing was unleashed, and it was awesome. We were the first to use automated one- and two-frame intercut editing for extended periods of screen time, as well as utilizing multiple superimposed layers of images and early 3D animation.

That was the classic Garcia approach to working with outsiders, straight people, and it was wondrous to behold how they blossomed, started having real fun, and showed us stuff that they'd never shown anyone else.

SO FAR, PART TWO

I had a pretty firm system in place with the facility to prevent uninvited guests from dropping in on us; we were working, it was a closed set, and the system worked very well until one day, Tom Davis and Dan Aykroyd burst into the editing suite through the door that only the technicians used to go back and forth to the machine room. I understood right away, Tom and Dan were not going to be rebuffed by the rules, so they found a back way in, using their famous faces and humor. Dan was one of the biggest stars in America at that time (*Ghostbusters*, *Trading Places*, *The Blues Brothers*), and I guess he and Tom fully expected everything to just stop so we could all party. They were boisterous and laughing, slapping Garcia on the back. The house technicians were gobsmacked, while me and my team were somewhat less impressed. Tom and Dan could see that this was not a typical Grateful Dead workplace, Garcia was hunched over the big mixing boards just like the rest of us, we were working. Garcia, as usual, always unflappable, indulged them for a bit, but as you might imagine, he was not prone to being starstruck, and considering the hourly rate at this facility, I wasn't going to allow too much fooling around. Garcia, as usual, always unflappable, indulged them for a while, but as you might imagine, he was not prone to being 'starstruck.' To shake things up, Dan jumped up and announced, "I can teach anyone to act in under five minutes!" He grinned and waved his hands invitingly. But we all just looked at him, there were no takers. We were working. So they were kind of deflated, settled down to watch what we were doing, but as always happens when visitors grasp what the actual work-pace is in filmmaking, which is glacial, to say the least, they got bored and eventually left. But I've always wondered, what if I had taken Dan up on his offer to teach me to act in five minutes? I've always wanted to play 'the bad guy' in a big thriller.

So Far was released in late '87. It went on to become the best-selling music video of 1988 and won the American Video Conference award, sponsored by the American Film Institute and Billboard, for best music video. They sent us a little trophy, like an Oscar, and Garcia, Sue Stephens, and I took it with us to the local pizza lunch spot near the Dead's office in San Rafael to celebrate.

Of course, the visual innovations of *So Far* are dated compared to present-day digital effects, and we knew that would happen, but we made a conscious decision to try to hit the culture of the time as best we could, and not worry about our place in history.

Chapter 9

ROBERT HUNTER

At the very end of 1986, or maybe the first week of 1987, I was working with Garcia at the band's Front Street studio in San Rafael on the sound mix for what would become *So Far,* the home video released in late '87 as a follow-on to their huge album *In the Dark.* We were alone for a bit, sitting on the Dead's own rolling chairs in front of their gigantic, fully automated, state-of-the-art Neve mixing board, taking a break, shootin' the shit, when Robert Hunter strolled in. Hunter was always shy, polite, an unassuming presence, a heavy smoker.

Garcia was a tad startled. Hunter seemed a little sheepish, I'm guessing because it was unusual for Bob (as Hunter was called) to venture into the recording studio. Visitors had to navigate through the crew hang-out room, positioned between the street door and the studio, and always attended to by at least two large, male members of the stage crew if there was work going on in the studio. You had to get by them in order to go into the studio, and they were expected to be at least slightly intimidating, in case someone just showed up, like a process server, or an angry spouse or girlfriend, or a fan hoping to meet, or kill, the band.

Hunter was a great lyricist, songwriter, and performer in his own right, and also an erudite student of literature and poetry. He published a translation of Rilke's *Duino Elegies* in 1987, released a dozen solo albums between 1974 and 1993, and coauthored songs with Bob Dylan, as well as Garcia and other members of Grateful Dead. He was a sophisticated, romantic, and sensitive person, and I think a lot of the off-putting and sometimes even grotesque weirdness of the layers of people and activity that Grateful Dead had constructed or tolerated around itself was maybe baffling to him (misogyny was rampant in the business in the '80s, for instance, and I'd seen some disturbing treatment of young female fans or groupies).

He and Garcia had met and started collaborating in 1961. According to the lore, they used to sleep in abandoned cars on a vacant lot, and were very happy about their lifestyle, trying to survive as folk singers. They'd made a pilgrimage back east to Appalachia to learn about old-timey music, and to meet Bill Monroe, pioneer of bluegrass.

Hunter obviously knew that his collaborations with Garcia were a big part of the Dead phenomenon, but somehow all the action was centered around the six guys, and he may have felt peripheral. Certainly, he was invisible to the mass media, in stark contrast to the members of Grateful Dead, although of course his role was understood among the true fans.

I always thought of them as two guys who met when they were nobody and nowhere, a normal state of affairs for young people, and they in some sense invented each other as actual creative forces. Then Garcia was absorbed, or taken over by, or chose to lead a group, the Warlocks, and then Grateful Dead. The Dead took off like a tornado, and Hunter was not in the band, even though his creative input grew larger and larger over time. Grateful Dead's fourth studio album, *Workingman's Dead* (1970), thought by many to be their greatest, was made up entirely of songs written by Garcia and Hunter, with Phil Lesh contributing to one track.

I had a huge sense of respect for Hunter, bordering on awe. As a nonmusical professional whose job was to interface with musical talent in their work in visual media, I had learned a lot, and cared a lot, about the songwriters, who were often totally out of the spotlight. And I had long ago concluded that Hunter was one of the greatest lyricists of all time, a GOAT as we now say.

I recall a chat I had with him in the run-up to Dylan rehearsals at Front Street in preparation for the summer 1987 Grateful Dead/Bob Dylan stadium tour. Hunter was occasionally difficult to engage, enigmatic, maybe prickly at times, and God knows I'm pretty strange. He offered the opinion that his own work suffered in comparison to Dylan's, because Dylan's lyrics were more accessible. By that I think he meant in the common vernacular, in comparison to his own lyrics, which he seemed to think were somehow more . . . complex? Enigmatic? Obscure? By that time, I was an expert on the crowd dynamic and appreciation at many, many Dead shows, and I was so thrown by his comment that I felt compelled to disagree with him and told him so. I said in just the one song "Desolation Row," Dylan made more obscure cultural and literary references that the average person could not possibly understand than in the entire output of many other songwriters. Hunter's work, by contrast, was very much rooted in the common language of English speakers. Songs like "Ripple," "Bird Song," "To Lay Me Down," "Cumberland Blues," "U.S. Blues," "Touch of Grey," and "Stella Blue," and on and on, express deep thoughts and complex ideas and plotlines in the most direct poetic language possible, which is why the public loves them. And it's a *big* part of why these songs land so hard in front of concert audiences. There's nothing in those lyrics that they don't already understand. They had a *need* to hear those words, and they loved them.

I believe Hunter is actually at the core of the Grateful Dead phenomenon. He is the final, innermost layer of the onion.

Anyway, as Hunter arrives, Garcia and I stand up to greet him. Garcia is happy and giddy (Hunter visiting the studio was not a common event), and I'm flushed with that "Oh my God, I can't believe I'm here" feeling that I had learned to recognize and deal with coolly. They shake hands and nod and laugh, I mumble something like, "I'll let you guys alone for a bit," and move to exit, which is my go-to strategy in situations like this. I had learned that the big stars were used to everyone trying to horn in on their lives, and they didn't like it. Horning in on anyone is the last thing I want to do, so it's my practice to excuse myself, and that strategy had always worked for me. I think because of that, the stars tended to trust me.

But Garcia says to me, "No, don't go, stick around . . ." I'm surprised but I deal with it. They light cigarettes and nod and laugh while catching up with small talk.

Garcia has a habit of inviting me to stay when I'm trying to excuse myself; it's happened quite a few times. Maybe he's trying to help others in the Dead scene get to know me, because he, or he and the band, have decided I'm a part of the team, and they know that the larger tribal team has a well-known resistance to outsiders. Maybe he knew I was shy and needed encouragement to engage more with people like Hunter. Maybe he wanted Hunter to get to know me better so that he could be somewhat inoculated to the bullshit that the tribal rumor mill could be expected to generate about me, given that Garcia and I were spending a lot of time together, working on big projects, but also just as friends.

Hunter asks what we are up to here, and Garcia explains: the *So Far* mix, and other stuff. Then there comes an obvious moment of truth. There's a break in the chat, and Hunter says, "I brought you something . . ." He starts rummaging in his shirt pocket, and Garcia is visibly excited: "Oh yeah?"

Hunter pulls out a single sheet of lined notebook paper, folded three or four times, and starts to open it up. Garcia is practically salivating. Hunter says, "Yeah, I just wrote this. Thought you might want to put it on the new record." Garcia is like, "Oh, too much, man . . ." He reaches for the paper, but Bob is still unfolding it. I'm just stunned, goosebumps. I am present at the birth of a new Garcia-Hunter song.

Hunter says, "It's called 'Black Muddy River,'" as he finally hands it to Garcia. There is a big moment when Garcia takes a deep breath, grins at his old partner, thanks him profusely, and then folds up the precious piece of paper and puts it in his shirt pocket. He then urges Hunter and me to sit down and kick back for a bit. I relax a little, feeling honored to be present with these two longtime friends and collaborators.

"Black Muddy River" went on to be the closing song on *In the Dark*, released just seven months later, in July '87, and the best-selling album of the band's career. It's one of those passionate, wrenching ballads about suffering and surviving that would often show up late in the second set of the band's shows, or even to end their shows—as did songs like "Stella Blue," "Knockin' on Heaven's Door," and "Brokedown Palace."

I think a joint may have gone around at that point, because the memory is a little hazy, and then they get to reminiscing. I do remember the subject of psychedelics comes up. They are talking about the mid-'60s, and I can participate because I have a true interest in what was going on back then in the San Francisco Bay Area. I've read a few books about it, and my interjections or questions come from my heart. I'm alone with the two guys who wrote everything on *Workingman's Dead*, and I'm gonna be shy? I don't think so. This is awesome!

So, when one of them makes an oblique reference to those days and DMT, and they start recalling, with fond chuckles and deep appreciation, a certain event, I perk right up. I was reading Dennis and Terence McKenna's *The Invisible Landscape* at that time, which Garcia had lent me, adjacent to our long chats about mysticism, philosophy, and psychedelics, including DMT.

DMT is short for dimethyltryptamine, which is one component of the entheogen ayahuasca. Ayahuasca has been used ritually for a thousand or more years in Amazonian Indigenous cultures. It's made from a plant and a vine commonly found in their habitat, cooked by shamans according to knowledge passed down, and used in serious communal spiritual practices that take many hours and can be quite harrowing at times. It very clearly serves a powerful purpose to the community.

DMT, in contrast, was isolated from ayahuasca recently in the West, solely for its psychedelic, or hallucinatory, properties. Nowadays it's commonly smoked, and the experience lasts for fifteen or twenty minutes. (I am just reporting here, I've never tried it.)

In the studio with Hunter and Garcia, there's a pause, cigarette smoke is exhaled. Hunter says to Garcia, "You remember the mahogany eagles?" Garcia guffaws and nods cheerfully. "Yeah!" Then Garcia says, "D'you remember the mechanical elves?" Hunter returns the laughter and happy nodding: "Yeah, I do!"

I am truly mystified, drawn in, curious. These guys are two of the most important psychedelic adventurers in my lifetime, so I feel compelled to ask, "Wait a second. You guys took some DMT?" They look to me and nod, and Garcia says, "Oh yeah, a bunch of times." I ask them how they took it—in a pill form? They say no, they smoked it. It came on real fast and didn't last long at all, like fifteen minutes or so, but in that time you were transported to another dimension, there was just no question about it.

"So, you're saying that you were both transported to this other place, where you both experienced the same things? Mahogany eagles and mechanical elves?" I ask, and they both nod and laugh. Garcia spells it out to me: "It was *not* a hallucinatory experience, like psilocybin, LSD, or mescaline, it was a *place*!"

I'd had experience with mescaline, magic mushrooms, LSD, and of course cannabis, but not DMT. I had heard DMT was different from all the other psychedelics, in that it delivered you to a different world, or dimension, which existed in and of itself, and was experienced by visitors in the same way as a real place, just as Garcia had said.

Garcia goes on to say that you would meet entities that you had met there before, and sometimes they remembered you. He says the entities were quite often disinterested in you and sometimes a bit hostile, in a trickster kind of way. They were very active, busy, constantly "doing things" that were inscrutable to the visitors. They were also often very funny. I'm dazzled by this conversation, the implications that the DMT experience challenged modern physics in a way that the other psychedelics don't.

Just then a mixing engineer returns from lunch and breaks the mood, and Hunter takes it as a signal to let us get back to work. He and Garcia share a fond goodbye, Hunter wishing him luck with the new song, and Garcia thanking him with a big grin.

Regarding my theory of Hunter being the engine driving the Grateful Dead train, I first saw the Dead in concert on August 4, 1967, at the O'Keefe Centre in Toronto. I was sixteen years old and had first tried marijuana just a few months before. Weed back then was far weaker than it is now, and I hadn't yet been exposed to any psychedelics. I first heard their first record, released in March of that year, pretty soon after. My good friend Mick Stern found it in a record store and was fascinated by the collage art design of the album cover. Jefferson Airplane headlined the Toronto show. They had exploded onto the scene with the hits "Somebody to Love" and "White Rabbit" coming out of every car radio that summer and inspiring a bunch of us youngsters to leave Buffalo and cross the border to Canada to see them. Their set was good, but what really captured me was the opener, Grateful Dead.

I remember "Turn on Your Love Light," "Good Morning Little Schoolgirl," and little else, but I vividly recall I was actually having my first religious experience, albeit a small one. I hadn't smoked any pot, so it was clearly brought on by their music—the idea of six soloing musicians, the long roaming jams. I was pretty stunned on the ride home. But given this was smack in the middle of the golden age of rock 'n' roll—the Beatles' *Sgt. Pepper* came out that year, and we had the Stones, the Who, Led Zeppelin, Dylan, and dozens of other hugely original and influential bands and artists blowing our minds for the next several years—I didn't pay much attention to Grateful Dead. I did see them at Woodstock, and yes, they sucked, and I've had the distinct pleasure of hearing Garcia joke about it with his bandmates when I brought it up to them sixteen years later. And yes, they thought they sucked too, but they were just laughing their asses off about it, even after all that time. Something like, "The stage was electrified somehow, it was raining, and every time we touched a mic or a mic stand we were getting these shocks!"

I started working in concert films in 1974, first as a camera operator, and then directing. I shot the Dead many times in cheap black-and-white video (all on YouTube today), without mingling with them. And then I did the big Radio City national broadcast in 1980, working directly with them with a big budget, shooting lots of comedy with Franken and Davis, and everything else. And then of course there was the fifteen-year friendship with Garcia. And during all that time I was able to see and hear and experience the band up close, from both within their bubble and as an outside observer in my role as director and producer, interfacing with the straight world of business and rapidly developing distribution technology. Part of my job is to understand how the artist is affecting the audience—why they are there and crazy happy—so as to heighten the experience for both them and the artist. In the case of the Dead, there was a huge and ever-growing legion of followers literally following them on the road, and of course an even larger group buying records and listening to them on the radio. This phenomenon always attracted intense local media interest wherever they went, but also in the national mass media, which hit a crescendo in the 1987 to 1990 period and afterward, right up until Garcia's death in 1995.

As an avid consumer of that mass media (it was part of my job), and also as someone who was learning more and more about what actually went on among the six musicians and inside their tribe throughout that time, I formed a pretty stable set of views.

The typical media item hosted by a local know-nothing reporter, often in a mocking or sometimes frightened tone, centered on the mind-altering drugs that seemed to permeate the concert experience. I subscribe to Andrew Weil's theory (see his first book *The Natural Mind*, published in 1972, recommended to me by Garcia) that human cultures from all over and throughout time have put three kinds of things into their bodies: water, food, and substances, the latter being everything that is neither food nor water and that has healing or mind-altering effects but no clear nutritional value—such as spices, caffeine, coca, cocoa, nicotine, alcohol, marijuana, opium and its derivatives, refined sugar, psychedelic mushrooms and cacti, ginseng, kava, and a zillion other herbal substances.

CHAPTER 9

Even the shortest news segments usually had a little time left over after they highlighted the substance practices of this weird subculture, during which they would talk about the Deadheads, the joyous young travelers living in their vans or camping, leaving a mess on people's front lawns, that sort of thing. Of course, local vendors and motels loved the band and their fans, but that's another story.

If the reporter had more time or more brains, they would move on to the guru that they perceived as the leader of the group, Garcia, and how the fans seemed to worship him. God knows Garcia was very generous with his time in giving these reporters some bit of chat, always positive and insightful, but often over their heads. From there a reporter would go on to how this whole thing was a bit of a cult, or a possibly threatening movement, because these kids seemed to care more about fun and ecstasy than going to school in order to get a great job. They would report on the phenomenon as a subculture, which I can sympathize with, but they'd present it like a dumbed-down David Attenborough examining the behavior of leaf-cutter ants.

If they had even more time or brains, they would focus on Garcia's guitar playing. You know, he's a guitar god, but usually they didn't actually sit through a few shows or live recordings to get a truly big picture of what it was about the music that was so exciting to fans. In a way, I can understand this. A Dead show was composed of many styles of music, spanning most of the different types of music that America has produced. Jazz is perhaps the most sophisticated American musical invention, and the least understood, and the typical Dead concert contained huge swaths of free-form improvisational jazz, or jazz-rock. And of course it's true Garcia was one of the greatest electric guitar players in American musical history, but he also played banjo, acoustic guitar, and pedal-steel guitar, and he recorded with and coproduced a huge number of records with other artists, including his own band, the Jerry Garcia Band, which did a lot of blues (never a strong suit for Grateful Dead); David Nelson and the New Riders of the Purple Sage; Jefferson Airplane; Crosby, Stills, Nash & Young; Bob Dylan; keyboardists Howard Wales and Merl Saunders; mandolinist David Grisman; the all-star bluegrass band Old & In the Way, featuring Peter Rowan, Vassar Clements, John Kahn, and Grisman, whose debut album was one of the best-selling bluegrass albums of all time; Robert Hunter; Ornette Coleman; Warren Zevon; and on and on.

As a musician, Garcia had an astonishing career, but it was more varied and adventurous than he is given credit for.

It's a sad fact that the media sphere didn't grasp what was truly going on at a Dead show. Yes, psychedelic substances played a role, which I would describe as a sacrament, a shared ritual among the gathered fans, who could be viewed as congregants. As Garcia and everyone else who was there at the Kesey Acid Tests in 1965 will tell you, LSD played a crucial role in the birth of Grateful Dead and the ensuing history of psychedelic rock and jam-band music. Back then, psychedelics were quickly demonized by a social and political establishment that was deeply frightened by the public revolt against the Vietnam War and the rise of the civil rights movement, and Richard Nixon started the war on drugs. (Note to political speechwriters and pundits: One cannot actually be in a state of war with inanimate substances.) Then, before we knew it, Timothy Leary was in jail, and LSD and other psychedelics were listed as Schedule 1 narcotics, a ridiculous notion. Tragically, everything was driven underground, and the leading lights of the movement were ostracized. I say *tragically,* because we now know the value of these substances in treating PTSD, rampant among the Vietnam veteran generation, and a wide variety of other mental health problems, and after fifty years in hibernation, society is finally accepting their positive value.

A good part of any Dead concert was crowd-pleasing country-and-western tunes, such as Merle Haggard; classic old rock, like Chuck Berry and Buddy Holly; some blues standards; Dead originals that fit in well with that material, like "Jack Straw" or "Bertha"; and a large group of Hunter tunes that could be described as nonsense, like "Mississippi Half-Step Uptown Toodeloo" and "Tennessee Jed." Other big elements of any show were a percussion duet by the two drummers, extended soloing within songs, and huge pieces of completely experimental and improvisational music referred to as *space.*

But there was a core part of every show, not all at once, but spread out over the three-hour-plus experience, where the players and audience shifted into another mindset. The best word I can come up with for it is *reverence.*

A Grateful Dead show was in many ways a lot more like attending a religious service than a rock concert. Many religions have ritual meetings where everyone sings and dances in a fun way. And then there are the serious parts of the service when the religious leader quotes a chosen passage from a revered text and discusses the meaning with the congregants—a sermon.

CHAPTER 9

I would describe the core message of a religion as the liturgy, the kernels of ancient and deep meaning that uplift the congregation.

In a Dead show, you knew it, you could feel it, when the liturgy was brought out to enlighten us. "The Wheel," "Eyes of the World," "Franklin's Tower," "Uncle John's Band," "Black Peter," "Bird Song," "Stella Blue," "Throwing Stones," "Let It Grow," "Ripple," "Estimated Prophet," "Wharf Rat," even rockers like "Touch of Grey," "I Need a Miracle," "Hell in a Bucket," "Scarlet Begonias"—this is just my personal list, there are many more—were the songs that raised up our souls, that got all of us, as a group, feeling the important things in life and the mystery of all that is. That's what sent us home, or to our hotel rooms, with a sense of big satisfaction, that the world was all right, pretty good, after all. (For additional information on the songs of Robert Hunter, see *A Box of Rain: Collected Lyrics of Robert Hunter*, Viking Penguin, 1990.)

All of those songs are gems of songwriting, and the artists who wrote the music, as opposed to the lyrics, deserve a huge portion of the credit for their greatness. And the band also knew how to perform the songs for maximum effect. At times it was awesome—and I mean the word in its purest sense: inspiring, actual honest-to-goodness awe. But when you get down to examining the liturgy, the actual message transmitted in the songs is held within the lyrics. And for the big majority of these songs, the liturgy is in and arises from the words of Robert Hunter.

That's why I believe that the innermost layer of the onion of the Grateful Dead phenomenon is Robert Hunter. In Garcia, Hunter found the perfect actor to bring his words to life, to put his words to music; and in Hunter, Garcia found the perfect muse and inspiration. All the layers of the onion that came after—the eleven total members of Grateful Dead, the developing following, the commercial success after ten years of playing, becoming the biggest concert draw in America for a number of years, finally achieving a hit album in their twenty-second year of existence, the bold and innovative pay-per-view and home video work, their incredible omnipresence on the internet today (you could probably watch their concerts and listen to their interviews until your eyes fell out and your ears fell off)—I think it all comes down to that core message in the liturgy.

Chapter 10

HELL IN A BUCKET

Grateful Dead's album *In the Dark*, and its first single "Touch of Grey" and companion music video, were released early in July '87. I was out on the road with the band for the month of July doing video reinforcement and recording of their historic stadium tour with Bob Dylan. By the time I came back off the road, "Touch of Grey" was the first top-ten hit the band had ever had, blaring out of car radios wherever you went, and the album was on its way to becoming their best-selling record, after twenty-two years as a band. *So Far*, the film project Garcia and I had been working on for three years, was nearing completion, and we both felt very good about it artistically. It was clearly destined to be a follow-up video release later in '87 to *In the Dark*.

I was back in San Francisco the first week of August 1987, working hard creating broadcast-ready live concert excerpts from the just-completed Dead/Dylan tour for use in a big mass-media event on August 8, an all-day MTV event boldly entitled Day of the Dead.

I got a call from Sue Stephens: Could I take a meeting with the band in Boulder, Colorado, ASAP to discuss producing a music video? Of course I said, "Of course!" And soon thereafter I was in the air on my way to Boulder.

What the band wanted to talk to me about in Boulder was the second music video to support *In the Dark*, which would be for "Hell in a Bucket," a tune written by Bob Weir, John Perry Barlow, and Brent Mydland. The plan was that we would conceptualize the video during my visit, I'd write it up and preproduce, and we'd shoot it in the Bay Area the last week of August. That would be, like, twelve days from then. But hey, I love a challenge. (You can just search: Grateful Dead official video *Hell in a Bucket* to see the finished product.)

In retrospect, I was so far down the Grateful Dead rabbit hole, living and working by a have-fun-first-damn-the-torpedoes ethos, and swept along by the band's astounding 1987 success on top of Garcia's astounding comeback, I felt anything was possible, and twelve days would be just dandy, thank you very much. At this point in my life, I was flying higher than I had ever imagined possible.

I scheduled an afternoon meeting in my hotel room in Boulder for the six guys and me on August 14, a day off for them between shows. We were all in a mood to charge forward, and I didn't bother trying to book a conference room or have a notetaker, so we all just jammed in my room.

I sit on the bed leaning against a wall, with my trusty yellow legal pad and pen in hand, still nerd-like. Weir sits on the bed, cross-legged, and the other guys are on the easy chair, the little couch I had, or leaning on the windowsill. We're all very conscious of the circumstances: The band is hitting a career high after twenty-two years together, they're all as excited and happy and fulfilled as could be. And me? Well, I'm happy as shit and proud of myself for being here, and in awe of them.

A powerful joint goes around, the room fills with smoke. By this time, I've finally learned to adjust to their normal state of consciousness. I'm comfortable, and there's much laughter and excitement. After we transition to the high, there's a moment of silence as we all recognize there is work to do. I'm very aware that it's just us in a small room, which I kind of like—it feels a little like summer camp or something—but I know Garcia is tolerating it, given his claustrophobia. And it's up to me to make something happen, get the job done.

With the joint going around the room, I pick up my pen and yellow legal pad and say, "So, what are you guys thinking about? How do you see this music video, what should be in it?" This is always my approach to working with artists on their music videos. I don't arrive with a vision after studying their song; I start with their thoughts and feelings, and we go from there (possibly my style was a reason why I was a good fit with the band).

Everyone looks at each other. Garcia is unusually reticent. I guess he may feel that since the first single and video from the record was one of his songs,

"Touch of Grey," then we need to hear from Weir first. I turn to Bob: "It's your song, I bet you have ideas. What should be in it?"

There's a moment of silence. What does Bob have to say, if anything? He's well-known for not loving to contribute to extended verbal exchanges about issues that have to be decided by the band or talk about the meaning of this or that creative move they're considering. You could say he's kind of nonverbal, and I have discovered over the years that some people, outsiders to the Dead scene, misinterpret this as a lack of intelligence. In the entertainment business of the 1980s in NYC and LA, talking a lot and fast had come to mean that you knew what you were talking about and had power and influence, whereas in truth it meant that you just had a huge snort of cocaine.

Then Bobby says, "A duck."

We all look at him, and there's some chuckling, because a duck is a funny thing all by itself. I ask him, "You want a duck in the video?" There's an explosion of laughter, which he joins in, and then he nods and proceeds to describe what else he wants, and I start taking lots of notes.

I still have the yellow legal pad from that meeting, and the first line of it is "a duck."

What followed was an amazing outpouring from Bob. He started off somewhat diffidently, but then picked up speed, egged on by laughter and ideas from the band and me. He had a fully formed vision of the video, and it was many years later before I realized his stunning authorship of the thing. Yes, technically I wrote it based on the notes I feverishly took during that meeting, but it was all his idea.

One of the more popular shows on TV in 1987, when there were only four networks, was *Miami Vice.* Known for its use of pop and rock music, bright colors, and stylish visuals, the show was a stunning reflection of late '80's culture. *People* magazine built and fed off the new celebrity worship, all about vanity and materialism, and network television followed suit. One of the leads of the show was Don Johnson, and his role made him one of the most famous men in America for a couple of years. He and his partner played on-the-make detectives, with plenty of money for great clothes and cars and stuff, lots of beautiful women were everywhere. Sophisticates on the coasts found it laughable, but also fun in a "meta" sort of way, as if maybe the creators of the show meant it as a joke—which they clearly didn't.

CHAPTER 10

Weir's idea was to basically satirize the entire materialistic and hedonistic ethos of the mid-1980s in the United States, using "Hell in a Bucket" and Don Johnson as the tools. I didn't fully appreciate it at the time, but this was an extremely bold and exactly right-on idea for the band to embrace in late 1987, what with the country still in the grip of Reaganism, and the "Greed is good" mantra from the movie *Wall Street,* released later that same year, being spouted unironically everywhere you turned. And in the year after the success of "Touch of Grey," a major national TV ad campaign by Citibank appeared, relentlessly pushing the tagline, "For those who want to succeed, not just survive!" (referencing the catchy chorus of "Touch of Grey": "We will survive!") Wow, a huge bank felt threatened by the idea that we could possibly be happy by just being alive and together with each other and dancing and singing, as opposed to grimly pursuing the expansion of our personal wealth. I was stunned, but there it was.

Now I can see that "Hell" was the perfect follow-up to "Touch," because while "Touch" was about surviving and thriving in hard times, "Hell" was a total embrace of all the indulgences of the most fortunate in our society at that time. It was jujitsu—take *that*—to all the critics. "We're Grateful Dead, we love it all, we can cover it all."

In the hotel room, Bobby says, "Yeah, I want to be wearing the pastel-colored tee shirt under the pastel suit that Don Johnson wears, a gold chain, y'know, the whole nine yards." We are all paying attention then, heads are nodding. He goes on, "And we gotta have some kind of brothel-type setting for me to interact with the dominatrix." I'm scribbling away . . . "And we have to have some animals in there." He's cut off by hoots and jibes from the others. "Wait, wait. We don't want any beastiality in this thing, do we?" Weir just smiles, enjoying it. Someone says, "Well, if you're going to have animals, we have to have a tiger," and Weir immediately nods and agrees. "Yes, a tiger!" I write down "tiger."

I can't say I remember how the rest of the plot or content of the video was generated on that day in the hotel room, but maybe it was something like this: Billy yells out, "Me and Mickey [Hart] could be driving the car to hell, with Bobby in the back seat!" And then Bobby might yell, "With the dominatrix next to me!" And Jerry might say, "What about the duck?" And Bobby would say, "The duck will be in the back seat of the car with us." And then he'd add, "It has to be a convertible, of course." And then Mickey would yell, "Yeah, a '63 Cadillac, the one with the biggest fins ever!" And Billy says, "Me and Mickey in devil outfits, with horns and shit!" And then Garcia adds, "Yeah, you should have a map, a map to hell, spread out between you, and you two could be arguing about the route." And Billy makes the point to me, the steering wheel has to have this thing called a Brodie knob attached to it that was hot for a while back then, so you could drive with one hand on the knob instead of two hands on the wheel.

We did get a '63 Cadillac convertible for the shoot, with the huge fins, pink, as it happens, and fully equipped with the steering wheel doodad, and also a tiger, and a whole lot of other shit. So, for the next two weeks I entered into this zone of get-it-done preproduction, happy as a clam. There was no problem with the money coming from Clive Davis and Arista. I was working so hard and moving so fast I really don't have much memory of it. We shot the bordello scene at the band's San Rafael studio and warehouse, we shot the bar scenes and the satanic party scene at New George's, and we shot the car scenes from a giant camera truck pulling a trailer with the '63 Caddy on it in a loop for several hours around Fourth Street in downtown San Rafael, the same terrain George Lucas used for *American Graffiti* (1973).

In August '87 I felt really great, in good health, despite the extreme work and turmoil in my personal life. I had the full-on positive energy of the band's sudden huge success (the Dead/Dylan stadium tour, "Touch of Grey," *In the Dark*, MTV's Day of the Dead, the imminent *So Far* release) as wind at my back, and everyone working and living in the Grateful Dead scene was energized.

I recruited all the extras we would need for the "Hell in a Bucket" video from the roster of Grateful Dead employees (ticket and merchandise offices, staff and management, tech, and road crews) to play the rowdy people partying and fighting in the bar scenes and celebrating and dancing in the satanic nightclub scene. The two-day film shoot brought all of us, the employees, the band, me, and the film crew, together in a huge two-day party. Looking back, I think that this was the reason why it was so much fun and why the music video was so successful. The song, the plot, all the action in it, and all the people appearing in it, were part of and grew from the Grateful Dead family, and the resultant "Hell in a Bucket" music video was as close as you could get to a Dead purist's worldview.

Before the shoot, I'm forewarned by the Grateful Dead office staff that Weir has just come back from some kind of rehab facility, or vacation, where he was drying out, that is, getting sober. I am totally used to this kind of thing, dealing with the talent throughout my career. I think that's great; he wants to be in top shape for the shoot, but the message to me is make sure there is no alcohol or drugs around during the shoot. I'm like, okay, fine, no problem, I want that too. I tell my staff to substitute fake liquor bottles for the real ones in the on-location bar and nightclub shoots, which is a very common and normal kind of thing to do in film shoots, and be alert to any possible incursions into our production from outsiders "bearing gifts."

The first day of shooting is the bar scene, where a tattooed Sue Stephens sits next to Garcia at the bar while he strums his guitar. Bob Weir in his Don Johnson persona leans on the bar next to them, with the duck on the bar in front of him appearing quite at home. Bobby shows a Polaroid of a dominatrix to his biker friend, and everything devolves into happy violence. Then we shoot the satanic nightclub scene, where Big Steve, in full devil costume, lip-synchs the lyrics, and the Grateful Dead employees and the whole big family, all in costume, sing and dance along. It all goes incredibly well. I'm blown away by how much the footage we get feels exactly like what we'd imagined and put in the script.

We take a break and then reassemble on Fourth Street, right outside New George's, for the night shoot of the Cadillac going to hell scenes. We had decided to do this by putting our '63 pink Cadillac on a trailer, with four actors inside: Billy and Mickey are up front, and the duck, Bobby, and the dominatrix are in the back seat. The trailer is towed by a large camera truck, with three tiers for the camera and sound people, the director and staff, and guests facing back toward the car on the trailer.

Garcia loves riding in the camera truck shooting the pink Caddy with me and the crew; he so loves the process of filmmaking. And the whole thing lives up to his essential criteria: Have fun.

As we pull the trailer through downtown San Rafael in a loop, maybe a half dozen times, blaring the music through speakers so that the actors in the car have a soundtrack and Bobby can lip-synchs, it becomes a celebration. The people walking by on the sidewalk start saluting us, singing along. Some of them realize that if they just hang out for a few minutes, the whole parade will go by again, and so the crowd grows.

In the front seat, Billy and Mickey argue over the directions to hell on a map between them, while in the back seat Bobby sings and the dominatrix (played by San Francisco model Allison Sullivan, cast for the part just days before, and killing it) tolerates him while they drink (fake) champagne, with the duck between them, cutely looking about. In succeeding takes, as we go through the verses, Bobby and the dominatrix flirt, and the duck is active, curious about the fake champagne going back and forth. It eventually puts its bill into Bobby's glass and has a nice pull on it.

The next day when I get to look at the rushes from the shoot, I see the duck drinking from Bobby's champagne, and it's absolutely priceless. I'm thinking, "Holy shit! This is awesome! Everyone will be amazed that we could train it to do that!"

In subsequent takes, the duck is slumped over, out of it. I figure it just got tired, and we are lucky that a tired duck just happens to look like a drunk duck, which is incredibly good fortune.

But wait! I get an irate phone call from the duck trainer, who is very upset. He loves his duck, and I know this because I'd had a nice interaction with him when we first met before the shoot, when he was explaining to all of us how to work with his duck.

He tells me that we got his duck totally drunk, and he is pissed off. I tell him it's impossible the duck was drunk, but he's adamant, so I tell him I'll get back to him. I make a few calls and discover that Weir had surreptitiously smuggled real champagne into the car scene (don't ask, I don't know), and we are indeed responsible for the duck's bad night out. During the pressurized edit of "Hell in a Bucket" (we had to get it to MTV ASAP), we discover that the duck-in-the-car subplot, where Bob and the dominatrix drive around while the duck samples Bob's glass, ending in the duck slumped over passed out, is subtle, but works spectacularly, hilariously, once you notice it.

I call the duck trainer to offer my sincere apologies, and take full responsibility for what had happened, explaining the circumstances, and prepared to make amends in whatever way he thinks appropriate. I ask about the duck's health, and he tells me that the duck is doing okay, recovering. I express relief, and then he explains to me that he had been training the duck for years using white grapes as a reward, and this is why the duck went so ardently after the champagne (and at that moment I finally understand the whole picture).

But now the duck will no longer respond to the grapes and is actually repelled by them. I repeat how sorry I am about the whole situation. In the end he doesn't ask for any recompense, he just says optimistically that he will train the duck with a new reward, and we are all good.

Whew! Dodged a bullet there.

The second day of the shoot is entirely at the Dead's huge warehouse and studio on Front Street in San Rafael, where we've built a beautiful red-velvety set for the bordello scenes. There's a four-poster bed covered in zebra skin, an upright piano, and various chains and whips lying around. And, per the script, there's a variety of barnyard animals, in addition to the omnipresent duck, and an actual nine-foot-long, four-hundred-pound Bengal tiger.

I've been briefed in depth about the tiger from the provider and the handlers, two big, tall, strong men, one of whom I vaguely recognize from the Johnny Carson show (Carson had the occasional wild-animal bit). It seems like we have it covered and it will be safe, but when it actually comes down to it, things get pretty hairy, at least for me.

We've put most of the shots in the can, saving the tiger stuff for last, knowing that we definitely want to minimize the time sharing the set with this huge animal, which is at this moment locked in a secure truck outside. The two trainers come into the weird bordello set to talk to the assembled talent, crew, and audience (there are bleachers off to one side for the Grateful Dead employees and their kids to watch the shoot, and Garcia has planted himself there).

They are very professional and reassuring, but they emphasize that the tiger is a wild animal—it isn't domesticated, it isn't a pet. One of them goes on to explain they will be tossing one-pound pieces of raw steak to the tiger between takes, so that he will never get any ideas while looking around at the barnyard animals and all the humans, which, the trainer points out, he probably views as just another type of monkey, a prey animal.

But they say not to worry, they will each be attached to the animal via heavy chain-link leashes at all times, except for the brief moments when the camera is rolling. I'm listening and starting to feel less and less serene. Occasionally on a film set, you are reminded that you are actually in charge, something I don't like to be reminded of or dwell on; the responsible part of the job was never the part I loved.

One time several years earlier I had been shooting a tribute to Count Basie and his orchestra, with Lena Horne, Stevie Wonder, Dionne Warwick, James Ingram, Joe Williams, Quincy Jones, and others, at Radio City Music Hall in NYC, one of the biggest and most beautiful "legit" theaters in the world. Radio City had an enormous stage with three vertically movable stage sections, and an orchestra pit that can drop down forty feet to facilitate the quick substitution of dancers and musicians. It was a very dramatic effect to watch a bunch of performers suddenly rise up in front of the audience and jump onto the main stage. I thought it would be a great idea to bring up a group of dancers that way to do their number. Naturally, there's a protocol carried out via headset among the stage managers, the recording trucks (which included me and the staff), and the talent handlers regarding the up or down position of the orchestra pit, in order to deliver the dramatic entrance on cue.

The script called for Dionne Warwick and Lena Horne to accompany Count Basie in his electric wheelchair to the center-stage mic, where he would receive his standing ovation. The two women would briefly sing his praises and then stand back a little while he spoke to the crowd. The idea was that he would never be left alone onstage, because the orchestra pit was down, receiving its load of dancers and leaving a gaping hole with a forty-foot drop in front of the stage. I had early on decided that I was not going to try to explain to Basie how he had to navigate in his wheelchair in order to avoid driving into that gaping hole.

Maybe you see where this is going . . .

On cue, Quincy and the orchestra hit the big intro music for Dionne, Lena, and the Count, but instead of the three of them, it was just the two women who headed for the center-stage mic. Alarmed, I jumped on the headset to the stage manager, yelling, "Wait, where's Basie? He's supposed to be with them!" There was confusion on his end; I guess he hadn't gotten the memo. He was like, "Where's Basie? He's right here standing by . . ." I was like, "Oh my God, what do I do?" We couldn't communicate with Lena and Dionne while they were talking to the crowd. I could have just called an abrupt halt to everything while we fixed the problem, creating chaos in front of a huge crowd of paying music lovers. The stage manager was useless. He explained, "Basie wanted them to introduce him and then he'd go out there on his own." I was thinking, "And you didn't think it was maybe a good idea to tell me about this development?" So I was stressing as the two glamorous women introduced Basie and turned to exit the stage just as he came zooming out on his wheelchair. They had a little smooch as they passed each other, and the crowd was on their feet, roaring.

CHAPTER 10

Lena and Dionne were gone, and Basie was drinking it in. Then he started maneuvering his wheelchair to the center-stage mic. I had never been so scared in my life. (Well, there was that time in college when I was selling weed from my dorm room and got ripped off at gunpoint and thought I was gonna die, but other than that . . .) But he seemed to be aiming himself toward the mic stand. I took a breath. With the spotlights shining in his eyes and the fact that everything was unrehearsed, did he even *know* about the orchestra pit? He got to the mic, the crowd still applauding, and looked around mischievously. Instead of talking, he started inching his chair toward the pit! My heart was in my throat, pounding, the only time I've ever felt that. He rolled up to the lip of the stage, stopped, took a long look down into the pit, then made a dramatic face at the audience. Everyone had a good laugh, and then he turned the chair around and went back to the mic. Back on script. Oh my God!

I don't remember the next several minutes or half hour, my heart still pounding, but the show went well. I was busy imagining the headline: "Film Director Arrested in Tragic Death of Jazz Legend Count Basie at His Own Tribute Show."

Ever since then, I've made it a point to always stress safety first in everything I've ever produced or directed. When you assemble the best, most creative and hardworking professionals, eager to help you make a good film or broadcast, they can get carried away on a tide of perfectionism. They need to be reminded constantly not to take unnecessary risks. Stifle your heroism, this is not a war for our national survival, it's just a fucking TV show or movie, okay? What's the worst that could happen? It might suck, but so what? We'll all go on to the next job. Or maybe some of us will never work again, so what?

That's a philosophy I discovered while working with Garcia, as it extends to his point of view: He never sweated whether the performance they were about to embark upon would be good or bad, or whether the show they just finished was good or bad, because it's a pointless waste of time. Stay in the moment, go out there and do the best you can, have faith in the process (very important to performers who do a lot of improvisation, like the Dead and jazz musicians). And if you walk off the stage after a show and you all think it sucked, you just laugh about it, shrug it off, have a drink, live to play again. Garcia used to say, to quote Samuel Beckett, "Fail better!" And to judge from the growth of their audience over the years, the Dead were very good at delivering the goods in live performances, despite the occasional poor show, which the fans were inoculated to. Many is the time that I was in the crowd, not working, and noticing that the band was kinda blowing it. The fans would routinely chuckle, light up a fatty, and talk to each other and party, until they gradually noticed that the band was getting it together and their attention would go back to the stage. When I was up in the cheap seats looking down on 20,000 fans, a point of view I occasionally like to get, I could hear the band struggling, and the crowd gradually reacting by turning to partying. The crowd hubbub would go up and up, kinda drowning out the band, and then when the band got their shit together, the sound relationship between crowd and band would reverse. There were many, many times when I witnessed a huge crowd reduced to absolute reverential silence—you could hear a pin drop—while listening to a killer version of "Stella Blue" or "Morning Dew." It was amazing.

Okay, back at the Front Street studio, where the tiger handlers are prepping us for the appearance of the beast, the handler doing the talking becomes stern, commanding attention from the thirty or so people present.

He says, "Absolutely no camera flashes at any time; if we see one, we're outta here. Do not make any sudden moves while he's in here, and under no circumstances should you approach him or attempt to touch him. He will be under our control at all times, because of the steaks and the chains. There's nothing to worry about, but we don't want to tempt fate, do we?"

Everyone is quiet, kind of sobering up. The outright party atmosphere of the shoot prior to that moment is over. "Okay, so when we bring him in here" (he gestures to the long corridor we had constructed for a motorcycle shot), "you may hear a kind of loud sound, like growling. But it's just the equivalent of purring, cuz he's a cat, and his purring is in a much lower scale and louder, cuz he's like four hundred pounds. Don't worry, the sound is nothing to worry about." Everyone is serious, listening, exchanging glances. I do notice that Weir has a cockeyed grin on his face. I know what he's thinking. He gets along very well with animals, plus he's just totally fearless as a permanent default position. That's just the way it is with him and Garcia, and also the other four guys in the band, to a less dependable degree.

The handler changes tone, summing up: "Okay, at this point we have to clear all nonessential personnel from the set. No children or their parents or anyone not actively working on this shoot can stay in here." You'd be amazed at how fast all those people beat a hasty retreat. When the handlers are satisfied that it is just crew and talent here, they excuse themselves and tell us to remain quiet, no sudden moves, they'll be right back.

Well, if they are trying to sober us up, they succeeded. Garcia is alone in the bleachers that everyone else has left, loving every minute of this. I can tell even from a distance how much he's relishing this. Meanwhile, the crew sort of withdraws to the perimeter of the set, along with the barnyard animals and the duck and their handlers. Weir and Allison, the dominatrix actor, sit down on the bed to stoically wait. Phil Lesh and Brent Mydland, in costume for their parts in the bordello scene, huddle on the far side of the opening of the corridor leading to the set, while I perch on a road box by myself on the other side of the corridor entrance. Then we all kind of freeze.

From our positions, no one can see down the corridor, but presently we hear the sound that the handlers had warned us about, the purring, getting closer and closer. It's deep and primal and scary, and accompanied by the sound of the jangling chain leashes approaching us. Suddenly to my left, maybe four feet from me, the giant head of the great cat appears as it enters into the room, the handlers behind it. The tiger pauses, glancing casually around the set, no doubt assessing all the monkeys standing and hiding and not moving, then continues into the set.

I am watching from the side as it enters, and it seems to go on for fucking ever, because it is really, really big, like ten feet long including his tail, so it takes a while for it to actually get into the room. Once the tiger is fully in the room, the handlers tug it to a stop and throw some raw steaks in front of it, which it casually devours in a few moments as we look on. I'm having some serious doubts by this time, wondering what the fuck I had been thinking. But I have to admit I'm also really excited, on a deeper level, to be in this position, living the life, at one with the Grateful Dead experience.

One of the barnyard animals on set, a pig, starts squealing and trying to hide, and then shits himself. Like, duh, he knows an apex predator when he sees and smells one, and he knows he is prey. This is a great icebreaker for all of us to jump to and be professional. The handlers signal that the tiger is happy; they will just wait while we scramble to get the pig off the set and clean up its little mess and clear the other animals off the set as well. And then we proceed to get the shots we need.

Once again Bobby shines as a lip-syncher and actor, and Allison, Brent, and Phil do great at their parts, along with the fire-eater, the sword-swallower, and of course the duck. We all gradually relax as we see how the handlers have control of the tiger—basically by throwing it untold pounds of raw steak every few minutes. We can see how he was just a big ol' friendly kitty cat. We get a shot of him lying on the bed just behind Bobby and Allison, his huge head barely two feet from their smaller heads, as they shared a toast of . . . champagne, of course.

The shoot is over, but we need to get some publicity stills. So, we position the tiger in the foreground on the floor in front of the bed, and Weir, Garcia, Allison, and I sit on the bed just behind it, toasting with glasses of champagne. I'm on the bed, in the shot (something I'm not especially comfy with), surrounded by the talent with the huge animal lying right in front of us, and Bobby decides to strike a dramatic pose, which included resting his left foot—he is now shoeless, for some reason—on the lower spine of the tiger.

Alarm bells go off in my head. "Oh my God, do you not remember what they said about *not touching the fucking tiger* under any circumstances?!" I'm suddenly flashing back to my Count Basie experience, only now the headline is, "Film Director Arrested in the Horrible Death-by-Tiger-Mauling of Beloved Rock Star Bob Weir."

But the tiger was not the slightest bit ruffled, the pictures were taken, and then it was gone, and we all went about the business of breaking down the set and getting the hell out of there.

Garcia had observed the whole day's shooting with avid interest. He just loved the hell out of the filmmaking process, just as he always had, going back to 1965. As the breakdown and loadout proceeded, I think he could sense how discombobulated I was after two solid days of madcap production. I was wildly happy, totally energized, but now facing the fact that it was over, and I had to come down. I was having trouble processing the fact it was over, and I think he could sympathize with me being an outsider he had brought into this peculiar scene of theirs. I still had a way to go to get used to their modus operandi, which was basically shoot for the moon, forget your fears, damn the torpedoes, and get used to how it feels when everything goes perfectly, and it turns out better than you thought possible. Relax, enjoy it, but learn to let it go, because tomorrow's another day, and that day may *suck.* So we smoked cigarettes and laughed until we noticed everything and everyone else was gone, and the security guy was turning off the lights and politely nudging us to get out of there and go home.

CHAPTER 10

I can unequivocally state that those two days of shooting were the most fun I have ever had in my entire life—not the happiest days or the best days or the most important, but definitely the most fun—and at the risk of bragging, I feel that I have to mention here that I have had a *lot* of fun in my life.

Chapter 11

LAWRENCE OF ARABIA WITH MACHINE GUNS

I was meeting Garcia at the Grateful Dead office in San Rafael, just after business hours one day at the end of March 1989, so that we could carpool to the Northpoint Theater (now long gone) on the corner of Powell Street and Bay Street in San Francisco to see the movie *Lawrence of Arabia* in its full glory on the big screen. It was a rerelease of the iconic 1962 David Lean film starring Peter O'Toole, Alec Guinness, Anthony Quinn, and Omar Sharif, and a must-see for all true lovers of cinema, as me and Jerry surely were.

We pulled into the lot simultaneously, greeting each other with masculine, cheerful fanboy behavior, because we were on an adventure to see a truly great motion picture. He was in good spirits, moving quickly as he did when he was feeling good. We agreed to take his car, as usual the biggest Beamer he could get. But before we got in the car, he said, "Wait a minute, I've got to load some CDs." In those days, the CD player was in the trunk, and you could load six or so CDs into it, then control it with a remote to play through the stereo system of the car. He popped the trunk and leaned inside as I waited nearby.

I quickly noticed something that gave me a jolt of cognitive dissonance: two black assault rifles with ammo magazines attached lying haphazardly in the trunk. I was shocked. It made no sense. Garcia? What? Then I recalled that I was a nerd from New York City, where no guns of any kind were legal, let alone anything like those. In NYC, if you were at a party with your friends and peers in the arts community and mentioned that you owned a revolver, people would move away from you.

I reminded myself I was not in New York anymore. Gun ownership in California was common, if not the norm. I remembered a time I was hanging out with Bill Kreutzmann at his place in Marin, playing pool in his rec room while high on LSD, when he asked if I wanted to see his guns, and I was taken aback. But I liked Bill, he was a very positive, entertaining kind of guy, and one of my clients, so I decided to be a big boy. We went up to his bedroom, and he dug out a box from the closet and proudly showed me three handguns, describing their attributes, and allowed me to hold them. Of course I asked, "Are these loaded?" And he gave the standard gun-owner response, chuckling and saying, "Well, they wouldn't be much good if they weren't, would they?" I chuckled too and handed them back gingerly, kind of frightened. The one I remembered was a small, dark brown, smoothly designed pistol—I think it was a Walther. That was part of my growing awareness that Grateful Dead, the actual guys in the band and the crew surrounding them, were maybe far more like pirates, or the Katzenjammer Kids (crazy destructive youngsters in a comic strip phenom that ran for most the twentieth century, when Garcia discovered it), than they were like peace-and-love flower children or dope-smoking hippies, the image the media loved to portray.

Peering into the trunk, I put on my best casual demeanor and asked Garcia, pointing at the assault rifles, "Uh, what are these?" He paused from his CD loading and looked up. "Oh, those are AK-47s, semiautomatic," he said as if he were describing butterfly nets or fishing rods. In those days, that was the gun you wanted to have in case you suddenly decided to join a mercenary army and go kill people. The version most popular today is the AR-15, a weapon of war.

He went back to CD loading, and I said, "Are we planning to hit a bank or something on the way to the movie?" He glanced up at me, like, "What?" Then he noticed that I was looking at the machine guns, laughed, and said, "Oh yeah, Parish told me that they're gonna be illegal soon in California, so I told him to get me a few." He slammed the trunk shut. As we moved to get in the car, I said, "What do you do with them?" He answered, "Me and Steve will go out somewhere you can shoot and it's okay, and we'll do a bunch of target practice and shoot up a bunch of shit. It's fun." And off we went to the movies.

So, we're in Garcia's big Beamer, he's driving, barreling south down 101 toward the Golden Gate Bridge to San Francisco, which involves a few big turns, and a major climb called the Waldo Grade leading up to the Waldo Tunnel (it's now named for Robin Williams). Garcia is a very confident and skilled driver, pushing the machine when necessary, changing lanes, keeping to the speed limit. I never once felt fearful while he was driving (something I commonly feel while in cars driven by others).

As we're driving, the car phone rings, and Garcia picks it up. In these days, before the cell phone shrank to pocket-size, car phones are a high-end addition to any car. It was a nicely designed handset nestled in the console between the two front seats, and when you picked it up to talk, it was just like picking up a phone at home. The handset was connected to the console by a curly wire, so I couldn't hear what the caller was saying. Garcia shows no hesitation about driving while also talking on the phone, and I'm not nervous either, because like I said, he's a very competent driver.

It's immediately clear to me that he is talking to a fellow band member, either Bobby, Phil, Mickey, or Billy. They have a distinct way of communicating as equals that no one else in the organization has. It is cordial at first, joking and needling being their default setting, but then it quickly changes to a business issue.

From hearing Garcia's side of the chat, I deduce that the caller is detailing how he believes a Grateful Dead employee is stealing from the organization, someone who is in charge of one of the satellite operations that produces an important amount of income, and also has built a special relationship between Grateful Dead and their fans—maybe the ticket office, which provides early access to low-cost shows; or the merchandise operation, which sells tee shirts, hats, calendars, and the like; or maybe someone working at the recording studio on Front Street. The person in question seems to be a member of their inner circle, going back decades.

I'm just trying to be impassive while the conversation is happening, not wanting to intrude or eavesdrop, but as usual, Garcia shows no sign of caring. I can't help but notice that he is listening like an indulgent parent: "Uh-huh." Pause. "Okay, so, you think he's stealing from us? How do you know that?"

This gets my attention.

Then he's done receiving information. He says to the caller, friendly but with a touch of both sarcasm and reproach, "So do you not have enough money? Are you making enough money?" He pauses for the caller's response, then says, "Well okay, good . . . so am I . . ." Pause for caller, then, "No, we're not going to fire him—" The caller objects, Garcia nods indulgently, smiling, then says, "Why not? Because if we fire him he will be let loose on . . . society! Where will he go, what will he do? We can't take responsibility for inflicting him on everybody else . . . What will he do if we don't take care of him?"

I'm suddenly transfixed by this conversation. I actually start to laugh, quietly. It's so foreign to me, the idea that a business owner when faced with the idea of theft from an employee, would just shrug it off, disinterested in the evidence or the proof, and play it for laughs instead.

But Garcia is like a grandma listening to a kid whine. He can't take it seriously. He says, "He's not equipped to take care of himself . . .What do you think it is, this thing we're doing? . . . There aren't any rules . . . We hired him, we created him, he's one of us."

But in that moment, I had a revelation: He was not playing it for laughs; he was actually quite serious and reminding his friend in the gentlest way possible that he was one of us, invoking the ancient tribal stance of solidarity first, and also the Christian code of empathy for the weakest among us, and the teaching that we must take care of each other first and foremost. Essentially the opposite of the idea that Garcia was the owner of a business, and an employee was stealing from him, which is of course the premise of a capitalist or ownership paradigm. That paradigm was largely birthed in the West by the Abrahamic religions, wherein God gave the earth to us to do with as we pleased. Contrast that with the sustainable paradigm of all of nature except humans, where there is no owning stuff or controlling resources for profit (see more about this in Chapter 3: The Zen of Jerry).

I felt a tremendous wave of shame as I sat there next to Garcia in his car. It was a profound experience that I will never forget, that changed me deeply. I had not really understood who he was or what was at the core of the Grateful Dead phenomenon until that moment. I mean, I thought I did, but not really, viscerally. It reminded me, in the moment, of the teachings of Jesus, and many other spiritual and religious leaders for thousands of years: If you have enough resources (in our modern case, money) to make you secure and happy with your family and neighbors, why would you seek to have more, rather than to share it with people who don't have enough, or maybe have nothing at all and live in desperation, to give them the security and happiness that you have? I was ashamed because I had resisted this understanding of Garcia and Robert Hunter and their whole subculture as being a real thing to them. It was not a strategy to engage their fans, or the public, or the media; it was at the core of who Garcia really was.

As he finished the call, my shame gave way to a wave of appreciation that I could now understand the reality that these spiritual ideas were in active play in the world around me, and even greater appreciation that I was playing a role in advancing these ideas in the work I was doing with Garcia and the Dead. I was suddenly overwhelmingly happy, teary-eyed, such that I felt I had to try to hide my feelings from him. Of course he could tell I was going through something. But so what? He was probably used to this kind of thing after hundreds of similar previous experiences, and it passed by the time we got to the Waldo Tunnel.

Jerry as Santa Claus, video production still from Ticket to New Year's *pay-per-view broadcast, December 31, 1987.*
Photo courtesy Len Dell'Amico's personal archive.

Chapter 12

BILLY, BOBBY, AND "THROWING STONES"

I was in my room at the Navarro Hotel on 59th Street across from Central Park (it was taken over by the Ritz-Carlton around that time and is now a condo-coop building known as 110 Central Park South), unwinding after a good Dead show at Madison Square Garden in NYC. It was maybe 11:00 p.m. or midnight, during the peak period for the band, 1987 to 1990, the best of times. The phone rang. I picked it up and it was Bill Kreutzmann. He was clearly in a good mood and invited me to his room for a drink, or food, or maybe some blow, I don't remember, so I popped over there. It was just the two of us, feeling good, kidding around. I always got along well with Billy. He is a warm, outgoing, good-time kind of guy, not complicated, direct. You could always tell what he was feeling, and if he had something to say he was not shy about it. He was the guy in the band, on the day back in January '85 when we made our deal, who pointedly told me, with intense eye contact, that I should remember that I work with and for all six of them and made me verbally acknowledge that I understood. Over time, I'd heard stories about his temper, how he could become threatening or intimidating in an argument, but I never experienced that side of him.

CHAPTER 12

But there was that time he and I and one of the band's engineers were sitting around the octagonal glass table in the kitchen at their office, just shootin' the shit in the afternoon, when the subject of drugs came up, specifically hard drugs of the type that everyone was concerned about with regard to Garcia (this was probably in '86, when he was still struggling with it). We were talking about our own past experiences with various substances, when I casually mentioned I didn't know anything about the class of substances known as opioids (derived from the poppy plant, such as opium, morphine, and heroin), or the whole class known as downers, the pharmaceuticals, from the benzodiazepines like Valium and Percodan and other synthetic opioids, because I'd never done any of them. I noticed that Bill was looking at me piercingly. I kept talking about how I'd never been attracted to substances that were numbing or painkilling; I was scared of them. I liked weed and psychedelics and stimulants. I noticed Bill was still glaring at me, like maybe stifling rage. I didn't know what to make of it. The engineer guy looked from me to Billy and back, as if he might have an inkling.

I later surmised that Billy may have heard the bullshit story that I was somehow supplying Garcia with his Persian smoking powder, or at least sharing it with him. If true, that could certainly have caused him to distrust me, given his relationship with Garcia, and if I were lying like a rug about it at that moment, could plausibly have made him very angry.

In that moment, as we were looking each other in the eye, I was mystified, but intuited strongly that I needed to just hold his gaze. I said to him, "What?" He dropped his stare and he relaxed, apparently thinking something over.

Again, looking back, I surmised that instead of confronting me with his anger, he suddenly realized that whoever had told him that story about me and Garcia and hard drugs was probably lying, and further, he could imagine the motive that this person might have had to lie about me. Anyway, the moment passed.

Even earlier, in '85, when I was still living at the Corte Madera Inn (now a Best Western) right on Highway 101 while working on *So Far,* I was still very much a fish out of water, alone, missing Veronica and our two cats at our place in Brooklyn. Somehow, Billy and his current girlfriend Shelley must have caught wind of my loneliness, stopped by the motel one night, and invited me to come meet them at the Pepper Mill, the motel's restaurant and cocktail lounge, which I was pleased to do.

The cocktail lounge was so prototypically mid-'80s that recalling it now makes me laugh. It was open very late and there was always a police or sheriff's car or two in the parking lot. The booths and the bar were dark, lit only by a large firepit that was roaring nonstop, all the time. The cocktail waitresses were uniformly young, tall, and beautiful, and they all wore the same revealing low-cut dress, slit up one side to way above the knee. Shelley, Bill, and I settled into a booth where we could gaze at the fire and ordered our drinks. They were jovial, playful with each other, and soon drew me out a little bit about what it felt like to be transported from my world in New York to this one. They sympathized and definitely made me feel better.

When it was time to go, they offered to walk me to my room in the warm night air. On the way to their car, past the shimmering swimming pool, past the hot tub, I joked that I hoped I hadn't gone on too much about my problems, saying something like, "Maybe I need a shrink." They laughed, and just as we were about to part, Bill stopped, got close enough to look me in the eye, which startled me a bit, and said, "I will be your therapist . . ." I must've gone wide-eyed, and he continued, "for . . . one dollar a year!" I burst out laughing. It was perfect, a perfect moment when I felt a genuine connection with him. But I did turn him down, and he was like, "Okay, I tried." We went our separate ways, laughing, and I was feeling much better than I had been a few hours before.

Maybe a month or so later, at the start of the third and final day of an expensive, high-stakes shoot at the Marin Veterans' Memorial Auditorium, an important step in creating *So Far*, it really wasn't clear that we had gotten enough material in the can to advance the project, and so there was a lot of pressure. The morning shoot yielded a great "Uncle John's Band"/"Playing in the Band" medley, and then the afternoon shoot, our last chance, culminated in an astounding "Drums/Space"/"Throwing Stones"/"Not Fade Away" medley. When the band came down on the last big climactic moment of "Not Fade Away" and the song ended, everyone present, including the film crew (who are not supposed to reveal their presence), burst into sustained cheering and applause. The guys in the band grinned and nodded at each other as they took off their guitars and stepped away from their drum kits and keyboards, and I knew that we had gotten what we needed from the shoot. It was one of the best moments of my professional life.

CHAPTER 12

I left the truck and went onstage to share the moment with the band and the film crew as the stage crew began the breakdown and loadout of the band's gear, and oh my, what a high it was. A bit later I was hanging with just the band in their dressing room when Billy came up to me, still wiping the sweat from his face with a towel, amazingly excited, and said to me, "I never knew that we could do that, hit that level of playing without an audience. I always thought that they provided the magic that took us there, but now I know that we can do that ourselves, just by ourselves."

Now, I've been blown away many, many times by wonderful, unexpected things that happened during my career or my life, but that moment was one of the best. Here was Bill Kreutzmann, a founding member of Grateful Dead, a band that had produced possibly more intensely high moments of musical ecstasy for more people than any other band in history, and he was telling me that until that moment, he deeply believed that they, the band, were dependent on the crowd, their fans, to bring them to that level, but that he'd discovered for the first time that they could do it by themselves. I was gobsmacked. I didn't know what to make of that. It implied that one or more, or possibly all of the guys in the band, viewed their own experience from a deeply psychedelicized point of view. That they and their fans and followers were in fact cocreating their live shows, as opposed to the standard model of a band playing to a passive audience. I have to say that was, and still is, a very compelling belief to me. Having shot sixty or so shows and also enjoyed another hundred or so shows as a fan in the stands, their concerts, at peak moments, did truly seem to be a cocreation of the band and the audience.

Many of Grateful Dead's records released between 1967 and 1990 were live performances, at a higher percentage than most other musical artists at the time. There was a widespread belief among their fans, and also within the band itself, that they just played better live than in a recording studio. I can't think of another act that this was said of (other than maybe Springsteen). There was an assumption that Grateful Dead only conjured magic when playing live, because of the mysterious role of the crowd, their fans.

Today, I can now see the importance of Garcia's conviction and determination to record the band with both high-end visuals and audio, playing live, truly live (which is decidedly *not* how records are made), but without an audience. That way we would be totally free to rehearse, stop and start takes, do multiple takes, and goof around, all without having to think about the experience of the audience, to see if the band could capture that lightning in a bottle they were known for in live performances. Instead, it would be for a new kind of creative product, made explicitly for the ages, but more immediately for the newly emerging visual mass media in the mid-'80s. This was an approach to film that they'd never done before and had rarely been done by anyone else.

Anyway, back in Billy's room at the Ritz-Carlton in NYC years later, the phone rings, and Billy picks it up, listens briefly, says "Uh-huh" a few times, then says, "Got it, we'll be right there," and hangs up. He jumps up, grabs his room key, and commands me to come with him. I'm like, "Wait, what's up? Where are we going?"

He gives me a wicked grin and says, "It's a code 240, we gotta go," and heads out the door. I scramble behind him into the hallway as I say, "What's a code 240?" But he's moving fast and just says, "A friend in need."

We arrive at a door, and we can hear that there's a party going on behind it, music playing. Billy knocks, a young lady opens the door, and he bounds in with me tagging along. We're in a large, smoke-filled living room, obviously part of a suite—in fact, Bob Weir's suite (he always has a suite so he can host parties). I can see Weir off in a corner; he has his bicycle upside down on a dining table, working on it with a tool of some kind. The room is filled with maybe eight young women, though they mostly look like girls, everywhere you look. No one is naked (yet), but some are only semi-clad. There aren't any males except for Bobby, and now me and Billy. It slowly dawns on me what a code 240 might be.

We go over to Weir, nodding and smiling at the girls perched on the furniture like so many pets, clearly happy to be there, laughing, singing along with the music, but also eyeing one another a bit warily. We get to Bob, and he pulls us in close and says, "Hey listen, could you help me out here until I figure out who I want to stay?" Billy grins and high-fives him. "Sure, man!"

Now, I've never been in this kind of situation before, but it seems that my and Billy's job is to lure some of these ladies into an adjoining bedroom to take some pressure off Bob, or later to help him clear the suite once he decides the time is right, maybe encouraging some girls to come with us back to our rooms. There's a knock at the door, and two more girls come in and greet everyone, squealing.

You see, I'm not, nor have I ever been, a lothario. I always feel pretty lucky with women, but I'm the kind of guy who wants to get to know someone a bit before getting naked with them. Y'know, at least a date or two so I can feel pretty sure they aren't psychotic or something. Whereas from the rock star's point of view, what's the worry? They don't want anything more from you than you want from them, and in the morning you'll both be gone. But I'm not a rock star, not even a musician, and I would never, God knows, misrepresent who I am or try to puff myself up in order to get laid. In other words, I'm a stupid, naïve young man slightly on the autism spectrum, and way out of my league.

Looking back, I feel like maybe I missed a lot of opportunities for casual sex with a variety of women. I've seen research and heard anecdotal evidence that many men, upon seeing the pearly gates in the distance, express regret that they didn't have more sexual partners when they were younger. I can relate to that, now that I'm old enough to imagine what it might be like to be even older and seeing the pearly gates in the distance, but every time I think it over, I come down on the side of my lived experience. I enjoyed some meaningless encounters and flings, and several deep, long-lasting, intimate relationships with women, including two that were exclusive cohabiting (which for me qualifies as marriage) that lasted thirteen and fifteen years. One of those long-term relationships produced a child, now twenty-five years old, and I feel pretty good about my choices. To pine for more when you know you have had so much compared to others, I now recognize as unevolved and neurotic.

Despite my reticence about casual sex, I did get pretty high in Weir's suite, and I was able to sit and relax and chat with the girls. I imagined I was in an avant-garde movie of some kind, and things eventually became a blur. When I noticed a male member of the sound crew arrive and signal that more reinforcements were on the way, I told myself that the girls and Billy and Bobby didn't really need me there anymore, and I took the opportunity to slide out of there and get back to my own safe, quiet room.

I did get to know Weir and Kreutzmann a little over the years. I socialized with them a bit and visited their homes, which I didn't do much of with Mickey Hart, Phil Lesh, or Brent Mydland.

I have some things to say about Weir that I've always wanted to share.

When the documentary film *The Other One,* about Bobby's career and life, came out in 2014, I got the impression from the publicity material that it was casting Weir as a number two to Garcia's number one, hence "the other one." There was discussion about what it was like to live and work in someone else's shadow. That whole idea was repulsive to me. I never did see the film, but I admit now that it was probably an irrational overreaction on my part. Go figure.

There was no member of Grateful Dead that was in anyone's shadow. They were all great musicians who had great and true respect for each other, and I've never seen another band that was as democratic as they were. They all participated as equals in important business and artistic decisions. Musically, they were like six soloists who were constantly weaving their parts together, thus the jazz comparisons. Watching them work from my special vantage point, a bunch of giant monitors showing me close-ups of all of them as they shot each other glances, or reacted to what someone else was doing with a big grin, you could never doubt the integrity of their process or their lofty musical goals, which they achieved some of the time but not all of the time. Sometimes they sucked, but more often they were truly astounding. And all of them, with the exception of Brent, were big characters, confident, comfortable with their own idiosyncrasies.

So that's number one: Bobby was not a "number two" guy.

Let's look at the facts: A typical Dead show was sixteen or seventeen songs, plus the extended improvisation of drums and space. Of the songs in a given show, one or two might be written or sung by Brent, one every few shows by Phil, there would be a bunch of covers, like "Mama Tried" and "Not Fade Away," and all the rest were fairly evenly divided between Garcia and Weir. They would trade off starting the show each night; if it was Garcia one show, it would be Weir the next show. And they more or less alternated lead vocal work from one song to the next. Bob and Jerry had pretty equal roles in terms of song time. Garcia sang mostly Garcia-Hunter songs, and Bobby sang mostly Weir-Barlow songs, with a lot of covers and songs authored by other guys in the band thrown in. That was their act.

And number two: Weir is totally underestimated as a songwriter. The songs he wrote, mostly with lyricist John Barlow, were a crucial part of the Grateful Dead concert experience. Many of them were part of the liturgy, the essential spiritual messages embedded within the show—songs such as "Estimated Prophet," "Lost Sailor"/"Saint of Circumstance," "Feel Like a Stranger," "Cassidy," "Weather Report Suite"/"Let It Grow," and "Throwing Stones." And many songs provided the essential kick-ass component of a Grateful

Dead concert, like "I Need a Miracle," "Hell in a Bucket," "Sugar Magnolia," "Truckin'," and "Playing in the Band."

Weir and Garcia both provided the music to a songwriting team, their partners providing the lyrics, a common and time-honored model for more than a century in our Western culture: Gilbert and Sullivan, Rodgers and Hammerstein, Lerner and Loewe, the Gershwin brothers, Jagger and Richards. One partner brought the music and the other brought the lyrics.

While Garcia was far more prolific, Weir was more original. The Garcia-Hunter catalog is full of amazing songs, mostly derived from Appalachian music, with roots in England, Scotland, and Ireland, while Weir's stuff sounds like nothing else around. As far as I know, there are no songs predating "Estimated Prophet," "Feel Like a Stranger," "Cassidy," "Throwing Stones," "I Need a Miracle," or "Hell in a Bucket" that sound like them and that could be referenced as plausible precursors. Those songs just seem to have come from nowhere and dropped into Weir's mind. They all seem totally original to my ear, with little or no relation to musical history, and they were powerful in concert and on records, maybe enhanced because of their originality.

Speaking of their act, Grateful Dead's total repertoire was more than one hundred songs, many of which were rarely played, but they'd all pop up every now and then, nevertheless. The regular repertoire was about sixty songs on any given night, some of which were played a lot more than others. Sixteen or so songs per show, sixty-song repertoire . . . So as a fan, you would have to attend five or six shows *in a row* if you wanted to be sure of hearing your favorite song.

This diabolical scheme, unique in the history of touring rock bands, as far as I know, was the key to their huge financial success. By promising their fans that each show would be different, a unique adventure, and making no bones about the fact that when they went onstage each night they didn't have a set list, they conditioned their fans to attend all their shows in a given arena-size venue, typically three in any given city, and to follow them on the road from one show or set of shows to the next.

A side effect of their approach was that they could not tell working professionals, like sound and lighting people, or say a director who's trying to film the show as best he can, what they were going to play on any given night, which made it much more difficult for those people to do their jobs. Most rock bands normally have predictable set lists. So Grateful Dead had to have these people in-house, not hired on a per-tour basis, so they could learn and absorb the entire repertoire. That allowed these professionals to relax, de-stress about the fact that they had no idea what was coming next, and enter the world of the moment, the psychedelic world that the band inhabited.

The other key components of Grateful Dead's business plan were to keep ticket prices low as a primary goal, the exact opposite of what you see in the business today, and to encourage fans to make audio recordings of their live shows and trade them around, which was counterintuitive to the argument that bootlegged recordings would hurt record sales. But it worked in a big way for the Dead, since the Dead's main source of income wasn't from their records, but from their touring and their merchandise operation.

So, this business strategy meant that fans would be glad to congregate in a given city for two or three shows in a row, for a long, long party, in order to experience the bulk of the band's regular repertoire at a relatively low cost. And the extensive collecting and trading of bootlegged recordings of all these live shows on audiocassette built a huge army of devoted fans over time, which persists to this day. Just look at the 2023 ticket sales of the band Dead and Company (Bob Weir, Mickey Hart, Bill Kreutzmann, Oteil Burbridge, Jeff Chimenti, and John Mayer), and also the proliferation of the many jam bands, such as Phish and Widespread Panic, that were clearly inspired by the original Grateful Dead.

Getting back to the Bobby/Jerry dynamic . . . I recall a time when Weir and Garcia and I were hanging out at the band's recording studio and warehouse on Front Street in San Rafael. It was late in the day, we weren't working, just fucking off, and Weir and Garcia were arguing over who the front man was for Grateful Dead. It had the feel of an accomplished routine, maybe something they liked to chew on for their own pleasure, or for the benefit of a newbie—that would be me—for a reliable guffaw. Or maybe it was spontaneous, and they'd never before discussed who the front man of the band was in their twenty-five years together.

It started with a discussion about a recent, less-than-stellar Grateful Dead show. The two of them were poking around in the ashes, trying to understand it, all in good fun of course, and trying to assess blame. Garcia muttered under his breath, "Well, *you're* the front man."

It took a beat before Weir absorbed that, and he responded, "*I'm* not the front man, *you* are—" And then Garcia looked at him and interjected, "Hey, man, you're at the center-stage mic, not me—" And then Weir took it up a notch, cutting him off with, "Yeah, but you're the lead guitar guy." Then Garcia said, "But you sing half the songs—" And Weir said, "But so do *you*—" And Garcia came back with, "Don't tell me all the girls are going crazy over *me*!" Weir broke down laughing, Garcia joined in, and I was astonished at this repartee and joined in the laughter. Whether it was an old gag or not, well, it sure worked for me.

Those two guys loved each other like brothers. That was my takeaway from my entire experience with them. When the band was formed in 1965, Weir was seventeen or eighteen years old and Garcia was twenty-three, so there was a five-year gap between them, which is not a lot among adults, but to a teenager, five years can be a lot. I think they had an older brother–younger brother kind of relationship. Maybe Garcia mentored Weir, but as far as I could tell, there was nothing but trust between them and an urge to enjoy and explore music and life together.

When I was tasked to do promo shoots to hype TV, cable, or pay-per-view shows or concert ticket sales, or to sit for interviews as the director alongside the talent, the two of them were the "go-tos." They just had a perfectly relaxed and instinctive relationship that generated warmth and humor seemingly effortlessly. You can see this in clips of them on the Letterman show and other media appearances.

They famously did their Christmas shopping together, hiring a stretch limo to take them around to various high-end Marin County boutiques and emporia to help them fill their Christmas stockings. I always imagined a sweet young girl, a daughter of Marin parents, working behind a counter parttime in the jewelry department at Nordstrom during the Christmas rush, looking up and seeing Garcia and Weir, very famous locally, approaching in black leather bomber jackets, laughing, and she's thinking, "Oh, shit . . ."

I'm quite sure Bobby never spent a moment thinking or worrying about whether he was in Garcia's shadow. It seemed to me he couldn't have cared less about what anyone else thought about him, in the positive sense, of having learned the lesson that it's counterproductive to a good life, and also really dumb to spend time keeping track of your own image. When you've built a career and a life in the entertainment business and achieved great heights, you should probably just keep your head down and keep doing what you're good at and thank the gods. And not coincidentally, I believe that this way of coping with your own image, when you're famous, was also Garcia's well-thought-out strategy. In many interviews over many years, you can feel Garcia's discomfort as the interviewer starts things off with a glowing description of how important or talented Garcia is. Garcia would cringe, deflect, or kid about it, not wanting to diminish the interviewer in any way, but impatient to get on to something more substantial to talk about than how great he was.

I did get to know Weir a bit over the years, better than any of the other guys in the band, save Garcia, and I came to appreciate him as a really solid, kind, thoughtful guy, as well as an amazingly talented musician, singer, and songwriter. And of course, he was very good-looking and in good shape all the time, and very popular with the women. I would have to say that Weir was the most consistent in supporting the brand; that is, making sure the live shows were as good as he could make them, personally, by being healthy and sharp at every show, dutifully participating in the business side of things, staying out of trouble (in the ways that count), treating his partners and all their staff and workers respectfully and kindly, not missing a meeting, remembering what he committed to earlier, and so on. The other five guys were a little spotty in that respect compared to Weir. Bob was just a tad more diligent.

He had his goofy, slightly blissed-out side, which I think led some people to underestimate him. I remember seeing him just before showtime on July 26, 1987, in Anaheim, California, while we were shooting the Dead/Dylan stadium tour. I knew that right after the tour ended I would be going immediately into postproduction editing mode, because Clive Davis, the band, and MTV had cooked up the nonstop, twenty-four-hour Day of the Dead programming on August 8, and I was going to provide a lot of hypercurrent stuff from the summer tour.

Weir is heading for the stage, and I'm heading to the recording truck, and I see him coming toward me, guitar in hand. He's wearing a Madonna tee shirt—she is having a huge moment that summer, with a new album and a big tour. I slow him down to have a word. I remind him, gesturing toward his chest, where Madonna's own chest is prominently on display, that we are shooting tonight's show for use in the MTV thing, and I'm wondering if he thinks the tee shirt is a good look for him. He glances down at his tee shirt, guffaws, and says, "Yeah, I think it's fine."

I nod and say, "Okay, it's part of my job to tell you that every time you appear on camera there's gonna be a significant number of viewers who will be looking at those Madonna hooters instead of you." He does a pantomime of seriously considering what I'm saying, then chuckles and says, "Well, I'm trying to meet her." I don't expect to hear that, so I have to laugh, and I say, "I'm sure that can be arranged without the shirt." We have a good laugh together, and he says, "I'm fine," and off he goes. It's there for the rest of time—Weir with the Madonna tee shirt.

Probably in mid-1988 or so, MG and I are sitting at the glass table in the kitchen of the Grateful Dead office just jawing. Things are really good for everyone during this time. Weir has just been through a quick rehab and detox. This is not uncommon in my experience all over the entertainment business. Like, hey, let's not make a big deal out of this; you've been burning the candle at both ends a bit, so take a week off, or a month, and come back rested, you'll like it. To me, the rehab-detox-vacation thing seems to exist on a spectrum, like everything else, but I'm no expert, having only done the vacation part of it myself.

Bob comes dynamically breezing through the kitchen wearing cutoff shorts and a polo tee, giving a quick hello and then breezing out of the room. He has business upstairs. He is obviously feeling good and looking good, what with a hit record and a hit single and video, y'know . . .

MG shakes her head and sighs deeply, saying, "Bob has finally become a God."

On a more serious note, through studying my notes and calendars from long ago to write this book, it's become clear to me now that Weir and Barlow's song "Throwing Stones" played a large part in my journey into Deadworld and ever since.

Garcia had sent me a set of mixing-board audiocassettes of the band's recent Greek Theatre stand in the summer of 1984. I took it as a howdy-do reminder and an invitation to a discussion, which led to a series of meetings with him on the road, which in turn started the ball rolling toward what would become *So Far.* I'd noticed a song on the Greek Theatre tapes when I first heard them that I'd never heard before that was intriguing: Weir and Barlow's "Throwing Stones."

When I went to visit Garcia on the road, I believe it was a Dead show at the Centrum in Worcester, Massachusetts, on October 9, 1984. I had time to kill before or after the meeting, and ended up onstage next to monitor mixer Harry Popick, enjoying the show from a great spot. That was the first time I'd ever heard that song live. It was electrifying. I could clearly understand all the lyrics. And the structure of the thing was amazing.

The song is a dark and scary vision of the current world with a solid dash of inspiration and hope. As soon as it ended I remember thinking I had never seen a clearer political statement from a rock band or popular artist as powerful as this one. And the lyrics were not peace-loving generalities, they were disturbingly specific. Immediately I was struck by two thoughts. The first was that song needed to be heard coming out of car radios, splashed across the late-night TV landscape, and all over MTV as soon as possible. My second thought overtook me like I was possessed: I was going to devote myself to a mission to make that happen. It was very clear to me, very simple and pure. I had the position and the skill set and a motive as strong as they come—that song and that band were destined to collide in a big way with our American culture, and I was duty bound to help them in any way I could.

"Throwing Stones" started a fire deep inside me. It gave me a touchstone, a higher calling, a hard and fast *reason* why I should push past all my insecurities and doubts and inborn disabilities to play the showbiz games that were necessary to compete in the big league of huge rock 'n' roll juggernauts such as the Dead. In those days, before the internet, record labels and radio were power centers, TV and cable were flexing their muscles, and there was seriously big money at stake in every move that top-ten recording artists made. The phenomena of Madonna and Michael Jackson in the 1980s attest to that. "Throwing Stones" connected the careerist part of me with the spiritual and political activist parts of me. My drive to work with Grateful Dead and Garcia was fueled by this fusion of motive—I felt it was my duty to get this song in front of as many people as possible, to play my part in the newly born ecology movement. Reagan had been elected in 1980, things were going in the wrong direction (he'd ordered the solar panels installed by Carter on the White House roof removed; why in the fuck would you do that?), and it was time to pull together our countermovement and start to take it to them.

It was three years and a few months later, November 1987, when it all came to pass. "Throwing Stones" was all over the goddamned place, including in a music video that I got to make, and also as part of a long-form, best-selling award-winning film, *So Far.* I am honestly amazed to say that for me this song resonates today more strongly than it did forty years ago. It was and still is a bit unbelievable to me, the interplay between my love of this song and my overall work with the Dead, but in particular with Garcia. It just felt like a perfect slow-motion alignment of a bunch of different forces, things going on, that brought such great artistic satisfaction to me. Kind of a gift to me, from . . . all that is. (If you want to see it, just search: Grateful Dead official music video "Throwing Stones," or Grateful Dead movie *So Far,* which has the longer, more amazing version.)

By the time we came to shoot the third music video from the Dead's hit album *In the Dark* in November 1987, I was swimming in the delirious zeitgeist of the big year we were having. And the song we'd shoot? You guessed it: "Throwing Stones" by Weir and John Barlow.

I wrote the script for the video. The guys in the band seemed to have a lot of faith in me at that point. The "Hell in a Bucket" video was a hit, and they liked what they were seeing of the forthcoming *So Far* home video, which had been in the works for three years at that point. I guess they were thinking, "Who knows, let's give this guy some more rope to hang himself."

Once again, it was like a two-week turnaround. What can I tell you, I like to work under pressure, and I like to work fast, maybe because my early experience was in live or live-to-tape concert shoots, where you only got one chance to capture a moment. But even when I later got to shoot single-camera film-style stuff, the idea of going past four or five takes of a scene struck me as dumb. Like this isn't brain surgery, let's get this done. I can't imagine going to twenty or forty takes of a scene. It just seems to me that if you're doing that you don't really know what you're trying to get.

I met with Garcia at the kitchen table in the Grateful Dead office about the proposed "Throwing Stones" music video, to talk over the concept. I wanted to suggest to him that he do some of the production design for the dystopian future I had imagined for it. I just wanted to see if he was game (a stupid question; of course he was game), give him some time to think it over, and then make a date for an in-depth meeting. Instead, he heard me out and asked a few questions about possible exterior locations.

I tell him I'm looking for a huge blank wall we can turn into a giant mural that will be a backdrop for the action. He says, "Grab a napkin," gesturing at a kitchen counter. I comply, and he pulls out a pen from his jacket pocket, sits down at the kitchen table, unfolds the napkin, and gets to work. I know when to shut up (sometimes).

In fifteen minutes, he sketches out the mural, which includes a terrifying humanoid ogre with black holes for eyes and mouth, fringed in flame, brandishing barbed wire between its enormous hands, with tiny human figures in the background begging for help. Scary.

Once again I'm astonished by this man's mind and talents, but I do a good job remaining calm. If he wants to do it there in the kitchen, that's fine. We talk over additional sets, decide to get the little kids we need for actors by asking band members and office staff for volunteers, and in under thirty minutes we have the entire concept for a third-of-a-million-dollars (in today's money) film shoot laid out from start to finish.

I take the napkin and get busy trying to find someone who can transfer the image onto a giant thirty-by-sixty-foot wall in, like, two days. We find our wall (at an abandoned school campus in Oakland), thanks to Lope Yap, my line producer. He also finds a local mural artist, a woman, who's game to transfer Garcia's napkin image onto the wall in the next two days, using a large crew of painters and a few cherry pickers. And you know we get these people to help us, in part, because of their feelings about Grateful Dead and their desire to participate.

The day of the shoot, Veronica and I go up to Garcia's house and get in his car. He is eager to drive, obviously turned on to do a movie shoot, even though it's like seven in the morning. I'm groggy, frankly, and glad to see that Garcia wants to drive and is definitely pumped to shoot a movie.

We climb into the big Beamer, Veronica in the back and me shotgun. Garcia lights up a huge joint and we get really high on the drive, against my normal principles, but he's so positive, whattaya gonna do? He puts an audiocassette into the car stereo, a hot-off-the-presses bootleg recording of comedian Jackie Mason on Broadway (I believe Mason and Garcia were both appearing on Broadway at the same time one month earlier, the Jerry Garcia Band at the Lunt-Fontanne and Mason at what was then the Brooks Atkinson and is now the Lena Horne Theatre). For all I know, Garcia may have caught the Mason show on a day off, or they may have met at a strip club and ended up on the Staten Island Ferry drinking whiskey and singing "Hava Nagila." Mason's stand-up act is just over-the-top hilarious.

The car rocks with waves of laughter, and we are all transfixed by the time we get to Oakland. I don't recall how we got there, exactly—there is no GPS then and Garcia has never been where we are going. Maybe I did my homework and had written instructions to feed him. But the magic of the drive is that we three never speak a word about the day's work ahead of us. It's just this huge cathartic outpouring of laughter. And Garcia's laugh, when he really gets going, is a great thing to behold. I've heard it compared to the laugh of Ed Wynn, the actor who played Uncle Albert in *Mary Poppins* (1964).

The big Beamer pulls into the exterior set and parks, the three of us spilling out of the car, pot smoke billowing around us. I immediately sense it doesn't look good, as we are wiping away tears from laughing and catching our breath. Everyone else is looking at us like, what the fuck? We aren't late, but everyone else—something like two dozen crew—has been there a while prepping the dystopian schoolyard set. There are also ten or so little kids on set (including the children of band members and office staff), who were a joy to work with, and Robbie Taylor, Grateful Dead production manager, who was acting as Bill Kreutzmann's stunt double.

Once we wipe away the tears and absorb the situation, we stand in awe of what we see. In the distance is the giant mural, a perfectly executed rendition of Garcia's napkin drawing, simple and terrifying. In front of the mural are mountains of smoldering ruins of a lost civilization, or maybe a bombed-out city, smoking tires, mangled furniture. Garcia is visibly staggered by the sight. We immediately snap back to the present, amazed at what a great job our production team had done, and they can all see how blown away we are.

Once again, the Zen of Jerry had struck: By completely forgetting what we were doing on the way to the shoot and not thinking about it, and then confronting the awesome set, we were suddenly energized. I tell you what, you can get mighty straight, mighty fast, in a situation like that. I was humbled and moved, and we got right to work. I had been fully prepared to take the first two hours of the workday getting to this result, but the crew took my plans and instructions and executed them before we'd even gotten there! And it had all started with those fifteen minutes and the napkin just a few days before.

Gold certification acknowledgment for video Ticket to New Year's, *1998. Courtesy Len Dell'Amico personal archive.*

Chapter 13

SNAPSHOTS FROM THE PEAK YEARS

I worked as hard as I ever had in 1987. I was on fire, and I was loving it. I shot two shows for HBO and I wrote a screenplay with my lifelong writing partner, Mick Stern (titled *You Can Have It*). Garcia was getting stronger every day, and *So Far* came together in postproduction. I produced and directed the filming and live video reinforcement of the legendary Dead/Dylan stadium tour, did two of the music videos—"Hell in a Bucket" and "Throwing Stones"—for the Dead's hit album *In the Dark*, and it all culminated in a live national pay-per-view broadcast of the band's New Year's Eve show from the Oakland Coliseum. The New Year's Eve show was a huge production that included recording the Neville Brothers' and Olatunji's opening sets, and with all kinds of comedy roll-ins and live interviews.

I was fighting off some kind of viral infection throughout December, but I knew I had no choice but to plow ahead. That New Year's event was another big hit for the band, the distributor was happy, and it was released on laser disc and videocassette to the home video market in 1996, a year after Garcia passed away, under the title *Ticket to New Year's*. I always thought releasing it then was a way to fill the hole of the missing traditional Dead New

Year's show, and to bring in some much-needed money for the struggling Dead family after losing Garcia.

The year 1987 also included the end of the cohabiting part of my relationship with Veronica. We'd been on the rocks for quite a while, my bicoastal travel not helping. I moved out of Brooklyn in midsummer and started living full time in Marin, as I do to this day. But she and I continued to work together. She was the editor of *So Far* and the two related Dead music videos and worked on the '87 New Year's broadcast and on and off on most of my other Grateful Dead projects until the end of 1991. We also worked together after the end of my time with the Dead on other projects, and we are still friends today.

I woke up on January 1, 1988, having put the New Year's show to bed just a few hours earlier. I was utterly exhausted, spent in every way, while at the same time profoundly satisfied and happy and grateful at all that I and all my coworkers and Garcia and the band had accomplished in the previous year. Those tumultuous feelings persisted for days as I slowly recovered from the virus. I had never felt anything remotely like this, the mix of exhaustion and deep satisfaction, before or since. I realized I had to change my ways.

Having basically accomplished everything I'd set out to accomplish, it was time to take a break, do a reckoning, start anew. I decided to change my diet, eliminating mammal meat, get real daily exercise, refrain from drinking alcohol before the dinner hour, and cut back on all substance use. I had always known that I wanted to get married and have kids, and here I was, age thirty-seven, so I resolved to focus on that. Stupid me thought, "Well, it shouldn't take that long to find the right woman, get married, settle down, have a kid . . . maybe a year or two." It was five years until I proposed to someone, took another year to get married, and five more years to have that first kid, by which time I was forty-eight.

By 1989, it had been three years since Garcia's recovery and inspiring comeback. The band was in top form, happy and comfortable after their hit record *In the Dark* and video *So Far*. Early that year the band asked me to produce a high-end shoot of their summer stadium tour, with lots of cameras, the ultimate in quality, and accompanied by a forty-eight-track audio recording operation. It would include live video-reinforcement screens using the latest tech for the fans in the cheap seats, and I was also tasked to put on some fun special effects to provide visual relief from the boring spectacle of six men in tee shirts standing there, as Garcia was fond of saying. He was my go-to rep for the band, as usual. Larry Lachman was brought in again, as he was on *So Far*, the '87 tour, and lots of other Dead concert work, to handle special effects.

I didn't question the band about why they wanted such expensive high-end production standards for what was essentially just live video reinforcement. I had learned from my 1987 stadium tour experience that Garcia and the band had their own reasons for how much money they wanted to spend on recording their shows. But I had a strong intuition that Garcia knew that was a period of peak Dead, with the band playing better than ever. I think his intent was to ensure that the band's archive for 1989 would include as many legacy recordings of live shows as possible, at the highest picture and sound quality possible.

The summer stadium tour would hit many big northeastern and midwestern cities in the United States, where the Dead were always a huge draw: Boston, NYC, Philly, Pittsburgh, D.C., Chicago, and all the smaller cities in between, what I thought of back then as the working-class heart of America. Buffalo, my hometown, especially loved the Dead. The rust-belt city had been in a long decline for more than a decade, its population shrinking. It was home to the Buffalo Bills NFL team, the unreliable Sabres hockey team, the State University of New York at Buffalo, and the Albright-Knox Art Gallery, but little else to sustain their civic pride. So they were especially grateful for the Dead, and I believed the band could feel their appreciation and responded with uncommonly good performances when they played there.

By the time of the '89 summer tour, I had assembled a wickedly skilled production team: camera operators and crew, production managers, all veterans of the '85 *So Far* sessions, the '85 New Year's broadcast, the '87 Dead/ Dylan summer tour, the '87 New Year's broadcast, or the '88 Rainforest Benefit Concert. Doing bare-bones concert captures, I needed to have a trained, experienced traveling team that was used to the Grateful Dead way of doing things—staying loose, going with the flow, improvising.

I'm going to take a minute here to tell you about what it's like to be on the road directing multicamera concert shoots. The shows included on the tour were at Foxboro, Massachusetts (July 2); Orchard Park, New York (near Buffalo) (July 4); JFK Stadium in Philadelphia (July 7); Giants Stadium, near New York City (July 9–10); RFK Stadium in Washington, D.C. (July 12–13);

and Alpine Valley Music Theatre in East Troy, Wisconsin (July 17–19). A total of ten shows, which taken together included a very large part of their entire repertoire, with multiple versions of several songs.

Long before we got out on the road, we had to do all the preproduction for each venue, many weeks of work to ensure that everyone on our team was on the same page as the band's crew and office operation. The travel and hotel arrangements had to be made, and we had to interface with the crews and operations at each separate venue to confirm what time our production trucks had to arrive, where they would be parked, security arrangements, and on and on.

We all understood that we were aiming for something higher than normal video reinforcement standards, which was obvious given that we had a huge broadcast-quality teleproduction truck, a separate multitrack audio truck, and seven cameras instead of the normal three. But we all understood as well that we needed to keep as low a profile as we could in order to avoid possible problems from local unions and promoters, who might have wanted a piece of whatever possible future products we were recording. In the predigital world of 1989, cameras were enormous and heavy, analog videotape recorders were huge, and videotape was expensive. You couldn't simply record the output of every camera and edit it later, as we do today with digital media, which is why there was a premium on live production crews and directing skills back then that would minimize expensive postproduction editing. Today, incredibly good cameras are small and lightweight, and you can basically make a multicamera film using your laptop.

We would arrive in a new city early in the day before the show was scheduled and do all our load in, setup, and system testing, while the other crews were bringing in lighting, sound equipment, and the band's stage gear and doing their own testing. It was often very hot, with everyone sweaty, running around, or it might be raining, so we'd have to cover the equipment and wait it out. We had to be hypersocial with strangers, including local police and fire inspectors, venue security people, and in Philly, mob guys with Dobermans claiming to be working with the local promoter and trying to get between us and the job, looking for payoffs. It was crazy, and we had to love it or leave it. If we were lucky, we got some food and drinks before hitting the sack, exhausted. The next day, show day, we'd pray it wouldn't rain, as most stadiums back then did not have roofs.

We'd have to race against the clock to get everything ready before they opened the doors and let the crowd in (it was all general admission back then, so there were mad dashes by fans to secure turf or seats, and there was basically no security at all, compared to today). It was barely controlled chaos, but it sure was exciting, and looking back I have to admit I kinda loved it.

There was some kind of meal backstage, a little break while the crowd grew and partied, and then about a half hour before showtime, everyone migrated to their work position, dolly and crane or jib operators, camera ops, lighting directors, and spotlight ops. My tech crew and I climbed into our truck and put on our headsets (headphones with a microphone so we could all talk to each other securely during the show), and went through a checklist, something like when airplane pilots are preparing to take off. It was a large virtual audio space, filled with constant creative chatter, which no one not wearing a headset was aware of. And when I was directing a live shoot, I had the music turned way up loud. I needed to hear it the way the crowd was hearing it, and so the people on headsets in the truck, including me, may have had to shout to be heard.

Maybe ten minutes before showtime, final instructions were given to security at the truck door that no one was to come in without the right pass. Then I'd go through a standard "Is everybody here?" I'd say, "Camera one?" And they'd say, "Yup," or "Check." Then, "Camera one dolly op?" And they'd say, "Check," or "Fuck yeah!" (probably a local hire).

I'd be looking at a wall of television monitors showing all the camera shots and what the recording machines were recording, so when I'd call out to camera five, they could just nod their camera shot up and down and I'd know that they heard me. I'd have to check in with the engineer in charge; and my technical director, who would be sitting next to me in front of the switcher, an enormous board of faders and knobs and buttons; and the shaders, who controlled the irises of all the cameras; and the people operating the tape-recording decks. During this part of the work was when I really started to get excited. It's so cool to be involved in a large technical undertaking dedicated to a rock band, with the audience having a great fucking time, and hopefully capturing it for future generations. Finally, I'd check in with my compadres in the multitrack audio truck, to make sure they could hear me and to talk with them before we got to the final countdown to the show.

CHAPTER 13

With two minutes to go, I'd say, "Stand by audio and video to roll and record," wait for their response, and then I liked to give a final pep talk to my camera crew on the headset to let them know that I was happy as shit to be there. I was loosey-goosey, and I wanted them to be relaxed and creative, not to worry if they had problems out there on the stage getting the shots I wanted. They were in the trenches, while I was inside a comfy little studio making demands on them. I'd tell them, "I want you guys to have fun, feel free to roam for shots. If you're hot (meaning their shot was going to program, either tape or broadcast) or on ready (meaning the shot was designated to be the next shot to program), you have to freeze; if not, fly around, show me things. You're out there, I'm not. You can see what's going on that I can't. Go for it, relax, listen to the music . . . and if you're trying to show me something and I don't notice, snap your zoom in and out and that will grab my attention."

At that point the houselights would have gone off, the crowd would be going crazy, and our trucks would be vibrating from their roars. The stage manager would be telling me that the band was about to go on, and I'd say, "Roll to record" to all the tape-deck operators. And it was off to the races.

We got to (my hometown) Buffalo on July 3, 1989, and went straight to work at Rich Stadium to set up for the show the next day. I had arranged for my two brothers, Ray and Fred, to work as production assistants, given their familiarity with local service providers. And I'd arranged for my parents, Fred and Shirley, to be treated as VIPs. My dad was sixty-nine and my mom was sixty-five. They'd never been to a stadium show, but they were music lovers and understood my relationship with the Dead. My mom liked their music; my dad had even made home recordings of her singing "Ripple." Dennis McNally, the band's publicist and biographer, graciously took care of them, bringing them to their seats and backstage.

It's nearly impossible to explain to someone what directing a live concert film is like, without that person actually being there and experiencing it. But once that person gets a seat in the production truck and can see all the monitors of all the cameras, and hear the music from huge loudspeakers, and puts on a headset and can listen to all the chatter between me and the camera ops and dolly grips and lighting people, it becomes eventually clear what it's like to direct a live concert film or broadcast and how it all works.

There is a large program monitor that shows the camera shot that is currently selected to go out to broadcast or to the huge screens in the stadium or to a master recording. Next to it is a smaller preview monitor that shows the camera shot that is selected to be up next. And there are other monitors that show what the remaining cameras are shooting. The director is responding to what all the monitors are showing and setting them up in the manner of a conveyor belt, so that the program is constantly changing, covering the action onstage from different perspectives.

I arranged with Dennis to bring my parents at the start of the second set to the backstage area where the recording vehicles were. I had earlier prepped my mom and dad as to what to expect. They would be entering a professional workspace, and they would be made comfy, but I would be fully engaged in my job. I was happy as a clam, talking on the headset with everyone, shooting the crowd cheering, the band tuning up, smiling at each other. It was really exciting. If you always wanted to be an astronaut when you were a kid, or a captain of a submarine, you'd love this. I was totally immersed.

I was only vaguely aware when Dennis brought my parents into the truck. There were two tiers of seating behind me and my assistants and the wall of monitors, meant for producers and guests to strictly observe only. Dennis knew that I'd wanted my folks to wear the headsets. I glanced around and stole a look at my dad halfway into the first song. He was an engineer by training, and an audiophile, and I could see immediately that he got it totally. He listened to the chatter on the headsets and saw how the monitor images danced and changed in response to my direction and understood that the final product was shown on the large program monitor. I don't think he had much of an idea what I did for a living before that moment. We waved to each other; he had tears in his eyes . . .

The band was great. The Buffalo show (released on DVD as *Truckin' Up to Buffalo*) is widely regarded as one of their best full concerts. As I got back to work, I was vaguely aware that the door to the truck was opening and closing, but I thought nothing of it. We were fifteen or so minutes into the second set when I felt someone tapping on my shoulder. That's prohibited behavior in our professional environment; if you are not on a headset, you are not allowed to interrupt the people working.

So, I shrugged my shoulder and waved off whoever it was, indicating, "Leave me alone." I went back to the action, but a moment later I got another tap. I turned around and saw that it was my mother with a concerned look on her face. I was startled and motioned to my technical director to take over for a moment. Mom had made her way down to my side because no one had thought it appropriate to stop her. I pulled the headset off one ear and turned to her to yell over the din of the music, "Mom, I'm kinda busy right now . . ."

She scowled and wagged a finger at me: "Do you have to yell at everybody? Why are you yelling?" I knew she was completely sincere and only concerned with my personal conduct, so I just had to cope. I explained, "Mom, it's okay. Everyone on a headset has to yell. They all understand; it's okay." I smiled at her and nodded until she relaxed a bit and signaled okay with her own nod. Then she went back to her seat.

For the 1990 and 1991 summer tours, we moved the video production out to the house mixing and lighting position, so I was with Candace Brightman and Dan Healy instead of in a truck. The main reason for this was the continued shrinkage in the technology and the desire to save money (we went with an eight-track audio recording system that Dan had perfected instead of a forty-eight-track truck). I now believe that another reason was because Garcia had concluded that we had already captured peak Dead during the '89 tour, and that whatever we would get going forward would be gravy.

It was very different being out in the middle of the house, compared to being inside a production truck. The mix position is on the floor, at the bottom of a huge bowl, surrounded by a sea of fans—sometimes as many as seventy thousand of them. It might be ninety degrees, it might be cold or rainy, but the mixing position at least had a roof. For the first time I could just look up and see the program we were creating on the giant screens, and I could experience as never before how the crowd reacted to the images. It was very gratifying. The special effects that Garcia had ordered and that we all labored to create were like a huge stimulant to the party going on all around us. There was no doubt at all about what was working and what could be improved, how to mix in the effects in the right proportion to shots of the band. Now I realized why all the Dead employees working in sound and lights began feeling a little resentful of the video as it was being integrated into the live event matrix starting in the mid-'80s. The Dead fans were very sophisticated, sensitive to changes in the sound level or the mix, or reacting to lighting changes, and now there was this new part of the experience, and sound and lights had to adapt to it.

It was sometimes weird to be working in the middle of what was a gigantic, barely under control, wild party. People were often half naked, high on all kinds of substances, yelling, screaming. You'd see the strangest things from our perch about fifteen feet above the floor. We workers had to fight our way through the crowd every time we had to get to or from the mixing position. It did have its own porta-potty, and it was surrounded by a ten-foot chain-link fence with one security person inside to glower at all the fans unruly enough to want to get inside the compound with us.

One time I arrived at my workstation on the second floor of what people were calling the tower (even though it was only two levels). The Dead had always minimized their footprint in the house, and now it had grown to two levels, which was still puny compared to other big acts. I had a little time to kill.

It was still daylight, and we were waiting for the first set. I was drinking a cup of coffee, looking down at the crowd. Some of them were looking up at me, so I waved. I noticed one burly young guy, shirtless, obviously very high, maybe from a combination of LSD and several beers, taking an unusual interest in the tower instead of the people around him. I stepped away to talk to my crew on the headset, then went back to people-watching.

This burly young guy was now plastered against the chain-link fence right below me, shaking it, as if testing it. I looked around; our security person was nowhere to be seen. Some of the people around the guy were yelling at him to stop, but he was laughing maniacally and started climbing up the fence right below me. Looking down, I realized that the main power distribution rack for the video was next to me on the floor. I decided to stay where I was rather than go look for security, but I yelled for help.

The guy kept coming up. I waved my arms and tried to get him to stop. The fans around him were all watching, some trying to talk him down, others laughing, encouraging him. He reached the top of the fence, his upper body entirely over it, his head at the level of my feet. He reached out with one hand to get a grip on the tower, I guess with the intention of climbing onto it. I watched his hand head straight toward the power distribution rack; God knows what could have happened if he'd gotten his fingers in there.

As his hand crept forward, I had to improvise. I placed my left foot over his hand and applied just enough pressure to make him notice and stop moving. He looked up at me, a crazed look on his face, laughing. He yelled something like, "What, you don't want me here?!" I tried to be unthreatening, but I wasn't going to take my foot off that hand. He screamed, "Okay, okay, I'll go!" He let loose with another maniacal laugh, and then pulled his hand away, threw both his arms up and out, arched his back, and launched himself back and out into space, falling onto the fence and making the whole thing rattle. I thought, "God, that must've hurt." Then he was on the floor, not moving, and people were surrounding him to see if he was okay. I thought, "God, I hope he didn't break his back." Then security arrived, a bit late. I had to get to work.

After the first set ended, I made my way through the crowd to go backstage. I ran into someone from the Dead's stage crew, who said to me, "So, you kicked someone in the face to get him off your tower?" I was incredulous. "Uh, no, I didn't . . . and it's not a tower."

Then I got the same thing from a bunch of other people backstage; it was weird. Some thought it was cool that I'd kicked someone in the face, and others were glowering at me. What are you gonna do? I've bided my time until now to finally make my case.

day's Examiner

The man who sells the A's — to the fans

Scene/Page B8

Things have changed at 'Peyton Place'

Michael Dougan/Page B8

Kuchen's mystery exit at Berkeley

Sports/Page D1

San Francisco Examiner

r No. 241  Tuesday, March 19, 1985 25¢ S

★★★ Streets edition Closing stocks

S. policy on draft upheld

with dying

ck out from
3 on a personal
ht take him, as
ournal, to "the
orever." Now he

s through to the
ndon him," says
my friends aren't
ry well. It took
o get here and

he's all the company I've had. Oh, people have called, and I've called a lot of people, but I think they're afraid to come see me. I understand, it's OK," Jeff wrote in his journal. Jeff King's story — of a disease that confounds medicine, that threatens to spread dramatically in the general population, and that poses a challenge to our humanity — has become a story of dying, of living with death, and of trying to find answers to a modern plague. Today, the last of three parts of "Living with dying/An AIDS journal" in a special four-page pullout section. It begins on Page A5.

Garcia in court

Examiner/Gordon Stone

It was sweet music this morning for Grateful Dead guitarist Jerry Garcia as Municipal Court Judge Raymond J. Reynolds gave him a chance to avoid criminal narcotics charges stemming from his arrest Jan. 18 in Golden Gate Park. Garcia is to enter a Marin County drug diversion program, which could lead to the dropping of criminal charges against him. "I feel pretty good about it," Garcia said. He said he would give a benefit concern "sometime this year" as a form of community service. "I want to do something above and beyond the diversion," he said.

Court says that prosecuting the protesters OK

Examiner news services

WASHINGTON — The government's former policy of prosecuting only men who publicized their refusal to register for the military draft was valid, the Supreme Court ruled today.

By a 7-2 vote in the case of a 24-year-old former Yale philosophy student from Pasadena, the court said the policy did not violate constitutional rights.

In other decisions today, the court said public employees are entitled to hearings before they can be fired, to determine if reasonable grounds exist for dismissal. The court also held that a 1978 federal law does not excuse states from repaying millions of dollars in misspent federal education grants.

Today's draft decision clears the way for the prosecution of David Alan Wayte, who had claimed his free-speech rights were violated by the government's "selective prosecution" of draft protesters. It also opened the possibility of prosecutions of other young men who, like Wayte, publicized their resistance to the military draft registration.

Draft registration — not the military draft — was reinstituted in 1980 in the aftermath of the Soviet invasion of Afghanistan. The law requires male citizens and resident aliens born after Jan. 1, 1963, and between the ages of 18 and 26 to notify the Selective Service. Some 12 million young men — about 98 percent of those eligible — have registered.

Wayte challenged the government's method of "deliberately selecting for investigation and prosecution only a class of vocal protesters against the law." Those prosecuted represent a tiny fraction of the more than 700,000 who have not registered.

Writing for the high court, Justice Lewis F. Powell said Wayte "has not shown that the government prosecuted him because of his protest activities." Powell said Wayte had shown only that the government was aware that its passive enforcement policy would result in the prosecution of vocal objectors.

The government has since aban-

— See back page, col. 3

ay

te
't be protected
il early 1987,
te safety
B1.

headed for a
te with President
that approval is
e success of new
A12.

elcomed
ent Raul Alfonsin
ith a declaration
"must not stand
communist
on Nicaragua."

Norris this is a
d take. He's
raining and taking
a drug
pert as well.

topped would-be
before they had

Hopes are high on compromise for Kesterson

SACRAMENTO (UPI) — Attorneys for San Joaquin Valley growers and the federal government say they are "optimistic" a way will be found to maintain production on 42,000 acres of farmland, threatened with a cutoff of irrigation water in the crisis over the polluted Kesterson Wildlife Refuge.

Their statements followed a 4½-hour conference yesterday in Sacramento. They declined to announce any details of the discussion, and said talks would continue.

"We have a feeling of some optimism," said Frank Richardson, solicitor-general for the Department of the Interior. "We hope it will be resolved soon."

Richardson said there would be no public announcement on the outcome for "several days." He said he is returning to Washington today.

Adolf Moscovitz, attorney for the 600,000-acre Westlands Water District, said that Westlands has no immediate plan to ask the courts for an order to keep irrigation water flowing.

"We are not going to court in the morning," Moscovitz said. Asked if a solution could be found he said "I earnestly hope so. I am optimistic."

Script writers go back to work

LOS ANGELES (AP) — The Writers Guild of America voted overwhelmingly to accept an $84 million contract ending a strike against movie and television producers. Writers percent of the 2,897 ballots cast last night at the Hollywood Palladium.

"The membership has spoken. We posed the possibility of a six-month

A 'down payment' on comparable pay

Jerry in court following drug bust. Photo by Gordon Stone, March 19, 1985.

Chapter 14

THE CURSE OF CELEBRITY

Some people are driven by their narcissism, and I am always wary about people like that. It's not healthy for them, and often working with people like that is just a world of pain. But if the person is, in fact, a huge star, then the business world (which I am a part of) will bend over and around them to promote their image, because of the allure of the money that could come their way. I don't want to dwell on this side of the entertainment business too much, but let's pick someone at random . . . say, Michael Jackson. An amazingly talented person from a very strange family, and it didn't end well.

If, as a hundred and fifty years of evolutionary theory and science suggest, all human traits exist on a spectrum and those traits are typically distributed on a bell curve, then just a tiny percentage of people at either extreme of a given trait—fearfulness, for instance—will be either extremely fearful all the time or have no sense of fear whatsoever, and the great majority of people will be in the middle of the bell curve, experiencing degrees of fearfulness within a variable and widely acceptable set of social norms.

I think the desire to be the center of attention, an aspect of narcissism, or the desire to entertain, enlighten, or even bring solace to the suffering, as a preacher might say they are doing, is one of those fundamental traits. I don't know what it is, but I imagine psychologists have a name for it. The "do you want to be famous or not" gene?

CHAPTER 14

Well, Garcia was one of those rare people who succeeded enormously as a musical artist *and* in the show business sense (related to fame, money, and the like) and who had absolutely no interest in being famous or being beloved by a large number of people, and no interest in making a huge amount of money. He was not attracted to the idea of attention or adoration; on the contrary, he found it repellent. And yet he was, even long before I met him in 1980, beloved by a large number of people, and famous—even though it was a constant source of annoyance and discomfort for him. He was what I would call the opposite of a narcissist. He actually worked hard to remain humble, and actively resisted every opportunity to acknowledge how great he was, and also, by the way, how wise and lovable he was.

It's not that he didn't understand his audience, his fans, or appreciate all the people around him for their roles in his life. He wasn't irritated by the attention, he didn't blame others for not being more sensitive to the facts about who he really was, as opposed to their image of him, and you would *never* hear anything like a "Poor me" statement coming out of his mouth, ever . . . It was just that his predicament was constantly perplexing to him, and sometimes even vexing, such as when he was forced to deal with an unpleasant situation brought about by someone who believed they were part of his life, maybe because they were enthralled by him, when he did not think of them in the same way.

It didn't help that he was very recognizable: a largish man with a largish head, wild, thick hair and beard, a huge, breathtaking smile, and signature aviator-style glasses. So even if he wanted to take measures to disguise himself to ease his movement through the world the rest of us take for granted, where we're all basically anonymous, it would have been difficult for him. He'd probably have had to shave off his beard, maybe get a nice crew cut, start wearing nice shirts and ties and business suits . . . But the notion is absurd; he was a defiant individualist first and last, and he liked to wear tee shirts and basic pants, with a long-sleeve flannel shirt on top if it was chilly, and that was it. For him, celebrity was not a reward in any way; it was the price he had to pay in return for the privilege to do what he most loved, playing and singing to a live audience.

I should point out that I never once heard him complain about that state of affairs, because he simply was *not* a complainer, and he was always the first to say how fortunate he felt with his lot in life. Still, I'd like to go into a little detail about what it was like to be him, from my perspective as a coworker and a friend, a witness to his process of coping with the *image* of Jerry Garcia as opposed to who he really was.

In mid-August 1987, I was in Boulder, Colorado, to meet with the full Grateful Dead band during their stand at the nearby Red Rocks Amphitheatre to think up and write a script for the second single and video release from *In the Dark*, the Weir-Barlow song "Hell in a Bucket" (see Chapter 10). After the meeting I stayed with the band as they moved on to Telluride, a tiny town in the Rockies being promoted as the next hot ski resort, for two shows on August 15 and 16. The Dead would share the bill with Olatunji, the great Nigerian bandleader and friend of Mickey Hart. There was also something called the Harmonic Convergence, a worldwide peace-and-love type event, happening at the same time.

It was a stunningly beautiful setting. The town laid out the red carpet for the artists and visiting fans. There was a big welcome parade. Bill Graham, a legendary promoter and music impresario, and the first big promoter to book the Dead, had bought a nice big house up on a nearby mountainside, a brisk walk from the town. I believe he thought Telluride was a great area for investment, and he wanted to be part of it, and I surmise that it was Bill who convinced the band to play there after their Red Rocks shows.

I remember the two Dead shows as being good and fun. They weren't the best musically, but the ebullience of the crowd and the natural beauty made it special, plus everyone seemed to be on acid or, shrooms, including me. One of the shows had a special moment when the band went into the intro for a song, and Weir and Garcia stepped up to the mic and started singing two different songs! This collapsed into musical chaos, and the two men feigned anger at each other. It was a riot. I think they were tripping. Upon consideration, I understood the mistake, because the two songs basically had the same intro. I'm sure it never entered their minds to have a set list after twenty-two years together.

Graham hosts a big party up at his house, a late-afternoon dinner affair under beautiful weather. Everyone showers appreciation on his new house, servers drift around with platters of hors d'oeuvres, and everyone sips fine wines. Graham is as happy as could be, mingling and welcoming his guests. A bell rings, and it's time to move outside onto the patio, where a very long table awaits us.

CHAPTER 14

No one shows any signs of moving, but I guess because I'm hungry I head out there by myself. Given no guidance as to seating, I sit in the middle of the table, avoiding the two chairs at either end. Classy tablecloth, linen napkins, lots of forks and glassware—really nice. Presently Garcia drifts out and briskly sits down directly across from me, a bit of a habit of his. It makes me a little uncomfortable sometimes, but it's also kinda secretly flattering. Graham is right behind him and sits next to him, and then the other two dozen or so guests fill up all the remaining seats. It's beautiful, and the conversation and wine flow.

When it comes time for dessert, I'm chatting with Jerry and Bill and I notice a server, a young woman prettily dressed for the part, glide behind them with a coffeepot on a silver tray. She's definitely a local and looks around nervously. She starts serving at the head of the table and then working her way down my side, passing behind and leaning in to offer and pour coffee. I become aware she is behind me to my left but isn't offering the person next to me coffee yet.

Instead, she freezes, as if a switch has been thrown. I look up at her. She is staring across the table at Garcia and Graham, three feet away, clearly starstruck. I glance at them; Graham hasn't noticed, but I can see Garcia making a little uncomfortable smile and wave, as if to say, "Yup, it's me. I'm just here, y'know."

Then I feel a sudden sensation of heat down my spine. I'm wearing a light-blue sport coat, it's the perfect temperature outside, so . . . I turn a bit toward her to look at her. She remains transfixed by the vision across the table as she continues to pour hot black coffee down my back. I think fast. I don't want to make a scene, so I try to help her. I don't need the coat, anyway. I wave and catch her eye, and the spell is broken.

She comes to, stops pouring coffee on me, says hello to the person to my left, and gets her shit back together, moving behind me and properly pouring from the right, completely unaware of what has just happened.

Kinda flustered, I utter, "Excuse me," push back my chair, stand up, and take the jacket off without turning around to reveal the back of it to anyone. Discreetly as possible, I turn it inside out, fold it lengthwise, and then drape it over the back of the chair, then sit down and try to regain my composure.

Looking back, it was no big deal, but it was so strange to witness close-up the momentary stunning effect of a close encounter of the celebrity kind.

Maybe she was a huge Deadhead and knew all about Garcia and loved him. I kinda hope so.

Whenever Garcia and I went out to eat together, which was fairly often in and around San Rafael and on the road (although on the road he was more likely to chill in his hotel room and order room service), or to a deli or a retail store or a movie, I was a close observer of his methods of coping with his predicament. He was a big tipper, to a fault. He knew that a lot of people recognized him, and some of them gave him a little nod and a smile, which he would just return.

Many of them were like, "Hey, Jerry! Good to see you!" That was a bit much, but okay. And some of them were like, "Fuckin ay, man! I love you, man!" Then you could feel him flinch a bit, but just carry on. He would even occasionally mutter to me, "Sorry about that . . ." I was mystified by that, but I guess he thought the intrusion was his fault. I learned to just say, "Hey, no, I get it, it's fine."

If we were going to a nice restaurant, I'd get reservations and try to lead the way to help mitigate the disturbance his presence made wherever he went. I'd try to get the attention of the maître d' or head waiter and help them make things smooth. If we moved fairly briskly, it cued strangers not to interrupt our progress or try to chat. Then once we were seated, it took the typical room about ten minutes for everyone there to murmur to each other about his arrival, and then things would be okay.

So at one restaurant, a waiter comes up to us beaming, though clearly struggling to cope. I think to myself, "Jesus, give Garcia a break; you're making him uncomfortable." Done with the hellos, he turns to Garcia and says, "So, what may I bring you to drink, sir?" Garcia turns to look directly at him, asks for water for now, and then politely says, "And please don't call me 'sir.'" You can probably guess where this is going.

When the waiter comes back to tell us about the specials, he closes with the wine request, saying to Jerry, "And you, sir. Would you like some wine?" I'm perking up, wondering what will happen next. Jerry takes a beat, looks directly at the waiter again—he isn't gonna be rude or annoyed—and just orders some wine, repeating in a level tone, "And please don't call me 'sir.'" The waiter smiles, takes a little step back, bows, and then leaves. We are having a good conversation, usually about films or politics; it's a packed house, our good food arrives, it's a good time.

CHAPTER 14

When it comes time for the waiter to see if everything is to our liking, we are happy and nod and smile at him, and he looks at Garcia and says, "Thank you, sir!" Of course, Garcia is looking straight at him, and he quickly and very firmly says, "Don't call me 'sir'!" The waiter stiffens slightly, and I'm desperately afraid he will answer by saying, "Yes, sir, I won't, sir," at which point I would burst out laughing, spewing wine everywhere. But no, he finally gets the message and withdraws without saying anything. And then what happens at the end of the meal?

Well of course, we ask for the check, the waiter comes back a moment later, and once again beaming, says, "The manager is happy to make this meal on the house." Garcia beats me to it, politely but firmly saying, "No, that's okay, thank you . . . but we'd like to pay." The waiter, a bit perplexed, withdraws, and as we're getting our stuff together to leave, another guy, probably the manager or the maître d', approaches us smoothly and says, "It would be our honor if you would accept the dinner as our gift to you." Okay . . .

So Garcia stops fidgeting. We are standing around the table again, looking right at the guy, and Garcia says, very friendly as usual, "Look, I have plenty of money. I can afford to pay for this very easily. Why is it that you're trying to give it to me? Why don't you find some people who *can't* afford it and give *them* some free food?" The guy is gobsmacked, and so am I, a bit. He then picks up the check and Garcia's credit card and leads us out to the cash register, where he nodded goodnight and beat it.

If you were a movie star, a well-known athlete, a rock star, or a model, restaurants, bars, hotels, and nightclubs wanted you to come back again, and soon, because they knew everyone who saw you there would tell their friends. Remember, this was back in the '80s and '90s; imagine how much worse it is now, with social media (which I consider to actually be *anti*social) all the rage. But that truism about celebrity culture was hard for Garcia to acquiesce to. I'm sure he understood the dynamic, but his working-class upbringing was deeply ingrained in him. The music that carried him from his youth to his own great success had its source in the common people: folk music, bluegrass, country and old-timey music, rural and big-city blues. And because he had absolutely no desire to escape his past, he could never shake his discomfort with getting special treatment. It was like collaborating with the giant bullshit machine each time you go along with it. I guess it could feel like a long, slow deterioration of the knowledge of right and wrong, justice and injustice. Hello, welcome to the real world . . .

But he did always have the biggest Beamer.

A month after the Telluride visit, in mid-September 1987, I was in New York to do promotion for the release of *So Far* on Clive Davis's brand-new Arista Records video label, 6 West Home Video. Davis conceived and created the label, I believe, for the main purpose of releasing the new Grateful Dead videos, which also included Justin Kreutzmann's documentary *Dead Ringers: The Making of Touch of Grey.* Davis had won the auction, which I orchestrated at the direction of the band, for the *So Far* rights with an offer significantly larger than any of the others—despite my mild objection that Arista had no distribution expertise in home video at all compared to the other offers. I was so wrong. Arista did a great job. Turns out that promoting a home video is not much different than promoting a record.

Dennis McNally arranged a screening of *So Far,* along with a press conference and photo op at Morgans, Ian Schrager's new East Side hotel in Manhattan, where everyone was staying while the band played Madison Square Garden. Garcia and I were very happy about the debut of our three-year-old baby, and confident it would be well received and sell a lot of copies. But as we watched the screening room fill up with reporters and camera crews, we looked at each other and agreed—we didn't want to sit through the screening of a film we'd already watched a million times in postproduction, twitching to every perceived reaction in the room while simultaneously dreading the postscreening press conference. So we decamped to the bar in the lobby, to return after the screening was over.

It's truly a fond memory of mine, sitting with Garcia at the tiny bar in the tiny lobby of Morgans in the late afternoon, not much hustle and bustle, everyone already upstairs at the screening. We had our drinks, fortifying ourselves for an extended encounter with the press, but also celebrating our achievement. We had codirected *So Far,* and we got the fucking thing done despite some bumps in the road, like Garcia's life-threatening coma. And like a newborn child, it was finally coming out to the public.

It was a great, warm feeling. Also, I think he was aware of how much I did not enjoy being the center of attention, and how I might have been apprehensive about lights and cameras and questions, and he wanted to help me relax. He'd been through this a thousand times. But in any case, we were both able to step away from the distractions and recognize this important milestone in our work and lives together on a personal level. *So Far* went on to become the best-selling music video of 1988 and won the American Video Conference Award for best long-form music video of the year.

Apparently the screening went well—people seemed to have gotten what we were trying to do. The press conference was also a success. The questions were good, and Garcia and Weir handled them with aplomb, always generating humor and goodwill; they were such pros at that. Clive Davis was beaming like a proud father, and I was struggling to survive, which I guess I did okay. You can see the news conference on YouTube if you're a glutton for punishment.

A month later, in mid-October, 1987, I was back in New York, working on a screenplay with my old friend and collaborator Mick Stern, and also to attend as many shows as I could of Garcia's eighteen-show residency at the Lunt-Fontanne Theatre on West 46th Street, Jerry Garcia on Broadway. That was the culmination of another long-held dream of Garcia's, finally brought to fruition with the help of Bill Graham. The performances included Garcia's current acoustic band (with David Nelson, Sandy Rothman, John Kahn, and Dave Kemper) and the Jerry Garcia Band (with Dave Kemper, John Kahn, Melvin Seals, Gloria Jones, and Jackie LaBranch) playing two sets per show.

Now it so happens that I had made a concert film for HBO the year before, shot in New Orleans, called *Sass & Brass,* built around Sarah Vaughan (known as "Sass" in the jazz business, and my personal favorite of all the great female jazz singers) and a group of great horn players, Al Hirt, Don Cherry, Dizzy Gillespie, Chuck Mangione, and Maynard Ferguson. It also included a backup band of Herbie Hancock (also the musical director), Billy Higgins on drums, and Ron Carter on bass, and Sarah's band of George Gaffney, Andy Simpkins, and Harold Jones.

When I noticed that Sarah was doing a stand at the Blue Note, the legendary jazz club in the West Village, at the same time Garcia was on Broadway, I thought her people would remember me and I could grease the wheels. Jerry's father was a horn player and the leader of a jazz band, and I'd bet Garcia would love to get out on the town in New York and see that show. It was the last show of Sarah's stand, and it was on a night off for Garcia from his Broadway gig.

So I made some calls to Sarah's people and the Blue Note management to buy tickets and alert them that we would be a party of four with a celebrity, Garcia. I wanted to be sure that we could be accommodated without causing problems for the club or Sarah, and to ask for their discretion and secure a good table. I asked Garcia about going to the show and he got very excited about it. He knew I was super discreet; it would not become a big thing, and no one had to know about it. I recruited Sue Stephens and Jackie LaBranch, a singer in Garcia's band, to make it a foursome.

It was a warm night when I met them in the lobby of their hotel. Everyone was upbeat and happy. I led the way outside, and because there was no limo waiting, we just grabbed a cab. Garcia was tickled that he was going out on the town in the Big Apple, just like a regular person, with two of his favorite women and . . . me. At the club, the front door people were polite, but not fawning, and we just grooved on in. It helped that most everyone there was Black and well-dressed, unlike the typical Dead or Garcia Band crowd, and no one seemed to pay Garcia any mind, which improved his mood even more. I noticed we were seated at a long table for six, and I encouraged the women to take the wall seats, while Garcia and I took the two middle seats so I could keep an eye on things. We ordered drinks. The place was packed and bubbling with excitement. Just before Sarah was about to be announced, I saw Clive Davis with another guy, younger, being led toward us by a staff person . . . Okay, I thought . . .

Davis, of course, is a towering figure in the history of the recording business, and he was personally presiding at that very moment over the platinum-level sales of *In the Dark*, the record he had waited for patiently for years. I had personally sold *So Far* to him, and of all the executives I'd screened it for, he was by far the most respectful and intelligent. He had all of his top staffers join us for the screening, played at top volume in a great room. He'd played it through all the way to the end, unlike some other guys (yeah, they were all men), who just wanted to see highlights. But I was also privy to the extremely unkind things that members of the Dead said about him in private. It would be years later when I figured out that they knew they were indebted to him; they'd owed him an album for years and just refused to make it, even though he had paid for it. For those California hippies, a genius businessman like him could be frightening.

CHAPTER 14

Anyway, Davis and his companion joined us at our table. The younger guy was a new country-and-western singer whom I didn't recognize or know about, and for all I know became the next huge C&W star on Arista Records. Garcia showed no surprise at Clive's arrival at all. He was his always-graceful, kind self, welcoming them. I was a little concerned that this development might have a negative impact on Garcia's enjoyment of being off his leash, anonymous, just a Sarah Vaughan fan, but it turned out that Davis and his companion were very polite, sophisticated, and were just there to dig on Sarah like the rest of us. Of course, it was possible that Garcia himself invited him to join us, but if so he didn't tell me. And why should he have? It was also possible that someone working for the Blue Note had a standing arrangement with Davis to tip him off if anyone interesting was going to be there, and it was even possible that it was pure coincidence that we were all there at the same time. I didn't know then, and I'll never know, so fuck it, it doesn't matter. I guess my point is, if you're that very visible famous person who actually craves no attention at all, you have to deal with not knowing who told who whatever about you and face the limits of knowing why things happening around and to you are happening the way they are. Where fame and big money are in play, I could see how that may be frightening at times. But Garcia was fearless, by nature but also by choice, and he had a chosen way of being in the world: that it was all good, whatever it was; we're all in this together, so enjoy it and spread the enjoyment while you can.

It was a great and memorable show, ending with Sarah's heartbreaking version of Sondheim's "Send in the Clowns" (which was also in the HBO show I'd done) and a standing ovation. Clive and his friend left, but I stayed seated, signaling that we should wait a bit and let the crowd thin. After a while I said to Garcia, "Would you like to go meet Sarah in her dressing room?" I'd okayed this with her people before. Onstage, she was an absolute queen, ruling over the musicians and the crowd, utterly confident and powerful, and funny. Offstage, she was as small and humble and charming and adorable as a person could be. The contrast had really thrown me off, but it made me love her. Garcia considered my offer for a moment, unsure. I could tell he wanted to, but then he said, "Ah, no, she's probably beat. I don't want to impose." I wasn't ready to give up. I mean, it's possible that she knew of his dad, or maybe actually knew him, but I didn't say that. I was just like, "C'mon, it's okay. I cleared it with her people already." He hemmed and hawed, and then said, "Nah, it's okay, let's go." And I gave in. And I still think about it today. Should I have applied more pressure, or presented it in a more appealing way? What the fuck. He couldn't argue in this case that he didn't want to make a scene or disturb someone else's routine. I think it was more his wanting to maintain his extremely humble view of himself, of his importance. If I were smarter, or more manipulative, I could have said, "It's okay. I mentioned you to her and she said she'd like to meet you," but that wasn't true.

Anyway, we cleared out of the Blue Note and ended up walking around the West Village, a very special place, full of partying people, clubs, restaurants, record stores, perfect warm night air. There were Deadheads flooding Manhattan for Garcia's Broadway show, and a few couples passed us on the streets happily yelling, "Hey, Jerry!" But by and large they behaved themselves. It was the out-of-towners who could be weird. New Yorkers pride themselves on their nonchalance around the famous, and there were enough of us that we could effectively protect him from too-friendly advances.

I remember him having a smoke, grinning, the ladies joking and laughing. We end up at the corner of MacDougal and Third Street and decide to go into the famous Caffe Reggio to get some espresso and cheesecake.

The place is not full, and we get a little round table. I sit Garcia so his back is to the door and most of the other people there, with the women on each side of him and me across from him, again, keeping an eye out. We order the cheesecake and coffee. Garcia is just so happy to be actually doing what everybody else does all the time, relaxing in public. Sue and Jackie are cracking jokes, and Sue and Garcia light cigarettes—you could smoke everywhere back then. I notice a young couple of Deadheads against the wall behind Garcia, and I can tell their antennae are up, as if they have a suspicion it's him, but they aren't sure. I look away. The food and drinks come, and Garcia smiles up at the waitress. I can see that the young couple now know it is him. They look like statues, with their eyes wide, their mouths open slightly, and their forks frozen in midair. I'm like, "Uh-oh," but what the fuck, they're harmless.

Garcia notices me glancing at them—nothing gets past him—and I quickly return to my cup and cheesecake, but too late—he stops what he's doing and slowly turns around to where he sees me glancing. The couple *really* reacts then, as if they're seeing a ghost. They slowly put down their forks, their mouths fall open more, and their eyes get even wider. I'm hoping they'll be funny or friendly, but it doesn't feel that way. Garcia nods at them nervously and smiles. Nothing. For them, maybe it's like it would be for a devout Catholic to stumble upon Jesus Christ at Caffe Reggio. Garcia quickly turns back to us, now sheepish, and we are all kind of on pause. Garcia tries again, turning fully around. Yup, they are still staring, a pair of statues.

He gives them a little wave, nods his head, and says, "Hey there." They remain frozen, as if struck dumb. He says, "Yup, it's me! No big deal." Then he gives up and turns back to our table, but you can see something has gone out of him. The little bubble we had going has burst.

I mean, what the fuck do people *want* from their idols? He actually invited them to say hello, have a little chat maybe before we went back into our own little worlds, but no. We got out of there pretty quickly after that. It was okay. Garcia recovered fully in the cab back to the hotel. Sue and Jackie made a big laugh out of it, as usual: "Man, you gotta watch out for the zombies in this town! They'll getcha!"

God, I am so glad I am not famous.

A year after Garcia's coma, he and I are in a seating area at a departure gate at the Burbank Airport, waiting to board a plane back to San Francisco after working in LA for a few days on *So Far.* It was a good working visit, with the project going well, and we are both happy and healthy. There are just a few other people in the seating area—businesspeople, commuters. We're standing instead of sitting, acknowledging that we'd be sitting for the next two hours (including all the boarding, deboarding, and taxiing time).

Along comes an older guy in business attire pulling his carry-on down the corridor to another gate. He spots us, or rather Garcia, and makes a beeline toward us. The guy greets Garcia boisterously. It's clear Garcia knows him, and they shake hands. "So what're you doing down here? Been a long time no see!" Garcia is relaxed; this isn't a problem. They talk about what they have been doing. Apparently, the guy has worked in the recording industry for a long time, and he knew Grateful Dead during their years with their first label, Warner Bros. Records.

Eventually the guy smiles slyly, lowers his voice, and says, "So I saw you OD'd and were in a coma . . ." Garcia winces a tiny bit at this sudden personal intrusion, but smiles and answers gently, kindly, "Well, no, actually, it was a diabetic coma brought on by a tooth infection and severe dehydration." The guy looks at him skeptically and cracks a devilish smile, making the up-and-down fist gesture that men use to imply jerking off—in this case, meaning Garcia is full of shit. He says, "Don't try to pull that shit with me!" Then he guffaws and starts to proceed on his way, saying, "Anyway, good to see you back on your feet!" Garcia nods, smiles indulgently, and says nothing, just waves goodbye.

I feel a sudden intense wave of anger, a very rare thing for me. I'm thinking, "He just told you what happened to him, to your face. Did you not hear that? What the fuck!" I say to Garcia, "Who was that asshole?" He just chuckles and sighs, "Oh just some company man from years ago. I forget his name; Smith maybe?" I'm still pissed.

Whether someone is a rock star or not, that was a really rude way to talk to someone. But Garcia had a high tolerance for that kind of behavior, and we boarded the plane like nothing had happened. I found myself wondering, "How does he do it?"

The curious thing about being famous is that everyone thinks they know all about you, but you don't know anything about them. It's a strange phenomenon. No one experienced this much before the twentieth century, but celebrity culture was cranked up a big notch in the 1980s. The idea of being famous for being a celebrity was born, fueled by things like *People* magazine and *Lifestyles of the Rich and Famous* on TV. You could now become famous without having any special skill, accomplishment, knowledge, or displaying any moral leadership. If you wanted to make a lot of money and had no qualms at all about drawing attention to yourself, you were good. And we've ended up with the Kardashian family and Marjorie Taylor Greene and TikTok and Donald Trump.

Garcia definitely paid a price for his unwanted fame and following. His life's experience brings to mind another figure who emerged from and then exploded in the American culture of the 1960s: Bob Dylan.

My mother turned me on to Dylan's first album when I was twelve. My first Dylan concert was at Kleinhans Music Hall in Buffalo when I was fifteen, where he did an acoustic set and then an electric set with the Hawks, a band that would later become the Band, and it made a huge impression on me. There were college kids heckling and booing him for going electric. I was stunned. The guy was an artist, his folk songs were great, and his blues-rock was great. What was their problem?

This was the beginning of the great collision between pop music and American political culture. Dylan's *Bringing It All Back Home* (March 1965),

Highway 61 Revisited (August 1965), and *Blonde on Blonde* (June 1966); and the Beatles' *Rubber Soul* (December 1965), *Revolver* (August 1966), and *Sgt. Pepper's Lonely Hearts Club Band* (May 1967) were seismic events in the lives of millions of teenagers. There were of course many other musical giants who were part of this moment (Van Morrison, Hendrix, the Doors, the Stones, etc.), but Dylan and the Beatles can stand in as representatives of the whole tidal wave. The Warlocks were formed in 1964 and Grateful Dead in 1965, releasing their first album in 1967, so that was the musical and cultural ocean they were swimming in as they came of age. Before that tidal wave, rock 'n' roll was just pop music, and after it, music identified with a youth culture that was clearly not happy with the establishment. The music reflected opposition to the Vietnam War, the rise of the Black Power movement, and the acceptance of taboo mind-altering substances (think Creedence Clearwater Revival's "Fortunate Son," the work of Stevie Wonder and Marvin Gaye, Hendrix's "Are You Experienced," or Lennon's "Imagine").

From that first Dylan album in 1962 up to today, I have always revered him as the greatest recording artist of all time—although, of course, there is no such thing, so think of me as a superfan. But oddly, considering my career, I never met the man or filmed him until 1987, when he teamed up with the Dead for their 1987 stadium tour, where I was by then part of their concert production apparatus.

Throughout the 1970s, you could see a cult of personality forming around Dylan, stoking weird stories and theories about him. Dylanologists often lurked around his townhouse at 94 MacDougal in New York, where he lived with his wife and children; they were known to go through his trash in search of, I don't know . . . clues? And by 1980, as the Dead became one of the top concert draws in America, you could see that some of the band's fans, the ones known as Deadheads, who followed them from show to show, thought of Garcia as a sort of guru, or even a god.

As a young observer and music lover, and eventually someone making a living in the business, I was aware of how these new gods were depicted in the media and how their music was impacting the culture, or at least the youth culture, in a way that earlier idols like Sinatra and Elvis never did.

I had no inkling prior to meeting and starting to work with Garcia in 1980 that he had any association with Dylan, personally or professionally. Dylan was based in New York, the home of first the folk revival, and then of hard rock and blues-rock. Garcia was ensconced in the laid-back, psychedelicized California music scene, along with bands like Jefferson Airplane; Crosby, Stills, Nash & Young; and the Eagles. But I *was* aware that both men suffered from the characterizations of them as leaders or gurus or gods among their fans and in the media.

It was November 16, 1980, when I first learned about the friendship between Garcia and Dylan (see Chapter 3: The Zen of Jerry). We had just done the Radio City live Halloween broadcast, and we were assessing the material in the living room of the Hepburn Heights house for a future home video release, which ended up being *Dead Ahead.* Garcia and I were rapidly getting to know each other at that time.

Grateful Dead manager Rock Scully, who shared the house with Garcia, graciously interrupted our work, as always with a slight dramatic flair, and asked to have a moment with Garcia in private. Garcia said, "Just come over here and talk to me." So Rock joined us in the conversation pit of the editing room, kind of reluctantly, I think probably because he wasn't sure how to treat me. Was I an outsider or an insider? He said, "So, you know Dylan is in town. He's playing at the Warfield tonight, for Bill Graham, with his new Christian thing." Rock chuckled, maybe waiting for a reaction from Garcia, which wasn't forthcoming, which seemed to make Rock a little nervous.

Dylan at that time was in his "saved" period (1979–1981), when his apparent or supposed conversion to evangelical Christianity led to widespread anger among his fan base, and the notion that he was somehow betraying his anti-establishment outsider status by becoming a Jew for Jesus swept the showbiz world and the mass media, even if that was not what he was doing at all. It was a really big case of what we now call *cancel culture.* The controversy laid bare the new concept that artists were somehow responsible for their public image, whatever that was, and that it was acceptable to attack them for daring to wander from that public image. I was shocked by how fast and how sharply the public turned on him.

Anyway, Rock went on to tell Garcia, somewhat sheepishly, as if he were sorry to bother him, that Bill Graham's people were asking if Garcia would like to sit in with Dylan at tonight's show. It was clear to me, as a silent observer, that Rock didn't think Garcia would want to do that, and also didn't think Garcia *should* do it. But instead, after a brief pause, Garcia asked just one question: "Is it Bill who's asking me to sit in or is it Bob?"

CHAPTER 14

Now I'm like, whoa, this is interesting, Bill was the promoter of the show at the Warfield, and an old ally of Grateful Dead, and Bob is, well, Bob Dylan. Rock was a little stunned, but he was also a very sharp cookie. He knew his place, and he adjusted quickly, "Hmm, okay, I'll call them back . . . and let you know." He hurried off to make the call and Garcia and me got back to work as if nothing had happened, though I was a little distracted, not quite understanding what was going on. A half hour later, Rock came back in, politely interrupting, knowing that he was expected to talk to Garcia about anything at all, despite my presence.

Rock said, "It's Bob who's asking." Garcia nodded and smiled and suddenly went into what I call his executive mode, which I'd never seen before. He held eye contact with Rock while he gesticulated each point. "Okay, great. Call Steve (Parish), tell him to go to Front Street and pick up my Irwin Tiger guitar and my practice amp, and tell him to meet me at the office, and have a limo pick us up there like at . . . what time is the show?" Rock jumped in: "I got it. I've already got the limo; I'll let you know the pickup time. Anything else?" Garcia chortled, "Yeah, make sure there's some food left there for me and Steve." Rock said, "Got it." He turned and exited efficiently.

Because of my prior experience, I'd learned to present myself to musicians and recording artists (no, not rock stars) as a dispassionate professional whose job it was to help them expand their work into the visual realms of TV, film, and live broadcasts. I never fawned or flattered or talked about my love of their work, never tried to wedge myself into photo ops or get too close to them. I treated them like they were regular people, thrust into difficult circumstances by their stardom, and I was there to help them cope with the demands of the new visual media.

I found that the less starstruck I was with them, the more seriously they took me and the more they appreciated me.

But after Rock left the room, I felt my inner dam breaking. I couldn't help it; I lost my cool. I said to Garcia, "So you *know* Dylan?" Garcia looked at me blankly, as if I'd just dropped in from Mars. I couldn't help it, as I said, "I mean, are you *friends* with him?" His demeanor changed suddenly, and he became reticent. "Well, uh . . ."

That was the one time when I scared Garcia. He thought he knew me, but then I revealed I actually was just another fanboy by how I reacted to that Dylan news. I think he was surprised by my behavior, because prior to that moment I had not shown any symptoms of showbizitis. He definitely backed off a notch, looking at me a bit sideways.

In that moment I realized I needed to correct my bad impression. I knew I had to be utterly honest and tell him my whole backstory about how my mom loved Joan Baez and Dylan and played their stuff in our house all the time, and that I grew to have an unusual reverence for him. Then I tried to make light of my own extreme interest in Dylan, and gradually Garcia relaxed. He could see I was sincere, that I was not a dangerous Dylan-obsessive. After all, I was extremely discreet in my interactions with clients. I tried to redirect our attention back to the work at hand. But then after a pause, Garcia said, referring to Dylan, "Yeah, we're friends." I nodded appreciatively but didn't say anything. He said, "We talk on the phone a bit now and then, get together as circumstances allow."

A few days later we were talking about Grateful Dead's unusually large repertoire, which included a lot of Dylan songs. Garcia got to talking about Dylan again. He knew about my avid but totally innocent interest, and I felt that he trusted me, that I was not trying to pull anything out of him. I have a vague memory that Garcia told me that he and Dylan had first met in the late 1960s. He told me a story about how he was in New York, playing a gig. It must've been in the early or mid-'70s, and Dylan had invited Garcia to join him on a little driving tour of New York City. Garcia climbed into the nondescript van, with Dylan at the wheel, and they'd driven around for several hours, with Dylan pointing out various theaters and clubs and hotels and telling Garcia about his own history with these places and his early mentors, Woody Guthrie, Dave Van Ronk, Ramblin' Jack Elliott, Fred Neil. Garcia was clearly relishing the memory. I was just stunned and in awe that these two musical giants were in fact close friends.

Dylan teamed up with Tom Petty and the Heartbreakers as an opening act for Grateful Dead for a summer tour in 1986, and he joined the Dead onstage for a few songs on July 2 at the Rubber Bowl (yes, that was its real name) in Akron, Ohio, just before Garcia's coma episode. In early 1987, with Garcia fully recovered, full of vim and vigor, the band held a large meeting at their studio on Front Street to discuss who they might want as an opening act for the big summer stadium tour to coincide with the release of *In the Dark*, their first studio album in seven years. I was amazed and humbled to see how many people in their operation they invited to this meeting, including me, all of whom could shout out their suggestions and talk it out. The degree to which the band treated their employees, their family, as stakeholders, people whose opinions they respected, was unlike anything I've ever experienced in my life in the entertainment business.

In the end, the band chose Bob Dylan. The resultant summer tour, Dylan and the Dead, was of truly epic proportions. At Garcia's guidance, we innovated daylight-visible video reinforcement screens for the people in the cheap seats in a stadium, which were like a quarter mile from the stage, used special visual effects to create an alternative to just shots of the band, and recorded all the shows at the highest possible technical standards for future use. I was privileged to watch the interactions between Dylan and Garcia and the Dead from my seat in the recording truck, and it was great to see Bob and Jerry hanging out backstage before shows or between sets, eating, drinking, laughing.

A year later, in 1988, Garcia and I went to see Dylan at the Greek Theatre in Berkeley. We stood stage right, behind the stack of speakers for the whole show. Just a couple of fans, loving it.

David Braun was Bob Dylan's longtime personal lawyer, and I came to know him when he represented a production company that I was a partner in during the 1990s. Braun was the president of Polygram Records for a while, and an important lawyer in the music industry at that time, representing Dylan, George Harrison, Neil Diamond, and others. He was known to be especially close with Dylan.

When Garcia died in 1995, I talked to Braun about it, and he told me that he had never, ever, seen Dylan brought so low. Dylan said this about Garcia the day after he died:

There's no way to measure his greatness or magnitude as a person or as a player. I don't think any eulogizing will do him justice. He was that great, much more than a superb musician, with an uncanny ear and dexterity. He's the very spirit personified of whatever is Muddy River country at its core and screams up into the spheres. He really had no equal. To me he wasn't only a musician and friend, he was more like a big brother who taught and showed me more than he'll ever know. There's a lot of spaces and advances between the Carter family, Buddy Holly and, say, Ornette Coleman, a lot of universes, but he filled them all without being a member of any school. His playing was moody, awesome, sophisticated, hypnotic, and subtle. There's no way to convey the loss. It just digs down really deep.

THE CURSE OF CELEBRITY

I often think back to that day in 1980 at the Hepburn Heights house. Garcia didn't hesitate for a moment to stand by his old friend—someone who must have known better than anyone else Garcia knew what it was like to be worshipped, adored, and ultimately objectified by strangers. So, Garcia said, "Hell yes, I'll sit in with him." It looked really courageous from where I was standing, but I'm sure Garcia didn't give it a second thought.

Sometime in early 1988, Garcia and I were reminiscing over a meal about the incredible journey he, and we—but mostly he—had been on between 1984 and '88. We were talking about the role of the mass media in the contemporary entertainment business. I brought up the January 1985 drug bust in Golden Gate Park that he went through; what a torture it must be to be famous and go through an enormous shaming or humiliating event, his hangdog photo on the front page of the newspaper, all the media attention, to know that everyone is gossiping and judging you and even condemning you.

He thought about this for a second and then casually said it was actually a very freeing experience, in a permanent way, because "once everyone knows your worst failure or secret, you're free of the need to hide things. You realize life goes on, and in fact a lot of the people in your life don't give a damn about all that shit, and you feel . . . liberated from some kind of weird subplot. Now that everyone on earth knows all about me and my habits, it's not a secret anymore."

It was a sunny spring day in 1991. I was killing time at the glass octagonal table in the kitchen of the Dead's office, when Garcia ambled in, hesitant, and I could tell right away that there was something troubling him, because he so rarely seemed troubled.

I say, "What's going on?" He pulls out a chair and sits at the table, toying with his BMW keys, his worry beads.

He sighs, hesitates, then tells me, "Ah, there was this guy kinda camping out in my driveway . . ." He turns away, reflective, and looks out the window. I feel a strong electrical signal pass up my spine to my brain, then I realize that was alarming.

I put on my emotional armor and try to be casual. "What do you mean 'camping out'?" "Ah, well, y'know, he's living in his car, on the street, and I see him out there for a few days, and then he's in my driveway . . ." At the time, Garcia is living in a nice house with a pool in the Dominican neighborhood of San Rafael, a very upscale neighborhood where he had moved after Brent

CHAPTER 14

Mydland's death. Seeing Brent's two little daughters at the funeral, fatherless, he'd realized that he should be with his toddler daughter, Keelin, and her mother, Manasha Matheson.

I'm thinking, "So you have no security, or even a gate up there, and there's your baby and her mom?" I say, "Ah, Jer, this is kind of serious. I know how friendly and open you are, but we have gotta do something about this, it's not safe—" He comes out of his reverie and looks up.

I go on, "We could call the cops, or talk to Steve and he could get some help from the crew, and they could just go up there and, y'know, read him the riot act, in a friendly way. But you can't just let this go on—" He cuts me off, "No, no, so, listen . . ."

He pauses to light a cigarette. "I finally went out there and knocked on his window, and he got out, y'know, just a typical young skinny guy, on his own . . ." He stops. I imagine the kid having what to him might be a mind-blowing moment, meeting Jerry, who is in fact at that moment just a happy, harmless suburbanite hanging out at his home trying to deal with what we'd now call a stalker, someone whom Garcia might have referred to as a wayward fan.

I say, "Yeah? What happened?"

He says, "I tried to calm him down, y'know. Just chitchat with him until he seemed, y'know, calm . . . and I brought him inside to sit down and maybe have a cup of coffee . . . so I could figure out what he was after, what he was looking for, y'know, to help him on his way . . . "

I'm thinking, "Oh my God . . ." I just look at him.

"Wait, when did this all happen?"

"Uh, the last coupla days, just a little while ago—"

Really alarmed, I cut him off.

"Wait, wait. Where is this guy right now?"

I stood up. "Is he at your house? Are Manasha and Keelin there?!"

Garcia looks up at me with a sad look on his face. "Sit down, man, take it easy. He left an hour ago. Manasha and Keelin have their own place now."

I'm greatly relieved and sit back down. I say, "Are you sure he's not coming back?"

Dismissively, like I was overreacting, Garcia says, "Yeah, yeah . . ."

"Jerry, you can't be so open to . . . these kinds of people. You gotta keep some distance. You don't know anything about this guy. He could be a psycho—"

He waves his hand, "Yeah, yeah, I know . . ."

I'm put in my place. Who the fuck am I to say . . . anything? But I try to be patient, because I can't know what it's like to be in his position, to be him.

He explains, "I talked to him. He was happy when he left; he's not gonna come back."

I start to relax a little. What's bothering him is not that there was a weird threat that has been made okay, but something beyond that . . .

I ask him, "What did you guys talk about?"

"Well, I could tell he was kind of . . . in a weird kind of awe of me, y'know? He had a weird look in his eye . . . So, I spent some time trying to express to him, talking about my life in a random way, I'm just a person, you're just a person. What's going on in your life? Like that. And he seemed to become more . . . present."

I'm taking that in, trying to calm myself, to comprehend what it must be like to be a very accomplished musical artist, highly sensitive and thoughtful and well-read, articulate, and then run straight into . . . the other side of the life you've built . . . the fans. Were you in some way responsible for what *their* experience was?

He continues, lighting another cigarette: "So I ask him, 'You wanted to meet me, and here we are, in my kitchen . . . Is there anything you want to talk to me about? Or do you need help with anything?" And we just sat there for a while, smiling at each other . . . and he's like, 'Y'know what? No, I'm good.' And he stood up and I walked with him to his car, and we had a friendly goodbye, and off he went."

I say, "Have you talked to anyone, Sue, Steve, the managers, about this?" I'm thinking maybe he should have. But he says, "Nah, it's okay. I think it's blown over."

He gets up and leaves, and if he'd been there in the office for any business other than stopping by for a sit-down in the kitchen, he's forgotten it. I sit there for a while, a bit shaken, thinking.

Looking back, what was troubling Garcia was not the young man or the incident. Garcia did not look at the world in terms of threats, and so he never felt threatened by anybody or anything. He was the most thoroughly fearless person I have ever known. It was the paradoxes it brought up when he was a popular musical artist in a huge rock band with its own subculture and how the mass media was amplifying everything. What part of all of that was his responsibility? What should he have done? Was that kid lost? Maybe. Did Garcia have any responsibility for that? (I'd say no.) Would that kid maybe end up benefiting from his experience with the Dead in the long run? Y'know, maybe find a cure for cancer? Possibly. Or become a homicidal maniac? Maybe. The fact remains that Garcia felt the need to deal with the situation. It impacted his life, and not in a good way. It gave him pause. I could see his perspective clearly: "Y'know, I'm just a hardworking musician, and the stuff we do is just songs. We do understand some of them carry a wallop of meaning in this world, but still . . . don't I deserve some privacy and peace and quiet when I'm living my day-to-day life? I know you see me as something more, possibly much more, than a working musician, but that's on you, that's in your head. It's not on me. I never asked to be worshipped."

The idea that the small talk that Garcia had with the fan, where they were just two people relating, gave the fan everything he was looking for, probably unknowingly. Some real personal contact with his idol, his hero, whatever. And maybe he learned, personally, deeply, that he and Garcia were on the same plane, both living in the same universe, and were both, in some way, one, in the way that everything alive is part of one thing, a spiritual belief I know Garcia embraced.

That story shows how kind he was, plain and simple kindness. He was a man of empathy, gentleness, and a generosity of spirit, willing to share himself with people in need, even strangers. But I also mean to give you, dear reader, a glimpse into the unseen underside of stardom. One that is specific to Garcia's case, a man famous for his music but also burdened with an aura of magic, mystical leadership. He was a living idol, and though he thoroughly rejected the idea of being a guru, it is also undeniably true that his life's work conveyed a set of deeply held spiritual beliefs, beliefs that moved people deeply, a lot of people, which they held in their hearts, and still do to this day, for their huge value in helping them on their paths through life.

Laura Kimpton and Jerry at Sue Stephens's wedding. Photo courtesy ©Sue Stephens.

Chapter 15

THE KIMPTON SAGA

I met Laura Kimpton backstage at a Dead concert (where else?). She was introduced to me by my good friend and business associate Todd Jackson, on the last day of July 1988, at Laguna Seca Raceway, near Monterey. She was twelve years younger than me, taking classes in photography and painting at the San Francisco Art Institute, the same school Garcia had gone to, and working as a bartender. She was an inch taller than me, five foot eleven, with wild blonde hair, deep blue eyes, long legs, altogether a striking figure. I was spending time with a number of different women, trying to have a more normal life than just work, work, work, and she was in no apparent hurry to get serious. We always had fun together. She had an adventurous personality, very outgoing. I thought it was a good balance with my more Spock-like traits. We both liked to travel, go to good restaurants, see movies, have a good time, have lots of laughs.

Laura and I were in Woodstock, New York, for a week or so in early October 1989. She was having fun and shooting photos, while I was working at a local recording studio on the final audio mix of a concert film I'd shot back in August for HBO at The Biltmore hotel in Los Angeles. The film was called *Caliente y Picante,* part of HBO's outreach to the Latino community. I had recruited Garcia to the lineup, which included Santana, Linda Ronstadt,

CHAPTER 15

Tito Puente, Celia Cruz (known as the "Queen of Salsa"), and Rubén Blades. When the job was done, Laura and I drove down to the city for some R&R.

We went out to the Hamptons for some beach time, then back to NYC for some Grateful Dead shows at the Meadowlands Arena in New Jersey. We also saw the Rolling Stones at Shea Stadium on October 10, where we saw Brent going down the aisle next to us with a tray of beers. We gave him a shout-out and he waved back. I heard later that the Stones and the Dead were in the same hotel for a few nights, probably the Ritz-Carlton, and that some of them actually got together—maybe to settle the disaster at Altamont? (Just kidding.)

We were back in our hotel room on the evening of Tuesday, October 17, 1989, settled in front of the TV with some take-out to watch the third game of the World Series, a matchup between our two Bay Area teams, the Oakland A's and the San Francisco Giants. A little past 8:00 p.m., just as the game was getting underway, suddenly all hell broke loose. The television image got weird and shaky, the audio cut out, and then the signal went dead entirely, to be replaced with an emergency-interruption kind of graphic. Holy shit! It was just like in the movies when some huge world-ending disaster hits.

Our first impulse was to look out the windows to see if New York was still normal, then check other TV channels, local radio. Nothing odd. Whatever had just happened wasn't happening in NYC. Laura tried to place a call to her father, Bill Kimpton, in San Francisco, but the lines were down. Remember, this was before cell phones, so we had to rely on the hotel switchboard—just an extra layer of panic to deal with when we were trying to reach someone. Then, within minutes, local TV and radio started reporting a big earthquake in SF, and so we knew.

Laura's family, her sister, her brother, her dad, and a bunch of besties were all in San Francisco. I also had a bunch of best friends out there, and a house—a house on stilts!—in Marin, with a cat living in it. We gave each other a long look. We were scared but resolved not to lose our minds and to stay calm, figure out how to get more information, figure out what we should do—stuff like call family and friends who were outside of the earthquake zone who might assume that we were in the earthquake zone, to reassure them that we were safe in NYC. Before this had all unfolded, our lives were a lot less complicated. We had tickets for a flight the next morning, Wednesday, for our return to San Francisco, in order to attend a big engagement party her dad Bill was throwing for Laura's sister, Marcia, and her fiancé that was scheduled for Thursday night.

Within a half hour, we were looking at helicopter and blimp shots of SF and Oakland. Conveniently, the blimps were there for the World Series. The aerial shots focused on the huge fires in the Marina District of SF, and a section of the Bay Bridge that connected the two cities and a section of highway in the East Bay that had both collapsed, as if they were made of cardboard. It looked bad, really bad. Pillars of smoke were lit up by the setting sun. We soon learned that the power was out and that all Bay Area airports were closed to all traffic for an indeterminate amount of time. In the good news column, Laura's sister, brother, and father were shaken but okay. We hunkered down, assuming of course that the Thursday party was canceled, as were our airline tickets, and that in the morning we would just go to work figuring out how to get back home as quickly as possible. But who knew? The damage to the airports would take a while to assess, and how long before there was power? The point being, we could be stuck in New York for days, or longer.

The next day, Wednesday, I just kept calling the airlines, asking when the first flight into SFO would be announced—there was little else I could do. They kept saying, "We don't know, but you can keep calling." Late in the day we learned that, incredibly, the Thursday night engagement party in San Francisco had not been canceled. This was my first inkling of the Kimpton family gene for boldness, though I was registering it at the time as craziness. Also, it was a bit odd that Laura was getting messages from the earthquake zone despite the telephones being out, as if via some sort of emergency network. She was vague when I asked about it.

Thursday midafternoon I called the airlines for what felt like the hundredth time. They put me on hold for a bit, then came back on with, "Can you be here in two hours?" I said, "Hell yes," and Laura and I packed our bags and made a dash to JFK. The plane was full of journalists, television reporters, and their crews—camera people, sound people, some recognizable national media stars . . . and me and Laura.

We landed at SFO at twilight to a surreal scene. There were no other planes taxiing, and the terminal itself was mostly dark. Silently, somberly, we all got off the plane. All those media people and their support crews, and Laura and I and a few other regular people, trudged through a deserted and darkened airport, emergency lights only, to the only working baggage carousel. We waited there, sharing that heavy, somber mood of concern and wariness at entering into a disaster zone.

We stood in front of the baggage conveyor belt, watching a slow, endless parade of standard corporate black suitcases, tripods, camera cases, lighting kits, over and over, until our bags finally appeared. We grabbed them, and because we didn't have to regroup with anyone like all the media crews, we got to the curb first to get one of the few cabs available to take us to downtown SF—where, surreally, the party was supposedly happening.

There was no regular traffic like us, only cop cars and fire trucks and emergency vehicles flying by, the sound of sirens all around. Our frightened driver was constantly pulling over for them, working hard to drive safely without any signals or streetlights, or lighting of any kind, just staying in the flow . . . very fucking eerie like we were suddenly in a sci-fi disaster movie, wondering why we chose to come back to this place.

On the way, Laura mentioned to me that her father was kind of well-connected, in a way that I hadn't heard from her before. It was as if she were trying to prepare me in some way for something, which I could not make sense of at all at that moment. I was like, "Oh, sure," because compared to everything else going on, it seemed like a minor detail.

Laura had not previously seemed much interested in talking about her family. It seemed to be a fraught topic, so I avoided it. I did know through inference and mutual friends that her father was involved in some way in finance or real estate development or the hotel business, who knows, and that her mother lived in Chicago with her stepdad. Laura had invited me to a lunch to meet her dad many months earlier, which I found slightly odd, since she and I were not girlfriend and boyfriend at that point in time. But I liked her and was attracted to her, and we were spending time together, and I thought, "Why not have lunch with her dad?" It was a pleasant lunch, mostly small talk, and looking back from decades later I think Laura maybe wanted her father to take a look at me before she made any more moves in our pas de deux.

As we approached the restaurant, I saw that there was a good deal of lighting out front, a generator, flashlights, the sound of partiers emanating from within, and what seemed to be a security detail: double-parked SUVs with their lights on, and two largish men in suits keeping an eye on things.

Hmm. We dove into the party, already in full swing, as if there was no disaster happening at all. There was music playing, waiters bustling about with platters of appetizers and champagne, the whole weird scene lit by candles and a few odd lanterns. On seeing her family, Laura shared a big hug with her father, and we greeted the engaged couple. Again, I had that feeling of being in a movie, a movie I was starting to like—something like a Tarantino movie.

Bill introduced me to Nancy Pelosi, then in her first elected term in Congress, and then to the soon-to-be mayor of San Francisco, Art Agnos, whom Bill humorously disparaged the minute he was out of earshot. I noticed other local luminaries in the media and the social scene, all very well-dressed and drinking, and I was starting to think . . . hmm, this guy refused to reschedule an engagement party for his daughter two days after a devastating earthquake, and a mayoral candidate and one of the city's congressional representatives show up, and all these other people . . . this guy must be a real big shot! (Decades later I learned from Laura that she had mistakenly taken a wrong turn into an adjacent room at one point during the party, walking in on a private meeting among the politicians and a bunch of other city power players who were discussing the crisis, which suggested to me that maybe Bill's party was the most logical place to get together that night.)

By the end of the night, Laura and I were heading home in a cab across the Golden Gate Bridge on Highway 101 to Marin. It was an eerie sight: Except for emergency vehicles zooming this way and that, the roads around us were totally empty, and all the towns of Marin were in complete darkness. I was emerging from the fog of the surreal events of the previous twelve hours and moving onto anxiety about what my house in San Anselmo, sitting on stilts high on a ridge, might look like, not to mention how my cat was. But it turned out that the house and everything in it was fine, untouched. The wine bottles on top of the fridge hadn't budged; Gumbi, an elderly female Siamese cat, was frightened but okay. It was a classic reminder that fate is often just random. One house is destroyed, and the one next to it is spared, a lesson that Kurt Vonnegut taught us so well.

Six years later, during the winter of 1994/95, I was living in Marin full time. Laura and I were married, after living together for five years, and we were loving it. I was doing freelance producing and directing and writing screenplays. It had been three years since my business relationship with Grateful Dead came to a close, but I was still friendly with Garcia and Sue

Stephens and other people in that world. Laura's dad, Bill Kimpton, was by this time wildly successful in the hotel and restaurant business; investment in his company was hot as a pistol. He had gotten crazy good press as the inventor of the "boutique hotel." His future was utterly secure, and he was looking around, hungry for the next fun thing to do.

He announced at our family Thanksgiving get-together that he was starting a philanthropic organization called the Mental Insight Foundation, to encourage and promote Eastern thought, specifically meditation as a treatment for depression, anxiety, and other mental or spiritual maladies (some of us present at that get-together would become members of the board of directors after Bill's passing in 2001). He supported the creation of Spirit Rock, founded by Jack Kornfield, a spiritual retreat in West Marin devoted to the teaching of insight meditation and mindfulness. Kornfield spoke movingly at Bill's memorial many years later.

Bill told me about his visit to Esalen, the fabled holistic retreat and educational institute located in the ancient forests along the stunning coastline of Big Sur, to see if there was anything he and Esalen might want to do together in the future. He tasked me with contacting Daniel Quinn, the author of the novel *Ishmael,* about a very wise gorilla who engages a human partner to explore deep scientific, philosophical, and spiritual subjects, to discuss making the book into a film. We had a great meeting with Quinn, but it turned out that Disney had an option on the book and was not currently interested in developing it.

By this point in time, I had evolved great respect and admiration for Bill Kimpton, my father-in-law. My own father passed away on New Year's Day, 1989, and I have felt the loss deeply ever since then. Jerry and Bill were the only two men older than me whom I really looked to, like mentors, for wisdom back then, although Bill was only fifteen years older than me, and Garcia was just eight years older.

One day, Bill mentions to Laura that he would like to talk to Garcia about potential business ventures and wonders if I would be interested in arranging a meeting. I'm a little mystified. What does a hotel and restaurant mogul want to talk to a rock star about?

I have a meeting with Bill. He's really loosey-goosey, just wanting to explore any fun things that might be out there. It isn't the pursuit of profit for him anymore; he only wants to do the things that he believes in and that will be fun and rewarding for him and everyone else involved. I am a show business veteran at this point, well schooled in history and politics, and in the navigation through the world of what is now called the one-percenters. To be honest, Bill's take on life is implausible even to me, but I have to take him at face value. He is who he is: He's sincere, and his approach to life is what led him to invent the boutique hotel concept and build his company from scratch into a hugely successful enterprise. And so, he is saying to me, "It's no big deal. Let's just take a meeting with Garcia and talk and see what happens."

I have a chat with Garcia and tell him about Bill's ask. He's initially confused, wondering, "What does a guy like that want with a guy like me?" He says he has "an innate fear of being with rich guys, captains of industry, you know," and I'm, like, stifling the thought, "Well you're a rich guy yourself, and you seem to have mastered the recording industry." Instead, I say, "No one's looking for any commitment here or anything like it. This guy is my father-in-law. I know him really well and I am vouching for his character and good intentions. He's a great guy. He's looking for interesting opportunities and he's got the money to risk on new ventures. There's nothing to fear here, so let's see what happens." Garcia thinks for a moment and then agrees to the meeting.

I am amazed to find myself in the position of possibly bringing these two men together. Whether it comes to something on a business level or not, I know it will still be really interesting.

At home, I tell Laura what's going on, and she's happy and excited. Casually, she asks if she can come to the meeting. I'm genuinely thrown by this, and it takes me a moment to comprehend. I say to her, "Look, it's a business meeting. How will it look if I bring my wife along . . . for what reason?" It's hard for me to express this, to myself and to her, but she takes it really well.

I make the arrangements with Sue Stephens and Bill. We will meet at her office, no agenda, just a hello-who-are-you kind of meeting, with Sue, me, Bill, and Garcia. Then I call Jerry to bring him up-to-date. He's still a little unsure of what we are doing, but he's game. Before we hang up, he says to me, "Can Laura come too? It might be more comfortable for everyone, cuz it's her dad, and I'm comfy with her too . . ."

Garcia and Laura know each other quite well by then, because we've all been together on many occasions (movie and dinner outings, Sue Stephens's wedding, Brent's funeral), and it's obvious they like each other, so his request to have her at the meeting makes good sense. So, I have to go back to Laura and say, quite sheepishly, "Change in plan: Jerry wants you to come to the meeting." She's happy to hear it, she doesn't needle me, and I'm appreciative.

Looking back, obviously, I should have just said to Laura, "I've changed my mind, I want you to come to this meeting." I would have scored huge spousal points, but I wasn't sophisticated enough, even in my forties, to see the strategy. Or maybe I was just too plain innocent, or stupid.

Sue was bright-eyed and bushy-tailed as usual when Laura and I arrived at her office, and Bill arrived a few moments later, very punctual, as usual. There was cheerful banter among us. We were not surprised that Garcia was late, because . . . well, it was Garcia. But after a while, maybe fifteen minutes, I got a little uncomfortable. For a rock star, Garcia was usually pretty good at being on time, and I was the person who'd arranged the meeting.

Sue's office was in a converted house directly across the street from the Grateful Dead office, which was also a converted house with an adjacent parking lot. I had a sudden impulse to go look at the parking lot, which was visible from an anteroom in Sue's office, to see if Garcia's car was there, thinking maybe he thought the meeting was at the Grateful Dead office and not at Sue's office. Also, Garcia had a habit of cruising that parking lot to see if the cars of people he might want to hang out with were there before deciding to venture inside. Maybe that had happened, and he got distracted.

So, I go into the anteroom and head for the window that has the view of the parking lot. I'm startled to find that Garcia is sitting there in the anteroom, smoking a cigarette. I go into improv mode, rolling with the flow.

Garcia greets me, "Hey."

"Oh . . . you're here!" I say.

"Yeah, I'm here."

I try to adjust, summoning empathy. I breathe, no hurry, smile, and say, "Well, everyone's in the other room. Are you good to join us?"

He stubbs out his cigarette. "Yeah, I guess so . . ."

I say stuff trying to reassure him that "no one is after anything, there's no goal." He stands up, nodding, readying himself, and manages a smile. He's clearly not in great shape emotionally, which I must struggle to process. He is a hugely accomplished musician and recording artist, universally adored, with a centi-millionaire waiting to chat with him about anything that he might want to do that might require investment, and yet he feels . . . reluctant? Waddup widdat, brother?

Once underway, the meeting is very pleasant, full of laughs. All of us quickly come to realize that everyone has only the best intentions. We recognize the oddity of the situation: Why would Bill want to have a meeting with Garcia?

When it comes time, Bill is brilliantly sincere and concise, qualities that I had come to understand and admire over the previous seven years. He presents who he really is, what he's interested in, and the stuff he wants to pursue in life. Projects that he knows something about, like restaurants, clubs, hotels, resorts, retreats, where he can bring his creative skills to bear, spiritually and psychologically. Positive ventures that can also be financially viable, just as the Kimpton hotels and restaurants are. Sue, Laura, Bill, Jerry, and I all have some Irish blood, and by the end of the meeting it's that sense of Irishness that prevails, the urge to be jolly and friendly and optimistic about the future.

We agree that Jerry and I would come up with a wish list of possible projects and that we'd meet again for lunch. Bill suggests we do it at Splendido, his new restaurant on the Embarcadero in San Francisco. After that, he wants to show Garcia his newest current project, still under construction—Bill's vision of a high-end luxury hotel: the Hotel Monaco.

Bill had explained to me privately that it was important to him that Garcia see him and understand him as a creative person, not just a money guy. Splendido was his creation, and so the Hotel Monaco would be too.

The appointed day rolls around, and I go to pick up Garcia midafternoon and head into SF for a late lunch or early dinner at Splendido. I meet him at his physical therapist's office in Corte Madera. I offer to drive, and he accepts. We take his BMW 8 Series, probably because it's roomier than my car. I relish the idea of trying out the legendary twelve-cylinder powerhouse. The trip to the city involves the long, steep climb up the Waldo Grade. The car takes it like it isn't there at all.

On the way into the city, we fall into our usual relaxed conversational mode. Garcia talks about measures he's taking, like physical therapy, to try to improve his health, and the fact that he no longer eats anything with a face, the first time I've heard that way of describing a vegetarian diet. To be honest, he strikes me as somewhat weaker than the last time I'd seen him, not just physically, but psychically, or spiritually (and the rumor mill had been grinding for several years about his substance-addiction problems).

CHAPTER 15

We talk about what we've been up to lately because we haven't been alone with each other in a while. He visibly relaxes as he talks about his recent visits with his first wife, Sara, and his separate visits with the child they have together, his first daughter, Heather, in the San Jose area. I'm a little surprised; this is the first time any of this part of his life, from 1963, before the Grateful Dead began, to 1967, has come up between us, but he smiles as he recalls the meetings with his first family. Heather is now a musician, among other things, playing violin in the Redwood Symphony, which he notes with satisfaction. He talks about some of her physical traits and behaviors that he strongly relates to and which endears her to him.

I think it's really cool that he's visiting with Sara and Heather, and I ask him how he feels about getting together with intimates from his past, and what motivated him to do it. He expresses an air of mature contemplation about his life, about how it's good for him, and maybe them (he can't really say, though they seemed to value it), to do this kind of assessment; a reckoning with his life.

At that time, I was forty-four years old, and Garcia was fifty-two, I was a newlywed working on starting a family, but he was way, way ahead of me on that score (with five daughters, counting Sunshine, MG's daughter with Ken Kesey). I didn't think of him as over-the-hill, except that he seemed to be viewing life as a limited thing, and he was doing what he thought necessary, given the limits as he saw them.

We stop by a place in the city. Garcia says a friend of his has a guitar he might want to buy, and I wait in the car as he goes in. I think it's odd that he brought his custom, hand-painted little attaché case with him. He emerges after a while, making us late for our meeting with Bill, but as usual, his demeanor is the same as ever. I suspect that he was actually scoring and that he is back on the Persian smoking powder habit.

But I also sense some unease or disgruntlement in him. He's not his usual happy, jocular self. I'm thinking, "Well, if this mood is like similar moods I've seen him in over the last fifteen years, maybe a project with Kimpton could reactivate his creative juices and give him a boost."

And maybe if his underlying problem is boredom, or a lack of challenges, as I had concluded in the past, it also might help him get out from under an addiction problem, if he currently has one. His mind is so voluminous and complex, he's constantly at risk of not having enough stuff to engage his intellect, which makes it easier to turn to substances for entertainment or diversion.

Another problem he has is that he doesn't have enough people in his life who are at his level of knowledge, intelligence, and wisdom. He may want to hang out with scholars, scientists, or writers (he had spent some time with Joseph Campbell), but the people who want to hang out with *him* are more likely to be eager fans, aggressive women, or hipster con artists looking for a piece of his action, which he can detect in five seconds and finds depressing.

As we cross over the Golden Gate, with its stunning view of San Francisco and the Bay Bridge, it must trigger a memory in him. He tells me about the parrot that had lived with his grandmother and grandfather when he was a kid, and that his single mom had managed a bar located under the on-ramp to the Bay Bridge. His grandmother had found a lost parrot on the street in the aftermath of the great San Francisco earthquake of 1906 and taken it home, and the bird took a shine to his grandfather. By the time Jerry joined the household, in the late '40s or early '50s, the parrot grew very close to his grandfather, and they were all in a stable long-term relationship (parrots are known to select a specific human companion as a mate, and they can live a very long time, often outliving their owners).

I think that is a very charming story. Garcia is smiling and chuckling. There's a pause, and then he goes on to say that when his grandfather passed away, the parrot was inconsolable, sank into a depression, and just wasted away and died. We sit there and sigh and murmur and shake our heads. Wow, life is so strange.

In the talks we'd had since our last meeting with Bill, Garcia recalled fondly the coffeehouse scene of the early '60s. It included places that were often a walk-down from street level in many American cities, where wine and espresso and bar food were served, poets would sit on a little stage and recite their work, and acoustic musicians and the occasional electric blues band or folk-rock act would perform. I recognized those memories as representing his underlying understanding of the evolution from folk music (Woody Guthrie, and later Dylan) to the Beats (Ginsberg, Burroughs, Kerouac) to the psychedelic movement (Kesey, Leary) and to the music that followed, born in San Francisco: Quicksilver Messenger Service, Jefferson Airplane, Grateful Dead, Janis Joplin and Big Brother and the Holding Company, and many others. Garcia's first work as a performer was with

Robert Hunter when they were nineteen or twenty years old in the early '60s. They played as an acoustic duo known as Bob and Jerry in the coffeehouses that he fondly remembered.

So, in the car on the way to the meeting with Bill, I find myself improvising a proposal. It will be called Casa Garcia, a small, low-key place in SF; no bar, but wine and beer and espresso and snack food, where people can go on any given night and expect to enjoy a comic or a poet or a musical act for a minimal cover fee. By lending his name to the place, Garcia will of course be an owner, and as a bonus he will always have a place to go on a moment's notice where he can play solo acoustic, or with Hunter or Dave Nelson, if they are available, or sit in as a guest with whomever is already on the bill. That last point really gets Garcia's attention. There'll be no need to make deals in advance with venues or schedules, just, "Well, I feel like playing tonight, so I'll just grab a guitar and go to my club."

Because I am, in fact, a businessman, having been self-employed forever, and calculations about potential risks and profits are part of my modus operandi, I quickly outline a few details to him, almost as an afterthought. The first club will be in San Francisco, and we will test it and improve it. If it is successful, we can then franchise it, putting Casa Garcia in other cities, starting with LA, Vegas, NYC, New Orleans. I point out that this is meat and potatoes for the Kimpton operation; they are already highly skilled at this. He smiles and nods, approving the pitch to Bill.

We are a little late to meet Bill in a little plaza outside of Splendido, but Bill is his usual charming self. We all sit down outside so that Garcia can have a cigarette, which is no longer allowed inside a restaurant in the city. The meal is enjoyable, there's minimal reaction to Garcia's presence from other diners, and Jerry and I pitch our idea about Casa Garcia. Bill receives it well, talking about the place we are sitting in and his role in creating it, and I'm thinking, "Wow, Casa Garcia might actually be something that happens."

It's mostly the two of them chatting, with me throwing out the occasional point or remark, and providing each of them with a highly trusted third party. I am a bit gobsmacked that these two are actually talking turkey about a business deal in front of me, considering my feelings about both of them. I have to pinch myself to pay attention instead of just wallowing in awe. And what I experience is a master lesson in the art of social skills from two masters, both beyond the need to worry about money, and experts in the single most important skill for those at the top of their game or their field: sizing up a potential business or artistic partner.

Then Bill abruptly announces the end of the dinner and whisks us off for a tour of the Hotel Monaco, his first, and flagship, five-star hotel under construction. We pile into his Jaguar. He's in full, excited tour guide mode, all energy and charisma, and from my place in the back seat I can see that Garcia is chuckling and enjoying being *not* the center of attention.

We arrive at the construction site, which has a large office trailer parked outside, with a string of lights hung between it and the entrance to the building. Bill parks the car right behind the trailer in a clearly marked no-parking zone, pops out and heads for the trailer, and we kind of scramble after him. He yells something about needing a key as he bounds up the few steps to the door of the trailer, and Jer and I pause on the sidewalk in front of the building. Bill's in the trailer for a few moments, enough time for several people strolling by to turn and look at Garcia, registering surprise. He deals with their smiles and waves with his usual grace and charm, although I feel a little wary standing there. Then Bill bounds out of the trailer and down the steps with a guy chasing after him, yelling, "Hey wait, you can't go in there. It's dangerous!" Bill yells back, "The hell I can't. I own this place!" He's got a big flashlight and he's laughing, and we join in and move toward the door. The trailer guy yells out, "Okay, okay, just wait a minute. You gotta put on hard hats!" Bill acquiesces and we wait while the guy goes back in the trailer and sheepishly brings us three hard hats that we awkwardly put on, a comic scene. Then we follow Bill inside.

As soon as we're inside and Bill shuts the door, I look around and I'm stunned. It's a huge, gutted space, mostly utterly dark, so I can't really tell where the nearest walls or ceilings or structures are. Everything is lit by work lights, what looked like strings of party lights all over the place, only brighter and longer, giving the space an eerie, fantastical vibe, like a scene from Fellini's *8½* (1963). Bill shouts, "Isn't this great!" like an excited little kid, and Garcia does, in fact, get it. He nods and grins, recognizing that Bill is as crazy as he is.

Bill then launches into a little tour of the triple- or quadruple-height first floor, describing that it "will become a lobby and a huge sitting room, and over here will be a full bar and café for casual dining, and then over here will be the Grand Café, a towering space for a full-blown fine dining restaurant."

CHAPTER 15

He's leading us around this one-acre space by flashlight, with warning signs and taped-off areas abounding. We're stepping over newly laid stone or tile of some kind, and there's wet cement, which I step into once or twice.

"I've got a designer putting in huge light fixtures hanging from the ceiling, inspired by this place in Paris, and I've commissioned this great local artist to build me some really playful giant sculptures that I'm gonna put over here, by the maître d' podium." Finally, he shines his light on the one feature that is actually already there, an amazing twenty-foot-tall curving marble staircase that would lead to the meeting and hotel rooms above.

"This is the one thing we're keeping from the building before we bought it. Isn't it beautiful?" He plays the beam of the flashlight up and down the sparkling white marble.

As we head back outside I glance at Garcia, and yes, he is impressed. Not by Bill's money or celebrity or influence, but by his character and creative urge. I'm thinking, "Home run, Bill."

I don't know how he learned to do it, to seduce, but later I realize, wasn't that the same skill Garcia applied to me when we first met?

Later, I'm driving the big Beamer back to Marin with Garcia next to me. He's in a good mood after our meeting with Bill, and I get the feeling to ask him about his disgruntled mood when I picked him up earlier, so I say, "Is there something you want to talk about?"

Maybe I do this because I believe he trusts me and he may want to get some things off his chest, I don't know.

He sighs and takes a moment, then says, "Yeah, it's my marriage, my wife. She's trying to get involved in my business, lawyers are coming in . . . I just wanted someone I could live with, go to movies with, stuff like that . . . but it turns out that she married me for my money."

I'm shocked to hear him talk about someone in this way. It's probably the only time, because he is always generous and gracious with everyone, and it feels kind of jarring to me. It also feels weird because it's well-known that Deborah Koons, his third wife, is wealthy in her own right. He goes on, "Yeah, I don't really have any money, but she thought I did, and she has this big house project going on in Mill Valley . . . and she needs money for it." I'm kind of crestfallen hearing this. I get the strong feeling that for him the relationship is over, even if they haven't yet started talking about separating or divorcing.

Later, heading home after dropping him off, I thought about how unfair it was that someone like Garcia, unfailingly generous and famously not interested in accumulating wealth, could be in this situation. It was common knowledge and gossip among Grateful Dead employees that after Deborah Koons married Garcia, she behaved as if she would be accepted by the Grateful Dead world as the new queen or something, and that she was surprised and upset at the pushback that actually happened. First, Garcia was not the king of Grateful Dead or Grateful Dead Productions; he was one member of a six-member band and one owner of the company among many. Second, no one in the sprawling organization felt any pressure or obligation to treat her any differently than they did the girlfriends and wives, and ex-girlfriends and ex-wives, of the other five guys (which, trust me, was a long list). Third, she would have to adjust to her place in the preexisting order of women and children whom Garcia was obliged to support, which was its own considerable list.

Fourth, and maybe most crucially, Garcia was not the kind of person who carefully managed his income in order to create ever-greater wealth. On the contrary, he deeply believed that money should flow like water and not be hoarded. From his perspective, which seems kind of curious in this current age of billionaires (though not in comparison to the psychedelic values propounded in the 1960s), hoarding wealth could only lead to mental illness and societal decay. He saw it as destabilizing a natural order: all the life on earth cooperating in a fantastically complex dance that kept the wheel turning, by sharing resources, not hoarding them, a sustainable vision of life. He had long since internalized the notion that if he needed money he could just get as much as he needed by performing and recording, and so, quite logically, he didn't worry about or have a need to hoard money or build wealth.

After we parted that night, I returned home with a wild mix of thoughts in my head. The possibility of a fun, very lucrative ongoing project involving both my new family, Laura and Bill Kimpton, and Garcia, was more than intriguing. Casa Garcia could be a beloved new aspect to the Grateful Dead culture, maybe ultimately with local Casa Garcias in every major city, helping to keep his legacy alive and keep that subculture going. And it could also be a revenue stream to help sustain my family and Garcia's after we were all long gone.

CHAPTER 15

On the other hand, it seemed that Garcia was back into the Persian smoking powder habit, which wasn't good, even if he was only chipping (meaning occasional use, as opposed to outright addiction). And I had a feeling of dark clouds surrounding Garcia, a feeling of negativity closing in on him from both his marriage and the recent decline, in my eyes, of his interest in and ability to play the music that he'd been doing for thirty years with Grateful Dead. It also occurred to me that if you are an addict and need cash to keep the pain at bay, sometimes your spouse may feel it necessary to try to cut off your access to that cash. I'd seen this happen before, and I believe that this is what was going on in his marriage, and rather than see it this way, he was choosing to just see it as a money grab.

Many years later, I realized that the slight tinge of concern I had repressed when Garcia told me he was visiting his first wife and daughter was because deep down I knew that he thought his time might be limited, and he was, in his way, trying to settle his earthly accounts before he died. With hindsight it was clear that was the case, but I would not let it reach the surface of my consciousness due to my fear. Later, in 1999, I had a similar experience with Bill, my father-in-law, prior to his passing. Laura and I and our newborn baby went up to his St. Helena estate for a family weekend, and I found Bill going through his storage room there, rigorously throwing stuff away. He was opening multiple bottles of aged wine to see if they were still good, not letting them breathe before he tasted them and then throwing them away. It wasn't logical; if you open a bottle at noon and decide it *is* good, what are you gonna do, pound it? There were signs everywhere that he wasn't well, and he knew it and kept it from us. I repressed the knowledge rather than deal with it in the moment.

From my present perspective, I've learned that people often have a feeling when their time on earth is coming to an end, even if they don't really know. It's natural to go into denial about this when the person is someone you love. It's just too painful to think about them leaving you forever, and so we sometimes conspire, the dying and the survivors, to delay the moment of honest acceptance, of a reckoning. We are all only human, so the fear of losing loved ones is nothing to regret or feel bad about. Maybe we can learn to accept the denial as part of the process and learn to see it earlier, so as to help the dying person in their transition to whatever comes next, and to help ourselves live with it.

Chapter 16

DECLINE

Grateful Dead and I parted ways amicably in the fall of 1991. After putting fifty or so concerts in the vault, they certainly had enough high-end concert film releases to last a very long time. And keeping me around was not cheap. You could get perfectly adequate video reinforcement (good enough for the big screens in the stadiums, but lower than archival quality) with fewer cameras, dollies, and jib arms (cranes), and a less expensive director. I think Garcia knew that they had finally put together a truly great band starting around 1985, after Brent Mydland had been with them for six years, and they just kept getting better.

Brent died after the Dead's summer tour in 1990 and was replaced by Vince Welnick. I think Garcia knew that the musical heights they had reached by 1990 were unlikely to be matched any time soon, if ever. So, the incentive to put concert films in the vault was possibly reduced in 1991. That begged the question, was Garcia seriously interested in the legacy of Grateful Dead, or his own legacy? And the answer was yes to both. He took cultural history very seriously.

He had an abiding and long-held sense of the place that he and Grateful Dead held in the much larger history of music as a powerful cultural force. He also understood their place in the age-old evolution of human consciousness, because of the part they played, and were still playing, in the emergence of the psychedelic experience in the twentieth century.

CHAPTER 16

His strategy all along was not to attempt to devise and create the ultimate, perfect film of a Dead concert, but rather to record as many concerts as possible at the highest possible technical standards and leave it to future generations to pick and choose from the collection, making their own custom concerts, and converting them into new, unforeseen media and fan-based art forms. That plan fit perfectly with the Dead's creative ethos: No two shows alike; let's trust in the band and the fans and the music to manifest itself. And thus, we had fifty concerts to study, or play with, or get high with.

I had never seen Garcia so disheartened as at the first band meeting after Brent died, in early August 1990. Everyone was upset, and there were raw feelings as various agenda items were tossed about, seemingly at random, while Garcia just stared at the table. Suddenly he spoke loudly, and everyone shut up. "Shouldn't we be asking, 'Do we still have a band'?" he said bitterly. I rose to excuse myself, knowing I had no role to play in answering that question. I muttered something like, "You guys need to talk by yourselves," as others were getting up to leave too. It was an awful feeling, sensing what they must have been going through. There were twelve total members of the band from 1965 to '95; three of them had died (all keyboard players), and others had come and gone, leaving the core four of Garcia, Kreutzmann, Lesh, and Weir, and Hart, who had joined in 1967. There were five of them there on that day, with no keyboardist.

Everyone knew that the band had their normal East Coast tour planned for September, and then a long-planned European tour set for October, which meant that if they didn't cancel all of that, they would have to search for, audition, select, and rehearse with Brent's replacement in the space of just four weeks. I knew what I thought immediately; the best thing for them to do would be to cancel it all, process their grief, take their time to find a new keyboard player and singer, and work with them until it was running smoothly. Whoever the new band member was, they would quite likely be with them for quite a while, including maybe making a comeback in December, and a New Year's run. Or maybe they could hire a temp for the European tour. But they didn't do any of that. They found Vince Welnick, formerly of the Tubes, worked him into the band in just four weeks, and that was it. Vince could sing a good high harmony, which was important, but he didn't play a Hammond B3 organ, a signature sound of Brent's, and I think that was a loss to the Dead's sound.

Of course, it was easy for me to say take a break—I'm a freelancer; I can do that. But Grateful Dead had a big, generous payroll, benefits, pensions, and other financial commitments, and the band members themselves had built up some pretty elaborate lifestyles, including multiple homes, expensive cars, former wives and children to support. The band maybe could get by for six months. Garcia certainly could; he'd just play gigs on the two coasts with his side band, the Jerry Garcia Band. But the rest of the employees, I don't know . . . unemployment insurance? It could get hairy.

Plus, they knew the chances of finding someone to truly replace Brent were probably pretty low, because Brent was truly a monster musician. He was ten or so years younger than the other guys, and had fully come into his own, I think, in '86 or '87. He'd contributed a great song, "Tons of Steel," to *In the Dark.* He had an incredibly versatile singing voice, played a mean piano and an even meaner Hammond B3 organ. He could play both instruments at once, with one hand on each, and he'd developed into a great improvisational jazz player. While playing live, he and Garcia would be situated ten feet apart at stage left, and their eye contact was extensive. You could easily see them feeding off of each other. I always made sure that I had the ability to shoot their close-ups across them, so the viewer could feel the energy going back and forth in their eyes and their grins. Weir and Lesh, by contrast, tended to look at their instruments. Garcia did make occasional eye contact with the drummers. Of course, Garcia had this uncanny ability to play the most astounding licks without looking at his hands at all; he'd be looking all around, anywhere but down—not all the time, but most of the time.

I had the absolute best seat in the house for the shows I shot, close-ups or medium shots of all six guys on screens in front of me, plus a wide shot or two, all of them changing at my direction. I could see the show better than anybody. I viewed my job as following the emotion flowing among the players and singers, the quick glance that meant "I'm going to throw this instrumental break to you at the end of this bar," or "everyone get ready for Bobby's big vocal return," so the viewer could feel what it was like to be standing on the stage, or ideally, to be one of the players.

In a multicamera video setup, each camera has a red light on the front of it that goes on when that camera is selected and is online, going out live or to tape, the idea being that performers will know where to look. I learned to disable all those lights, and when a musician would ask me where to look, my answer was always the same and very simple: Ignore all the cameras completely; look wherever you feel like looking, like we aren't there. It's *my job* to be in front of you at all times, to anticipate where you're going, and the real goal is to catch the feelings going around among you. It should be an intimate feeling, like we're spying on you—in a good way.

For me, peak Dead was from 1987 to 1990, four years of very consistently great shows, with 1989 being the zenith. If you don't know much about the Dead, skip the albums, except the ones recorded live, and if you only have time to catch two or three live concerts, pick from the 1989 stadium tour. Two or three should be in a row, because that's how you're going to be exposed to the largest variety of tunes from their repertoire of a hundred or so songs, and because any two consecutive shows will have the largest variety. For example, the three shows from Sullivan Stadium in Foxboro, Massachusetts (on July 2, 1989), Rich Stadium in Orchard Park, New York (July 4, 1989), and JFK Stadium in Philadelphia, Pennsylvania (July 7, 1989). Or the two shows from Giants Stadium in East Rutherford, New Jersey (July 10–12, 1989), or the two shows from RFK Stadium in Washington, D.C. (July 12–13, 1989), or the three shows from Alpine Valley in East Troy, Wisconsin (July 17–19, 1989). All are available at low quality on YouTube or Amazon Prime, or better quality on DVD in secondary and used video markets.

The new 1991 band with Welnick was not bad. It was about what you'd expect from five guys who'd played together for fucking ever and were breaking in a new guy. To complicate things, they also brought in Bruce Hornsby on occasion to play grand piano downstage left (Brent and Vince's usual spot), moving Vince onto a riser next to drummer Mickey Hart, and they did this, as far as I know, without rehearsing much with both keyboardists together. The result was that Garcia stepped back a little to make room for two keyboards instead of one, and it ended up sounding like what I called New Age Dead (New Age was a trend in music at that time and included lots of romantic flights of fancy—not a bad thing, just a bit far from the rock, country, and jazz roots of the Dead).

The largest show the Dead ever did, in terms of how many people saw it at one time, including live in concert and on TV or in theaters, aired as an episode of the ABC network television program *ABC in Concert*, produced by my friend Phil DeGuere in 1991. It was another benefit for the rainforests, a cause the band supported. It was shot on June 16 and 17 at Giants Stadium in

Jersey and aired a week or so later. As I recall, we got about three million sets of eyeballs for that one. That was the last big production I did with the Dead. I did a couple more small ones at the Shoreline Amphitheatre in Mountain View, and then I went on my merry way.

I did stay close with Garcia and Sue Stephens and my other friends in the Dead scene, and I decided to make my home in Marin County permanently and started commuting to LA instead of New York. The band, or maybe it was just Garcia, very kindly kept me on the all-access backstage pass list and provided me with free tickets, and I enjoyed going to shows as a civilian. But to be honest, the great moments I'd look for in the shows became fewer and farther between in 1992 and 1993. An obvious reason was from the loss of Brent, but also Garcia seemed to be . . . losing interest, maybe? Or possibly declining in some other more subtle ways.

We still hung out, going to dinner and movies and stuff, but we didn't talk about how the band was doing, and he never wanted to talk about his health, just as he never did the whole time I knew him. This was a guy, to reiterate, who had the striking character trait of *never* complaining about *anything*, except for one time, and once only, when he complained to me that he didn't think he got enough recognition for his songwriting. That is unquestionably true—he didn't. I think it was because the critics and media and the business couldn't see through the forest of the counterculture—the drugs, the crazy fans, their treatment of him as a guru or a god—and see the trees, which were the songs. Mostly it was the songs written by Garcia and Hunter that were at the center of the whole thing. They provided the liturgy, if the Dead phenomenon was and is to be considered a kind of spiritual movement. If you talk to musicians and songwriters, they know. A lot of those songs are getting covered today by other artists, and Dead and Company is out on the road, selling out stadiums, playing those songs as well.

I recall a band meeting I attended in early '91, my last year with them, when they were planning the year's tours. Garcia was in an uncharacteristically sour mood (recall that this was their first year without Brent). At one point he kind of stopped the talk for a moment and addressed the room: "Am I the only one here who hates doing stadium shows?" Boy, that put a damper on things. It was clear to me that for the first time in my experience, Garcia's tolerance for being the leader, the decision-maker, the one whom everyone turned to for the final word on anything under discussion, was coming to an end. The burden had finally become more than he wanted to carry.

A stadium show might cost a bit more than an arena show, but it brought in typically four times the profit. It was a very hard thing to resist. The Dead had done better than anyone else in designing sound systems that were up to the task and innovated large-screen video reinforcement that they *had* to have, because there were paying fans a quarter mile from the stage. But from a musician's point of view, the experience was daunting. It was hard to control the sound they heard on the stage, plus there was the heat, the rain, the wind . . . you name it. The stadium crowds were more remote from the stage, and at the same time much more likely to become a giant, rowdy beast, sometimes crazy, putting people in danger. You could look out from the stage and see people being dragged away by security for God knows what reason, people losing their minds from weird drug combinations, the occasional life-threatening crush of people up against the fence right below you.

Weir had perfected a thing when something like that happened where he would stop the show and have a chat with the crowd, friendly but firmly telling them that the people in front were in distress and that everyone had to take a step back. Then he'd lead them in a chant: "Okay, one, two, three, take a step back," and he'd have to explain that everyone out there had to do it in order for it to work, not just the people up front. It was a simple case of physics, but, you know . . .

But once again, the Dead were trapped by the size of their own operation, their generosity with their people, and their insistence on keeping ticket prices down. Jesus, I remember them selling tickets for, like, $30, whereas today you have tickets starting at $400 and going up to $5,000. But it wasn't my place to suggest raising ticket prices. So, for the Dead, if they weren't going to do stadium tours, how were they gonna make up the shortfall?

It was obvious to me that one way out of their dilemma was to do more electronic touring—doing a show at a local venue, like the Shoreline Amphitheatre in Mountain View, and sending it out across the country via pay-per-view on cable TV. That would allow them to collect all that additional revenue without any additional cost to themselves, as we had demonstrated with our summer solstice '89 broadcast from Shoreline. Then they could have reduced their dependence on stadium shows, and touring in general.

The band and management knew this, from the presentations I'd made to them about the numbers that came in for each of their electronically distributed events. But one of the quirks of their business structure was that they paid many of their key staff people, like the stage crew and the roadies, largely in tour bonuses, accounted for as show expenses and therefore paid in part by the promoters rather than via regular weekly paychecks by the band. If those tour bonuses were reduced, it would have ripple effects on their workers, though not on the band itself. I provided information to the band and management, but not advice on business strategy; that was not my job, unless they asked me to.

The last time I saw Grateful Dead live was at the LA Sports Arena on December 10, 1993. Despite the fact that Branford Marsalis sat in with them, the great majority of the show just wasn't getting to me or moving me. It was sad, or I should say I was sad, because the crowd seemed okay with the show. The guys weren't jelling like they used to, when they'd all be playing completely different stuff, and it came out sounding like one perfect thing—or for at least half the show that would happen. Not that night. It wasn't like I *decided* not to see them again, but I didn't. I think in hindsight it came down to me not wanting to face what seemed to be a decline in Garcia's talents, in his ability to play guitar and sing songs like he meant it.

From a new distance, I heard reports after '93 that the decline was continuing. There were lots of stories and rumors, but for me it was just a headshaker. Maybe Garcia was back into the Persian smoking powder or imbibing too much of it. But then I remembered those days when he was definitely doing it, and it didn't seem to have much of a negative effect on his playing or singing, or his memory (I heard that in 1995 he was using a teleprompter for help with the lyrics).

And then came the tour from hell: the summer stadium tour of 1995, the band's last shows. There were also the terrible news stories of death threats against the band from the irate parents of runaway kids. And there were the out-of-control fans, who seemed to be more than ever driven to be present for the craziest partying any of them had ever heard of, instead of the music or the spiritual liturgy. There was some kind of roof collapse at a campsite near one of the shows and two kids died. The last time I saw Garcia was shortly after that, at Sue's office.

So, what happened? What went wrong between 1991 and 1995? From Garcia's point of view, there was the obvious loss of Brent, and the subsequent dissolution of the perfect band that he had worked on most of his life to achieve. If the band around him could no longer reach that exalted state, then he just might have lost interest in the project. I had learned that his *engagement* with things outside himself was the most important thing to him. He had this huge mind that demanded that he be interested in something, and if he didn't get that engagement he started to decay.

There were all kinds of rumors and conjecture swirling out there. In '92 or '93 he'd had some sort of heart attack, or cardiac event, which caused me to pay him a visit at his house out on Lucas Valley Road, where he was living with Manasha and Keelin at the time, just to wish him well and see for myself how he was doing. He was all, "Aw shucks, it's no big deal." In his last cover story and interview for *Rolling Stone,* he told the interviewer that his doctor had told him that he had maybe two years to live if he didn't change his ways, but then there was no follow-up discussion of what the problem was (heart disease?) or how exactly he might like to change his ways—the most obvious being substance abuse: a heavy cigarette addiction and possibly the Persian smoking powder habit.

The band had switched from using stage monitors (speakers facing each musician that could be individually mixed by the onstage monitor mixer to provide the sound each musician preferred) to an in-ear monitor mix provided via earbuds (a technical innovation sweeping the industry in the 1990s, because it eliminated screeching feedback), which could also be adjusted by the monitor mixer to each musician's preference. The key difference between the two systems was that the sound coming from the audience was not limited by the old stage-monitor system but *was* limited by the new in-ear system. The stage mixer could add the level of the audience into the earbud that each musician preferred, but in the old system it simply wasn't possible to avoid the sound of an audience losing its mind. If the interaction between the band's music and the response they were getting from the crowd was actually a factor in what they played, how it developed from moment to moment, particularly in the improvisational segments, and how good or bad it was, it could have been negatively impacted if they could no longer hear the audience as well. Further, the new tech meant that each musician could just tune out one or more of the other musicians if they didn't find what the other guy was playing was good or useful to them. With the old system, each guy could hear a clam (musician speak for a flubbed chord or note) the other guy made, or on the other hand something novel and brilliant he did; in the new system, not so much. After going to some shows after the transition, I got the impression that the in-ear system was harmful to their long tradition of listening to each other and to the audience.

I've scuba dived a few times. When you're learning how, the instructors stress the importance of returning *slowly* to the surface, because if you rush you may cause neurological damage, something to do with the role of nitrogen in your blood. Between 1991 and 1995, Garcia had taken up scuba diving, and he told me how much he loved it: going to Hawaii, being within a hundred feet of a giant whale underwater, experiencing a different world. He explained that it was totally stimulating and compared it to his introduction to psychedelics. I could easily imagine him on a scuba adventure, exuding total confidence in his skills, as he always did. How the guides with him might be intimidated by his persona and presence, how they might be reluctant to remind him of the dangers or to try to slow him down. There's a chance that Garcia, being relatively unsupervised on a dive, made the mistake of surfacing too quickly and suffered some lasting neurological damage. I've seen this dynamic before, with stars and super-rich people, where the minders assume that their clients know what they're doing because they're rich and famous, when in fact they *don't* know what they're doing. For young people working at a beach resort, it might be hard to actively intervene in the potentially dangerous behavior of a resort guest. I mean, after all, Garcia was past fifty, rich and famous. He must have known what he was doing . . .

There was also carpal tunnel syndrome that he was dealing with, something you might expect would happen to someone who made their living operating his fingers at an incredibly taxing rate night after night. The syndrome affects the main nerves that run through the palm of the hand connecting the finger muscles to the wrist and forearm. I've heard that Garcia sought help from medical specialists in this area, but I don't know if that is true, and we never talked about it. I recall visiting with him on a sunny afternoon, probably in early '87, at the Hepburn Heights house after his coma and incredible recovery, interrupting what he called his daily practice. He had his Tiger guitar strapped on, which he took off and put on a chair, and there was a music stand with a big practice book open to a page of arpeggios. I have a little background in reading music, and I hazarded a guess: "Thirty-second notes?" I asked, and he said, "Yeah." I shook my head, like wow, imagining him sitting there practicing arpeggios for what, hours every day? He seemed to read my mind and said, "Yeah, you think this shit is easy? I have to work my ass off to keep being able to do this." He wasn't pissed about it or anything; he loved playing music, God knows, but this is part of what he had to do. On some other occasion, I did a dumb thing and acted like a fanboy, asking him if I could hold the Tiger guitar for a moment. He gave me a quick glance, like, "Oh, I thought you weren't a fanboy," but invited me to hold it anyway. I remarked, "Man, this thing is really heavy." It was custom made for him by Doug Irwin, and it was stuffed with electronics concealed behind little panels. He chuckled, "Yeah, it's heavy, you bet, and I gotta stand there for three hours holding it at every show. It's hard work, physical work, sometimes in the heat and humidity." He shook his head ruefully, like, "It may look like magic to the crowd, but a big part of it is just plain, sweaty, hard work."

And there was the obvious fact that Garcia was diabetic, something that I didn't know until the coma, which was triggered by a severe untreated tooth infection followed by dehydration in the heat of the summer tour—probably the show in Buffalo on July 4, 1986, and the two shows at RFK Stadium in D.C. on the July 6 and 7. I don't know much about diabetes, and he clearly had a spectacular four- or five-year run after his recovery from the coma in 1986; it is complex and manageable, but not curable. It has a genetic component, a person's diet and sugar metabolism have a lot to do with it, and it can get worse as a person ages.

Garcia also had coronary heart disease, another complex condition—possibly genetically related and possibly related to lifestyle choices like diet and substance use. It's a condition that restricts blood flow to the heart, which he'd had for a long time, but that I never knew of. I sometimes wondered why he never had bypass surgery or a heart transplant; only his doctors or family could shed light on that, and if they have I'm not aware of it. It wouldn't surprise me if Garcia simply had a revulsion to the idea of radical invasive surgery, on emotional, intuitive, or spiritual grounds. The medical establishment has always been unanimous about the danger of smoking cigarettes when you have coronary heart disease. Garcia was a lifelong heavy smoker who never really quit, as far as I know. It was also obvious that his Persian smoking powder, the combination of the depressant morphine and the stimulant freebase cocaine, would be very bad for your heart, sending it contradicting signals.

Finally, there was the big elephant in the room hiding in plain sight, difficult to look at, hard to talk about: Garcia had no fear of death at all, just as he had no fear of anything, as far as I could tell in knowing him for fifteen years.

Chapter 17

GOODBYE

It was mid-July 1995, a beautiful afternoon, and I dropped in on Sue Stephens at her office on a whim, just to visit with her, chew the fat. It was widely known that the just-completed Grateful Dead summer stadium tour was a serious train wreck. There were credible death threats against Garcia and the band; out-of-control demand for tickets to the shows, leading to fans attacking and breaching a security fence, which led to the cancellation of a show; fans just camping out wherever they found themselves; the narks, police or federal agents targeting Grateful Dead shows in order to make arrests (basically using the band as bait); and a fatal accident caused by a roof collapse related to Grateful Dead fans at a nearby campsite at one of the concerts. Sue and I were chatting about the summer tour. She was philosophical as always, taking it in stride, always finding the humor in even the darkest times. This was three and a half years after my business relationship with the Dead had come to an end, and almost two years since I had last seen them live, but I remained friendly with Garcia and Sue and other band members and office staff.

Garcia had only a few weeks to live on that July day, but of course Sue and I had no inkling of that. Looking back now, though, I believe that he did know that he was in his last days.

We are shooting the breeze, and in comes Garcia, a bit diffidently, as was his habit, like, "I hope I'm not interrupting anything?"

CHAPTER 17

Sue and I are a bit surprised, but obviously happy to see him. We know about his habit of cruising by the office to see whose cars are parked there, and then coming in to visit if he likes what he sees.

He looks pretty good, considering what we've heard about the tour. He's wearing a windbreaker, and he smiles shyly, clearly pleased to see us too. I invite him to grab a chair and join us, making a crack about, "So, the tour from hell, eh?" He settles into the chair, smiling and nodding, and lights a smoke.

"Yup, it really sucked." It's clear that he's very affected by it, sighing, slumping, and shaking his head, and Sue and I just shut up and empathize.

When he's ready, he brightens and sits up in his chair and excitedly tells Sue about a dream he'd had about Sue's former longtime boyfriend Fred, known as Big O (he was very big).

Big O was a part-time road manager for the Jerry Garcia Band, and someone who went way back in the Dead scene. He had passed away several years earlier from AIDS.

Garcia says that Fred was in a wheelchair in the dream, as he was when we last saw him, but now he was in an ethereal place, bright, misty, seemingly boundless, suffused with feelings of joy and love, and he was glad to see Jerry and welcomed him.

I'm struck by the boldness of Garcia's description, and how it's clearly important to him to tell us—but really Sue—about this dream. Sue always engages with him easily and directly, and so she nods appreciatively. Here was the luminescent Garcia, as he had always been, still here . . .

For the next hour or so we all kibbitz about nothing special. We touch on the new Casa Garcia project with Bill Kimpton, for which the next move was for Jerry and I to write a more formal proposal. But mainly Garcia rambles through his memories of the past, some of them the deep past, using the story of Big O as a jumping-off point.

He is rueful, happy, and relaxed as he tells the stories, seeming to enjoy getting this stuff off his chest, or just being with friends. We laugh a lot. I never expected to see him that day, but I'm very happy I did, and to bear witness to the history he was ruminating over.

He talks about the first days of the band, starting when it was known as the Warlocks, in 1964 and '65. How they were kind of a jug band, and then Pigpen joined, and they moved toward electric guitars and the blues. He recalls how they used to play something like four or five sets a night, for twenty dollars or something, a pittance. Their first serious gig was at Magoo's Pizza Parlor in Menlo Park. He laughs as he remembers it all. He tells us about how a guy claiming to represent the musicians union (Garcia mocked his way of saying it as "the yoooonion") demanded that they join and pay up, and we all have a good laugh at that.

Then there's a pause, a silence, as we all just appreciate the moment, happily . . . life.

Garcia gets up, collects his cigarettes and lighter, and puts them in his pocket, saying, "Well, tomorrow I'm gonna go down to Rancho Mirage, the Betty Ford Center," and he turns away, heading toward the door. Sue or I make some noises like, "What? Wait a minute . . ." But he isn't about to discuss it, saying, "Yeah, this is what I've got to do, this is what Deborah and everyone are telling me to do."

I remember having a sudden feeling of alarm. I know a little about the approach at Betty Ford, which is basically to aggressively reshape their clients' daily lives to instill a sense of humility, what I would call a you-got-to-clean-your-own-toilet approach, so that you could build a new idea of yourself from more of a blank slate. I feel immediately that this is not a good fit for the man I know, so vast in his knowledge and talents and accomplishments. But as he moves toward the door and he's saying goodbye to us, I know that in that moment I could not and should not say anything to change his mind.

Just before he leaves, he turns to us and waves goodbye, calling out, "Seeya!" Sue and I wave and wish him well and say goodbye.

And that was the last time I saw Jerry.

Chapter 18

NO FEAR

Garcia and I used to talk about the various religious and philosophical teachings on the nature of consciousness and death, including those from Siddhartha Gautama (known as Buddha), Jesus of Nazareth (Christ), the Greeks, the enlightenment thinkers, Carl Jung, Alan Watts, Joseph Campbell, and the scientific and psychedelic contributions of the late twentieth century from people like Fritjof Capra, Tim Leary, David Bohm, Rupert Sheldrake, and the McKenna brothers. We were in complete agreement that when pondering the question "What happens when we die?" we must first accept the obvious answer that we simply don't know, and probably cannot know. That means rejecting the reductionist scientific assumption that we cease to exist, that there is nothing at all after death. When you ask for a definition of *nothing,* the scientists don't have one. That's because there is no observable or measurable example of *nothing*; it is merely an abstract concept cooked up by the human mind, useful poetically and metaphorically, but not rationally.

On the other hand, it can be assumed as true that the wide variety of fabulist descriptions of a life after death, the afterlife, are just made-up stories to help us live in a world that we could not explain, stories that help us cope with the loss of loved ones and our fear of death. Those stories have also helped to establish and enrich vast religious institutions and whole civilizations, from the ancient Egyptians to the modern Catholic Church, current fundamentalist megachurches, Scientology. It's only been a handful of generations since we discovered and have come to accept that evolution is how humans and every other living thing on this planet came about. We don't need imaginary narratives anymore, but old ideas die hard, especially if they are lucrative and helpful to those with wealth and power.

We have also learned, only in the last few centuries, that many phenomena in nature occur across a spectrum, rather than in separate discrete units. For example, what we call the *light* that we can see is actually made up of an infinite spectrum of electromagnetic wavelengths, some of which we've given specific names to in order to represent discrete colors, such as red, orange, yellow, green, blue, indigo, and violet, which span the range of visible light that humans can see. The visible light spectrum is itself part of a much larger spectrum of electromagnetic radiation, which includes infrared and ultraviolet light (both undetectable to the human eye), radio waves, microwaves, and gamma waves.

We've also learned that most of what we observe in nature is the result of field phenomena that are not detectable by our senses. For example, for many centuries people have known that if you placed an oblong piece of iron ore on a leaf floating in water, it would consistently point north. No one knew how or why this was true, but it worked, and it made possible navigation over the oceans. Now we know that the iron is responding to an invisible field, the earth's magnetic field, a "fabric" of nature that envelopes the entire world, and indeed permeates the entire universe, something that we had absolutely no concept of just four hundred years ago. Our new knowledge of magnetism led to the discovery of electricity, which is now totally integral to human civilization all over the world. So now we have field theory gradually replacing all the previous, more "mechanistic" conceptions and explanations of cause and effect.

It is an accepted scientific fact that every single living thing on earth today evolved from, descended from, one single-celled organism that lived, not symbolically or metaphorically, but literally, about four billion years ago, called LUCA (last universal common ancestor), which means that all of the currently living five to ten million plant and animal species on planet earth today (and the trillions and trillions of individual living things) are all descended from that first organism, which means that everything alive today on planet earth is related to every other living thing on earth, from bacteria to birds to trees to fish to us. This is a hard thing to truly accept and internalize: that all life on earth, in its infinite variety, is related and shares common ancestors, just as you and me are related to our grandparents, and not just in a religious or spiritual way, but literally. It's hard to imagine a more profound idea, but this is where our recent inventions—rationality and science—have brought us.

Everything alive on earth today came from something earlier that was alive, our parents, grandparents, their grandparents, back a million years to the primates, the bonobos, or chimpanzees that we evolved from, all the way back to that first living thing, LUCA. Before I was born I was an embryo, and before that I was an egg in my mother and a million sperm in my father, and when I was born and survived, my mother and father lived on, in me, and when I had a child, they continued to live on, in her, through me, and thus be it forever, into the past forever back to LUCA, and into the unknown future. This is kind of an astonishing concept, but it is accepted science today, and I believe it is far more awesome, beautiful, and spiritually moving than the teachings of our established religions, which are rooted in our understanding of the world before the Enlightenment in the eighteenth century, before our discovery of rationality and science.

So it turns out that "everything" is actually one thing (a growing certainty in Western physics, though an ancient belief in the East and to many Indigenous cultures), and we Western/modern humans have created an elaborate and destructive system of beliefs over the last ten thousand years or so, disconnected from nature, *allthatis*, wherein we are all separate from each other and separate from every other living thing on earth, the biosphere that has been here for billions of years before we came along, and further, especially in the Abrahamic religions of the West, that it is all here for us to consume, in sharp contrast to many ancient and Indigenous cosmologies that hold, quite simply, that all life is sacred, and teach us to share in and help sustain all life, like every other single living species on this planet.

There are no "divisions." There is no "separateness." Everything, *allthatis*, is one thing. We humans have invented all the separations and divisions, but we have also, paradoxically, at the same time developed insight into this deep reality, the "oneness," over thousands of years, which still exists in ancient, Eastern, and Indigenous cultural belief systems. And now, in the past seventy years, we Westerners have rediscovered the usefulness of psychedelic substances to help us reconnect to the true reality.

Then you have the scientific axiom of "conservation of mass and energy," proposed in the nineteenth century and proven in the twentieth, that matter and energy are two manifestations of the same thing, and they can neither be created nor destroyed, but they can and do constantly transform into one state or the other, apparently infinitely and forever—case in point, Einstein's theories, which included the equation $E = mc^2$. So maybe we have to now consider the possibility that the energetic component of every person, sometimes called "the soul," may be conserved, in a new form, at the moment when it is separated from the matter of the body, which we call death.

So you put all this together, and you get what Garcia and I shared a belief in: that it is most likely, probabilistically (which is all we have to go on, given the state of contemporary physics), that given our unknown level of ignorance (do we know a lot about the universe, or a little?), that life, consciousness, and mind are most likely field phenomena, and that our fear of death is mostly likely rooted in the uniquely human obsession with storytelling, of turning all experience into stories, with a beginning, middle, and end (which possibly evolved as a result of our extraordinary predictive abilities as a species, which gave us a big survival advantage), when in fact the world around us, *allthatis*, most likely does not have a beginning, middle, and end, as evidenced in the fact that no other species on earth suffers from a fear of death, an imaginary state of annihilation, and don't tell me that it's because all the other species are not sufficiently intelligent, or aware, when we now know that whales and dolphins have brains much larger than ours, have survived here on earth for millions of years longer than us, and that many other species, all the other primates, such as bonobos and chimpanzees, and birds and octopuses and dogs and cats, exhibit many of the same characteristics of intelligence and culture and awareness and love that we do.

It makes perfect sense to fear the death of loved ones, family, and friends, if you have the ability to imagine it, as we humans do, because we know from experience that it will be painful for us to lose them, we will miss them, long for their presence. But it is not rational to fear your own death, when you know that you do not know what comes after it, and there is plentiful evidence to believe that you may well be moving on, in a physical, energetic sense, into a new state of being, as opposed to a literally unimaginable state of "nonbeing," annihilation.

The "mind" is not a product of the brain, nor does it reside exclusively in the brain. Mind is probably a field phenomenon that exists, at least in part, outside of ourselves and is generated and shared in ways that we don't yet understand. The brain is most likely a type of "tuner," an organ that interacts with the mind and mediates between it and the sensory input of the individual "owner" of the brain, in the same way that our blood, heart, and lungs interact with the air we breathe, or the way our digestive system interacts with the food we consume from our environment. Garcia and I often talked about how we humans don't know what "consciousness" is (this is referred to as "the big problem" in science), but that it is probably not a product of the mind, but something that is shared by literally all living things (a single-celled organism must be conscious, since it can sense and move toward a food source), and there is even a school of thought in contemporary physics that consciousness may be a basic or fundamental force that is everywhere and at all times present in the universe, a part of the "substrate" of *allthatis,* alongside the four known forces: electromagnetism, the strong nuclear force, the weak nuclear force, and gravity.

So, it's more likely than not, or more likely than any other explanation, that life is not simply linear, that it begins at birth and ends at death, a belief system or tradition based on the uniquely human concept of linearity and produces the fear of death by fundamentally misunderstanding what life is. Life is better understood as an eternal "turning," or a wheel with no beginning and no ending. Life is a wheel. Or as Robert Hunter expressed it in "The Wheel."

The wheel is turning and you can't slow down
You can't let go and you can't hold on
You can't go back and you can't stand still
If the thunder don't get you then the lightning will
Small wheel turn by the fire and rod
Big wheel turn by the grace of God
Every time that wheel turn round
Bound to cover just a little more ground.

The Wheel words by Robert Hunter
Music by Jerry Garcia and William Kreutzmann
© 1971 (Renewed) Ice Nine Publishing Co., Inc
All Rights Reserved, Used by Permission of Alfred Music

CHAPTER 18

Garcia's lack of fear of death was not just a character trait, or a manifestation of an exceedingly optimistic mindset; it was also the result of a lot of reading and thinking about and discussing with others the history of science and the goings-on in contemporary physics, quantum mechanics, the recent proof that "spooky action at a distance" is real (seemingly denying the supposed limit of the speed of light), recent speculation about multiple or even infinite other universes, the idea that time may be nothing more than an invention of the human mind.

In short, it is the idea that we should put rationality and love for each other and all of life at the "top" of our spiritual belief systems, as the guiding lights, the primal organizing principles.

Sue Stephens told me, almost casually, a few weeks after Garcia's passing, that he had stopped by her office on his way to Serenity Knolls, the drug and alcohol treatment center in West Marin, a few miles from the office. This would make her the last person he spoke to before going away to die, excepting the staff at Serenity Knolls. He told her that he was feeling the urge to score, and that he didn't want to give in to it, because he didn't want to "go out that way" (that is, apparently, die by overdose), because it was not "classy." And something more, about how his family would have to live with it, the way the media would treat it, so he was going out to Serenity Knolls, which he reminded her was the abandoned camping place that he and Hunter and the early Warlocks would go to crash when they had no other place to sleep.

The meaning, the implication: that he was aware of and cared about his "mode of passage" and how it would be interpreted, and therefore aware of his legacy, Grateful Dead, and his role in the ongoing subculture. And that he was aware that his death was imminent, apparently from what he knew from doctors, but perhaps more importantly, what he felt within himself, from his heart, from his mind and spirit, such that he could proactively decide how his demise should come about, in the next few hours. Die in his sleep at the old campground or die while sucking on the pipe one last time.

And according to Sue, he left her office with a smile and a wave, just like he left the last time I saw him, on his way to Betty Ford just a few weeks earlier, no trace of dread or fear.

It's been reported that the Serenity Knolls night watchman noticed no sound of snoring from Garcia's cabin, a sound he was used to from earlier rounds he'd made, and he did a welfare check, and found that Garcia had gone home, and that he had a smile on his face.

Jerry Garcia was NOT a tragic figure. I've seen him portrayed or described this way a lot in the nearly thirty years since he passed. Dying young (fifty-three) does not make you a tragic figure. He accomplished more in his short life than most anybody else I can think of. He was the farthest thing from a tragic figure. He lived his life his way, always following his ideals, and leading a huge bunch of others toward those ideals. Since he was not the slightest bit interested in fame or money or getting credit for accomplishments (an exception for his songwriting complaint), you have to look at what he obviously loved, and lived for, and that is music and the power of music to bring joy to people and bring people together, and if you measure his life by that standard, he was wildly successful, playing for huge numbers of people with a variety of bands, recording a huge number of records with all kinds of artists from all over the musical spectrum, and those records, and concert films, are forever.

I think he is best understood, and revered, as a great musician and songwriter, yes, but also as a spiritual leader, showing us the way to a better world; the only other figure that comes to my mind for comparison would be Bob Marley, though Marley died younger and never reached as many "followers" as Garcia and the Dead.

Now he certainly did not consider himself any sort of person to be followed, or a person others should look up to as a role model. He knew he had lots of faults; he knew he wasn't the best family man or husband, or maybe not even a good one, the father of five daughters (if you count Sunshine Kesey) who was not able to fully participate in their lives. I remember an interviewer bringing up what was a trope to Garcia, something he rejected, that "Some of your fans seem to think of you as a guru, or almost a God," and Garcia cuts him off, shaking his head ruefully, "Those people should talk to my kids." And I remember at the reception after the funeral where we had all put Brent in the ground, sitting down at a table to recover a bit, Laura next to me, Garcia and Weir across from us, lots of sighing and teary eyes. Garcia, who I recall was living alone at that time, says, "I've gotta move in with Manasha and my kid, I've gotta try to be a father to Keelin ... " He shakes his head and looks down, refers to Brent's daughters with his wife Lisa, Jennifer, two, and Jessica, five, " ... Seeing those two little girls, now fatherless, God ... " Bobby and Laura and I appreciate what he's saying, empathizing, " ... I was never that good at being a dad, I've got to try to do this."

But spiritual leaders are just as flawed as anyone else, it's just that they have the wisdom and the courage to say stuff and do stuff that can show the rest of us a way out of the woods, a possible path to the greater good, and this is an exceedingly rare type of person.

On June 23, 1988, James Hansen, a NASA scientist, addressed a United States congressional committee and sounded the first alarm bell about the danger of human activity burning fossil fuels and raising the level of CO_2 in our atmosphere, resulting in the heating of the planet, now known as climate change. The Amazon rainforest is the largest "absorber" of CO_2 and producer of oxygen on our planet, and human activity was, and still is, destroying it.

My friend Randy Hayes, the founder of Rainforest Action Network and a leading activist on climate change, recruited the Dead to play a benefit concert at Madison Square Garden in New York City in September 1988, and I was charged by the band to design a live video reinforcement that would accompany the concert. The Dead, at the zenith of their cultural visibility, participated in a panel discussion and news conference, along with Randy, other activists, and the mass media, at the United Nations, which I attended as an observer. I remember being afraid that some skeptical members of the press corps might pounce on band members Hart, Weir, and Garcia, and confront them as showboating drug-addled rock star dilettantes, but after introductory remarks by Hayes and others describing the horrific destruction of the rainforest from out-of-control extraction capitalism, and the disastrous effect this has on the Indigenous people who have lived in those forests in a sustainable relationship with them for thousands of years, here's what Garcia had to say:

"Somebody has to do something, in fact, it seems incredibly—in fact, it seems pathetic that it has to be us, y'know [laughter] . . . this is not our regular work, y'know what I mean? We've never really called on our fans, the Deadheads, that you people probably know about, to ... align themselves one way or another as far as any particular cause is concerned ... because of a basic paranoia about leading somewhere ... when we don't want to be the leaders, but this is, we feel, an issue that is strong enough and life-threatening enough that inside of the world of human games where people regularly torture each other and overthrow countries and there's a lot of murder and hate, there's the larger question of global survival and, and everything else . . . I think we want to see the world survive to play those games, even if they're atrocious . . . so the sense of this is, let's take a break in the stuff that we normally do and address the earth's survival, and hopefully we'll include our own in there."

I was blown away. In a short opening statement, Garcia deftly killed off that one expected press reaction, by admitting that it was pathetic that it had to be them, Grateful Dead, that had to be there that day. Absolutely brilliant. Wise spiritual leadership.

I once heard that someone said about Garcia in his last years of decline, or after he went home, that he "loved heroin more than music." This isn't the stupidest thing I've ever heard, but it's in the top ten.

I would say he loved Grateful Dead and all that it entailed, the long history, the records, the live shows, the fans, the huge subculture, and on and on, he loved that more than he loved life itself. And when it became clear he was exhausted and needed a break, in 1992 and after, he didn't just say, "I don't want to do this anymore," he participated in the band's decision to keep on going. He could have said no, but he was determined that he was not going to be the guy who said, "Let's put Grateful Dead on ice for a while" (that had happened in the 1970s for a year or two, I'm told, and it had traumatized their whole scene). And he would never be the guy to put an end to Grateful Dead by walking away from it, and as long as no one else in the band led the way, then they would go on, despite the obvious decline from '92 onward in their music, and he would just keep playin' in the band until he dropped dead, which is what happened.

To me, this story is about a man who knew who he was, what he stood for, what he wanted, and the consequences of his actions, and was willing to accept them without flinching. It was not a tragic story; it was a heroic story.

EPILOGUE

In June 2023, as I was working on this memoir, my Gen Z daughter, Kiley, mentioned to me that Dead and Company, the current iteration of Grateful Dead, with Mickey Hart, and Bob Weir from the original band, plus John Mayer, Jay Lane, Oteil Burbridge, and Jeff Chimenti, were going to play three shows at Oracle Park in San Francisco, a beautiful stadium by the bay where the San Francisco Giants baseball team plays. It was billed as the last shows of their Farewell Tour, though of course one must be skeptical about farewells in show business.

I had seen several earlier iterations of the Dead after Garcia died, and I remember especially liking the one that had Joan Osborne in it. But by the time Dead and Company came along, I was a bit distanced from the whole thing, so I had never seen them. I asked a couple of people who'd seen them over the years, "Who's this guy Mayer? Is he any good?" Some of them were positive about him, but a little guarded, I think maybe because they knew of my friendship with Garcia and feared that I might not want to hear too much praise for his replacement. That was not true at all, but I could understand it. But I never saw them.

Kiley prevailed upon me to go see the show on July 16—purportedly their last ever—and I thought, "Well, I probably should," because my old friend Mickey Hart was around eighty, and Bobby was fast approaching, and so . . . you know.

The crowd of fifty thousand or so was deliriously happy while still pretty well-behaved, compared to what I'd seen in the '80s. There were young people, old people, families of three generations together, people in bizarre outfits or innocuously dressed, some crazy, high on various substances, or maybe just acting out. It was great.

The band was absolutely spectacular. I was blown away. Halfway through, I was thinking, "Jeez, how come no one told me how great they are? I could have gone to a bunch of shows." But then I thought, "Well, you're seeing their last show, it's gotta be a high point." Mayer is an amazing guitarist and a good singer, and though nothing like Garcia stylistically, his treatments of the songs were fantastic.

And the songs, or the liturgy as I've called them earlier: "Bertha," "Loser," "High Time," "Althea," "Bird Song," "Franklin's Tower," "Eyes of the World," "Cumberland Blues," "Brokedown Palace"—all Garcia-Hunter songs. They only did a few Weir songs, including "Estimated Prophet" and "Sugar Magnolia." I was struck by how Bobby chose to highlight the Garcia songs rather than his own. And the crowd was just ape-shit happy, singing along joyously. I was transported, like seeing my whole life flashing before my eyes before I died—only it was just a big part of my life, and I didn't have to die. And the crowd, God, it was so good to see so many people of all ages going crazy over these same old songs, made new again in good part due to the work of Mayer, Oteil, and Chimenti. And Weir was as dependable as always.

In the car on the way home, I said two things to Kiley. If Garcia was somehow looking down on this, if he could be aware of it, he would be absolutely ecstatic, he would be loving it, to see that what he devoted his life to was still going strong.

And I said to her that what he gave us didn't go away when he went home, or even stop for very long; it just changed its form and continued to live on. And like all living things, it will continue to evolve, as long as we are here to be a part of it and help it grow.

Jerry and Len posing together while working on "Jerry's Kids," San Francisco, CA, October 1980. Photo courtesy ©John Werner.

AN AFTERWORD: A FEW WORDS ABOUT THE TITLE OF THIS BOOK, *FRIEND OF THE DEVIL*

"FOTD," as it is referred to by fans, is of course a Garcia-Hunter-Dawson song that first appeared in concert and on the Grateful Dead album *American Beauty* in 1970. The title is meant as a bit of a wry joke at the expense of my beloved friend, the subject of this memoir, whom I believe would appreciate the irony.

In the song "Friend of the Devil," the narrator, a desperate character on the run, says, "A friend of the devil is a friend of mine." He's telling us that he's in so much trouble, so far off anyone's radar, that there is no one he would turn away from if they might offer a modicum of hope to him, including a friend of the devil, or even the devil himself.

This down-and-out-character storyline is a big part of the Garcia-Hunter songbook, as in other songs like "Wharf Rat," "Black Peter," "Mission in the Rain," "Stella Blue," and "Black Muddy River." Some of them create sudden eruptions of redemption, joy, and love out of the misery; some of them just offer us insight into the necessity of empathy for the suffering, or an understanding of the role of the randomness of fate, teaching that we must not look down on others who haven't done as well as ourselves and could use our help. Hey, many of us were born on third base, without having to hit a triple. These are everyman American themes—think Steinbeck, Guthrie, Vonnegut, Kerouac, the Beats, Ginsberg, Kesey.

No one I know believes in the physical existence of the devil, or Satan, though of course hundreds of millions of people do. But so what? Lots of people think the world is flat. The devil has always been a powerful archetype: a living, evolving symbol passed through many different cultures for millennia, especially in the West. But before he was recast as the archenemy and nemesis of God by the growing religion of Christianity in its first thousand years, going back many more thousands of years to ancient Eastern, pre-Christian cultures (and still to this day in many Indigenous cultures), the devil was just one name for a character known as the trickster.

Christianity promoted the devil to the role of Satan, a figure the Hebrews had no concept of, an utterly dark and evil force powerful enough to share the stage with God. But many people nevertheless continued to rely on the archetype of the trickster and an adjacent character, the joker, to fuel our perpetual demand for satisfying myths, storylines, and narratives, to shake things up. He was tolerated for his entertainment value, exposing our hypocrisies, delivering karmic comeuppance to guilty bad actors, making us laugh at our own foibles. All of that played a crucial role in our ability as a species to tolerate the antisocial, psychopathic behavior all around us, and learn to understand and accept it as part of our shared human existence.

Tricksters are extremely important to the storylines of mythic beliefs. They provide the crucial destabilizing forces or events that move the narrative within the otherwise static, permanent, or perfect mythic world. They provide a counterweight to the necessary but oppressive assumptions of the dominant established belief system.

Think of the trickster as the Greek and Roman gods of mischief, Hermes, and Mercury. Think of the ancient myth of the Greek Titan Prometheus, who stole the knowledge of fire from the gods and gave it to man and paid a price for it. The trickster as a hero in folklore may often triumph by outwitting his opponents, like Br'er Rabbit or Bugs Bunny, or by means of superior intellect or secret knowledge, like Yoda or Loki.

So, the devil in "Friend of the Devil" is more devilish than evil, a trickster, which is why we can readily accept him when he appears in the song as nonthreatening. He might even be there to help you when you need him, like by loaning you that $20 . . . just remember, he comes back two verses later and takes it back, and then vanishes in the air.

Garcia was keenly aware of his and Grateful Dead's relationship to that cultural history of the archetypal trickster. He was always eager to talk about the band's relationship with the psychedelic subculture of the 1960s (Kesey and Leary), and also how they'd descended from the Beat culture of the 1950s and '60s (Burroughs, Kerouac, Cassidy, and Ginsberg), and from folkies like Pete Seeger, Woody Guthrie, and country-and-western performers like Merle Haggard.

Ken Kesey's Merry Pranksters could easily have been called the Merry Tricksters, and Ken and his famous crew perfectly personified the idea of the trickster performing within, and interacting with, our current society.

Garcia and Hunter and the early Grateful Dead were in the same cauldron of psychedelic adventure as Ken Kesey and the Pranksters and their Acid Tests, and then Bill Graham's promotion of them, and the birth of the Fillmore in San Francisco (still operating to this day). These were all key parts of the cultural evolution that was going on in postwar America, flowering in the 1960s, getting good and weird in the '70s, then struggling in the roaring '80s, the happy '90s, and on and on. The spirit persists to this day.

It's hard to conceive of it now. When Grateful Dead appeared on the scene in the mid-'60s they were wildly successful, with an audience high on acid, like themselves, and appreciated by a lot of the general public. But there was a big part of American culture that was deeply perplexed and threatened by what was going on with popular music (the Doors, Jefferson Airplane, the Beatles, the Stones, Marvin Gaye, Dylan), Tim Leary and his LSD religion thing, and a lot of other stuff, like the Vietnam War, race relations and the Black Panthers, even assassinations and urban riots. It was all cast in the mass media as a confrontation between middle-aged privileged white parents and their wild and revolutionary teenaged and young adult children, who might even forge alliances with Black people.

So yes, a long time ago a lot of people thought of the Dead as the devil, as they definitely did of Keith Richards and Mick Jagger (now two of the wealthiest and most beloved musicians of all time, and both happy eighty-year-old grandfathers). I mean *Grateful Dead*—what does *that* mean? Scary.

And so, my choice of a title is a bit ironic, maybe. Consider that my friend, who, as part of Grateful Dead, the band with that weird name, was once thought of as scary to many people, is now universally accepted as a spiritual ideal, an icon of openness, acceptance, love, wisdom, conviviality, and generosity. And I believe that as time passes, the positive spiritual essence of Garcia and Hunter and the Dead's vast project will become more and more widely known and understood.

"Space-Time" by Jerry Garcia. ©Jerry Garcia Art.

APPENDIX A: THE ART OF JERRY GARCIA COMMENTS BY ROBERTA WEIR

Roberta Weir is a long-time San Francisco Bay Area resident and well-known artist and gallery-owner/operator. Garcia described her to me as his "art teacher;" she set up figure model sessions with him, taught him etching technique, and she was his primary art dealer and consultant starting in 1990. After his passing in 1995, I asked Roberta to evaluate my collection of his artwork, and what follows below are her comments on the Garcia works selected for this book, drawn from her assessment of the total collection.

"Space-Time"

Drawing in pen and transparent markers, in black, gold, and gray. Soiled on reverse. Dated on reverse by Len Dell'Amico "7/12/85." (5 x 8.5") Subject is a crossroads of time and space, a motif that introduces the theme of the collection.

Design sketches by Jerry Garcia for the film So Far, *1987. ©Jerry Garcia Art.*

APPENDIX A

"Duck Spaceship"

A series of six drawings.

1) Ink drawing on white drawing paper, probably drawn with a nylon-tip pen. Stain in the far right of paper. (5 x 8.5") Introduces the duck character, which in succeeding drawings is developed as part of the mechanical-organic form of a spaceship.

"Metamorphosis"

2) Ink drawing on white sketchbook pape, probably drawn with nylon-tip pen. A partial sketch, of a duck's head with curving beak, a beginning of a mechanical form. (5 x 8.5")

3) Ink drawing on white sketchbook paper. (5 x 8.5") Development of the preceding sketches using the duck motif as the fore section of the spaceship; some of the forms are items that held sentimental and formal attraction for the artist: specifically, the Buick-type car chassis atop the duck head. Two radar instruments protrude from the windshields of the car form; other allusions to cars in the exhaust pipes at the sides. These juxtapositions of elements of life-forms and machines recurs frequently in Garcia's work.

4) Ink drawing on white sketchbook paper. (5 x 8.5") Duck head embellished with another face on its forehead, with eyeballs on stalks, a clownish nose, and receding chin. Duck eyes appear drawn the way cartoonists represent a dead duck, horizontal lines, or crosses. Exhaust pipes, various mechanical apparatus; a form at the bottom of the drawing that suggests a hat. Upper area shows arched windows and radiator-like flanges.

5) Ink drawing with sepia-toned transparent marker used for accent. *On white drawing paper, torn from sketchbook. (5 x 8.5")* The duck motif played out—the duck is sleeping or dead, overwhelmed by the elaborate craft in which it is embedded like a hermit crab. A visual stream of consciousness in which many types of architectural and mechanical inventions coexist. Towers and turrets of European and Asian design, fishtail '50s car parts, headlights, exhausts, radar scope/antenna. This drawing shows the artist's enjoyment in allowing juxtapositions to occur without inhibition and is typical of Garcia's way of working, a spontaneous outgrowth of linked images without premeditation.

6) Line drawing in pen on white wove paper. In addition to pen line, transparent markers in yellow, gray, and red. (5 x 8.5") With the duck motif dropped, the mechanical aspects dominate; organic elements are limited to the shark fins at the side of the ship, the face suggestions at top section. In relation to the duck, the entire construction can be viewed as a mechanization of the duck face, with the stalk eyes projecting from the eye area in the bill.

"Keep Out" by Jerry Garcia. ©Jerry Garcia Art.

It is typical of Garcia to see faces everywhere. Often windows are the eyes, and the remaining face-forms develop out of this feature. Looked at biomorphically, the entire machine, with ears protruding at the top, also resembles a dog's face, with a ball-like dog nose at the bottom of the page, not complete because the drawing was created from the top down, without premeditation. It is interesting that it is one of the drawings where the design is symmetrical, since Garcia favors asymmetry There is only one departure from the perfect symmetry; the exhaust pipes being on the right and windows in the corresponding section of the ship on the left.

The entire form can also be viewed with the major pipes as arms, whereupon an amazing, armored praying mantis–looking alien warrior appears.

Also representing, because of the skirted figure image, a destroying female archetype. It only requires the viewer to consider these subjects, and they are easily seen.

Can also be viewed upside down, showing a baby elephant with two trunks. Garcia frequently turned his page around and upside down when working; to see all the images in a work, it is helpful to check different positions of the paper.

"Keep Out"

Drawing in black on cream paper, cut from sketchbook. (3.5 x 4.5") A scratchy ink style rendering of a mechanistic character in an architectural setting with stairs and archways. A door at the base of the figure is marked "Keep Out."

Len's additional comments, June 2024: Looking at this work again, after rediscovering Roberta's critiques, I see things I never saw before. "Keep Out" is not part of the production sketches for *So Far*, it is clearly one of the purely creative drawings that he gave me, and it is clearly dark, going to a dark emotional place. Once I could see the seated figure that Roberta pointed out, I was free to see the "Keep Out" sign as hovering over the torso, or heart of the seated figure. The figure is in a dungeon. The giant head of the figure appears to be encased within some kind of isolation or torture device. And there's a tube connecting the heart area of the figure to the brain area of the figure. It looks to me as if the artist is confronting his substance addiction (the smokable substance enters through the cardiovascular system and then invades the brain), which in turn serves to repel any who may want to intrude, thus, "Keep Out." I also see a possible tiny self-portrait in the top of the tube connecting to the head.

"Pyramids"

Ink drawing on a white sketchbook page with extensive coloring in transparent markers: red, pink, green, cerulean, and yellow. (5 x 8.5") An interior of pipes, snail forms, metal globes with faces, and intertwined and looping forms through which can be seen an open-air landscape of perspectival stripes-like, road markings, leading to a distant scene of pyramids.

"Pyramids" by Jerry Garcia. ©Jerry Garcia Art.

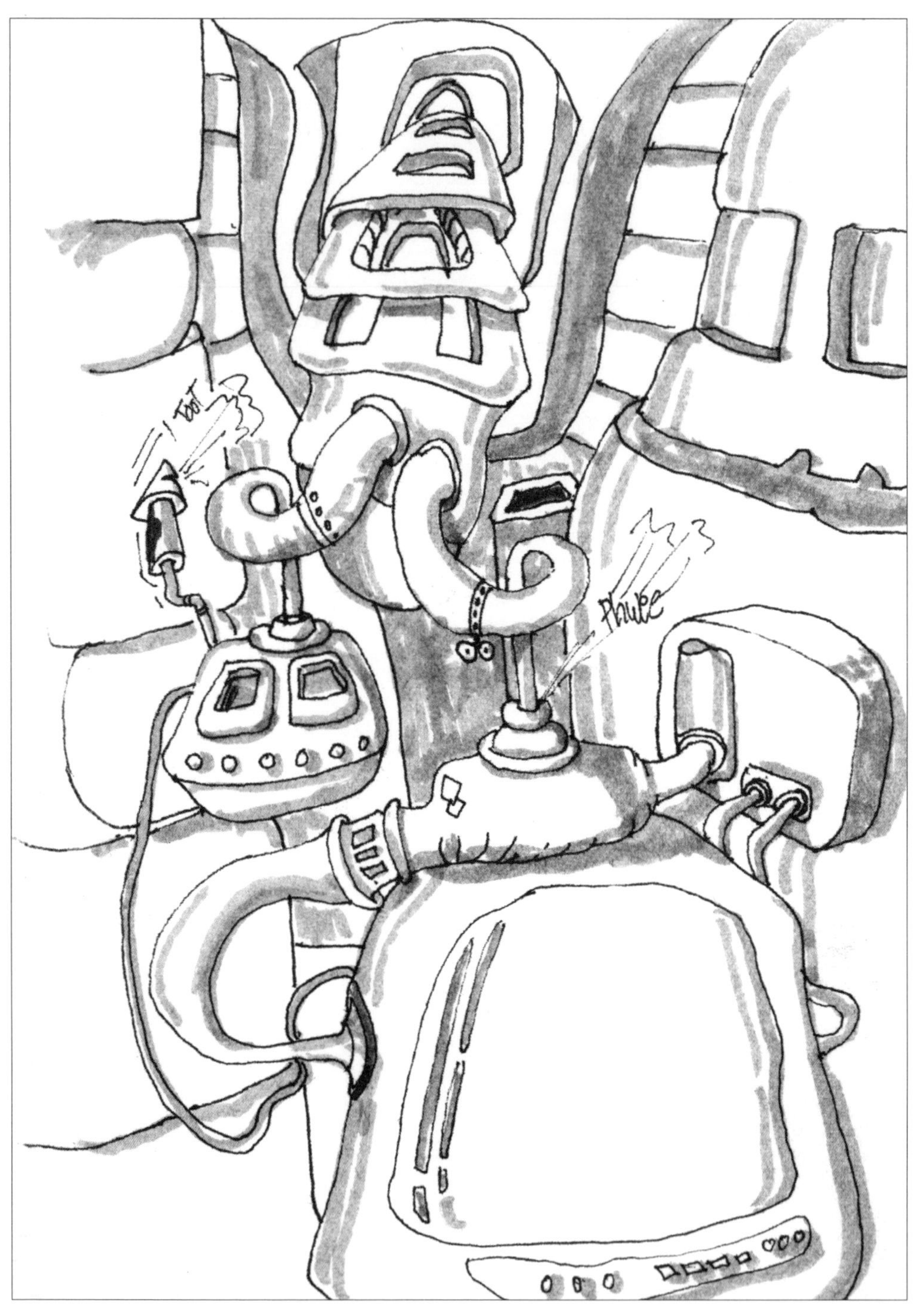

"Spaceship Interior" by Jerry Garcia. ©Jerry Garcia Art.

"Spaceship Interior"

Line drawing on wove paper. Shading and accents in transparent gray-green marker. (5.5 x 8.5") One of the most complete and realized drawings in the series; eccentric and humorous, expressing the artist's vision of machines as extensions and metaphors for the body. In a humorous way, expresses the idea that what is most intimate is also most alien, a paradox I have observed in much of the artist's work, and in his own comment to me that the body is "just a thing."

The composition is vertical, and attention is nicely directed upward by arrows of mechanical-industrial parts from the center, and then moves down again toward the foreground, at the base of which is a soft television. Also, numerous faces in the machine parts, a soft retort. A steam whistle at left emits a puff of smoke and printed "toot" while the retort's puffs are interpreted as "phwee." At the very center, a pair of eyes belonging to a snake draped over one of the curly tubes at the center.

Bizarre, funny, unique.

"Alien Monsters Looking at Tiny Spaceship on a Lake" by Jerry Garcia. *©Jerry Garcia Art.*

All images from the collection of Len Dell'Amico, courtesy the Garcia Estate.

"Alien Monsters Looking at Tiny Spaceship"

Line drawing with shading in transparent gray marker. Sketchbook page. (6 x 8") Grotesque faces; head upside down, eyes on stalks, etc., amid gears and towers; a body of water in the middle-ground with the ship visible.

APPENDIX B
FUN FACTS ABOUT *SO FAR*

The soundstage state-of-the-art recordings for *So Far* were made in April and December of 1985. Some of those sessions were combined with pieces of the 1985/86 New Year's live national broadcast to create *So Far*, released in late 1987.

I had a rough cut of the proposed release of *So Far* in March of 1986, constructed by Garcia and me, with a "slop mix" and no "cutaway visuals," just the band playing the music. It came in at one hour and fifty-one minutes. In a band meeting, I submitted it in the form of a "rundown," a big chart showing all the songs, the sources, the transitions. My co-director, Garcia, surprised me by proposing a much shorter version, something closer to one hour in length, in consideration, in his view, of the market, which was broadcast television, cable, and home video. I think he was wary of presenting something that represented their live shows, which were long, in a "small-screen" medium. (Of course, now, with six-foot TVs and huge sound systems commonplace, their concert films play very well at home, not to mention pay-per-view broadcasts in theaters, such as the annual Garcia birthday event in August, held across the country and called "Meet Up at the Movies.")

I was a bit let down about the radical shrinkage of the show (*So Far* as released in 1987 was fifty-five minutes, as compared to the one-hour and fifty-five-minute first proposal), because of all the work that had gone into that one hour of material that we were going to cut out in one fell swoop. But I had to trust in Garcia's intuition.

So Far was released with the following rundown:

"Uncle John's Band," "Playing in the Band," "Playing in the Band jam," "Lady with a Fan," "Rhythm Devils," "Space," "Throwing Stones," and "Not Fade Away."

All of this music was recorded at the April 1985 soundstage session at Marin Civic, or at the New Year's Eve broadcast from the Oakland Coliseum, on December 31, 1985; the film starts on the soundstage, segues to the live show, goes back to the soundstage, and then back again to end at the live show.

Here's the one hour that was cut out of the original 1:55 edit:

"Fire Jam," "West L.A. Fadeaway," "Hell in a Bucket," rehearsal session for "Tons of Steel" (7 minutes of the band working on vocal arrangements), "Man Smart," "Woman Smarter," "Tons of Steel," "She Belongs to Me," "Lovelight," and "Brokedown Palace."

"The Fire Jam," "West L.A.," "Hell," and "Tons" rehearsal were all filmed at the December '85 Marin Civic soundstage shoot; "Man Smart" was shot at the live show, segued into "Tons of Steel," which then transitioned quickly into the "Tons" performance from the December soundstage shoot. "She Belongs to Me," the Dylan song, was from the April soundstage shoot, and "Lovelight" and "Brokedown Palace" were from the live New Year's show.

I put this on the record because I want all the serious fans and scholars to know that this material exists, "in the vault," and it might be of interest to some of you out there, to maybe try to resurrect the original, longer version of *So Far*, or only to one day hear and see the Dead doing these songs, rehearsing, fooling around.

I also remember clearly having great versions of a medley of "Brown-Eyed Women" and "Jack Straw" from the soundstage, and great takes of "Brother Esau." We also did something like thirteen takes of "Day Job" at the December soundstage shoot, for those of you who are gluttons for punishment.

INDEX

G

H

I

J

K

ACKNOWLEDGMENTS

Many thanks go to: Kiley Dell'Amico, Fred Dell'Amico, Mick Stern, Mario Santilli, Randy Hayes, Richard Fugini, Andy Ross, Edward Ash-Milby, Susana Millman, Jay Blakesberg, John Werner, Ebet Roberts, Stephanie Mohan, Image Flow Photography Center (San Anselmo, CA), Laura Kimpton, Aaron Hoffman, Tom Engleman, Greer and Blythe Daly, Jon Blaufarb, Johnny Navas, Pat Woods, Michael Worden, Michelle Ritter, Paul Grippaldi/Digital Revolution, Tom Engleman, Trixie Garcia, Carolyn Adams Garcia, and Sunshine Kesey.

ABOUT THE AUTHOR

Len Dell'Amico has spent his entire working life in the film and television business, editing, writing, but mainly directing and producing concert films and music videos with such artists as Sarah Vaughan, Herbie Hancock, the Allman Brothers Band, Linda Ronstadt, Ray Charles, Blues Traveler, The Neville Brothers, Carlos Santana, Reuben Blades, and Bonnie Raitt.

He met Jerry Garcia in 1980, when he became Grateful Dead's "video and film guy," and their friendship lasted for the rest of Garcia's life. In partnership with Garcia, they produced the historic first national pay-per-view broadcast in the USA, from Radio City Music Hall in New York in 1980, the best-selling, award-winning home video *So Far* in 1988, a series of ground-breaking live concert broadcasts from 1987 to 1991, and two classic music videos, "Hell in a Bucket" and "Throwing Stones" to promote the band's hit album *In the Dark*.

Dell'Amico currently lives in Fairfax, Marin County, California, where he continues to do freelance screenwriting, producing, and directing, with a special interest in the environment and sustainability issues.

His most recent feature film is *Welcome To Dopeland*, currently streaming.

Visit lendellamico.com

weldon**owen**

an imprint of Insight Editions
P.O. Box 3088
San Rafael, CA 94912
www.weldonowen.com

CEO Raoul Goff
VP Publisher Roger Shaw
Publishing Director Katie Killebrew
Executive Editor Edward Ash-Milby
VP Creative Chrissy Kwasnik
Art Director Allister Fein
VP Manufacturing Alix Nicholaeff
Sr Production Manager Joshua Smith
Sr Production Manager, Subsidiary Rights Lina s Palma-Temena

Weldon Owen would also like to thank Bob Cooper , Karen Levy, and Peter Stoneman for their work on this book.

Text © 2025 Len Dell'Amico
All rights reserved. No part of this book may be reproduced in any form without written permission from the publisher.

Cover Design by Michel Vrana

The stories in this book reflect the author's recollection of events. Dialogue has been re-created from memory.
Every effort was made to credit photographers correctly. If you would like to update a photo credit, please contact the publisher.

ISBN: 979-8-88674-168-1

Manufactured in China by Insight Editions
10 9 8 7 6 5 4 3 2 1

REPLANTED PAPER

Insight Editions, in association with Roots of Peace, will plant two trees for each tree used in the manufacturing of this book. Roots of Peace is an internationally renowned humanitarian organization dedicated to eradicating land mines worldwide and converting war-torn lands into productive farms and wildlife habitats. Roots of Peace will plant two million fruit and nut trees in Afghanistan and provide farmers there with the skills and support necessary for sustainable land use.

ACCESS ALL AREAS
ACCESS
ACCESS ALL AR
Grateful Dead
JUNE·JULY TOUR
LEN DELL'AMICO
Dell'Amico
NAME
Fall
1989
Winter
ACCESS ALL AREAS
1984
LEN DELL'AMIC
ACCESS ALL AR